PRAISE

LILIANA'S
INVINCIBLE
SUMMER

"Cristina Rivera Garza wanted to shed light on the life of her sister, killed thirty years ago. Her book, part of a larger call for justice by women in Mexico, helped locate the suspect. . . . [*Liliana's Invincible Summer*] is the record of a woman who, against the odds, refuses to be forgotten."

—*The New York Times*

"Not everything can be put into words, especially grief and rage, no matter how precise and skilled the writing is. The beauty of this book is that it reaches for that truth regardless, and in doing so, Liliana becomes indelible. She is so fully realized that by the end, the reader is also mourning. I will be thinking of Liliana for a very long time, perhaps forever."

—*The Washington Post*

"Women across the world are killed at shocking rates by men, usually partners or former ones. . . . Anger at this lack of accountability seethes through Ms. Rivera Garza's book. Her main goal, however, is not abstract analysis of femicide but to chronicle a life lost to it. . . . [It's] absorbing and poetic."

—*The Economist*

"A searing account of grief and the quest to bring her sister's murderer to justice years after the fact . . . Reminiscent of Natasha Trethewey's *Memorial Drive*, Rivera Garza's memoir is both a master stroke and a critical inflection point in her country's brutal, patriarchal politics."
—*The Boston Globe*

"Rivera Garza carefully controls the nearly savage emotional landscape, making few false steps in her choices of when to speak, when not to, when to admit defeat, when to step in with a historian's training, when to cede the story to their parents, when to have Liliana's friends explain how it was. . . . One of the most painful scenes in the book, one that made me cry, is the one in which Cristina tells her parents that Liliana is dead. . . . This is the moment the yowl belongs to."
—*The New York Review of Books*

"The Mexican virtuoso's searing, propulsive memoir probes the murder of her younger sister. . . . Rivera Garza recreates Liliana's death at the hands of a violent ex-boyfriend, opening a Pandora's box of bureaucratic demons and igniting a cold case that rallied a nation to the cause of domestic abuse."
—*Oprah Daily*

"*Liliana's Invincible Summer* is a blueprint of one woman's murder, but it is also the story of hundreds of thousands of women throughout the globe. I was shaken and alerted by Cristina Rivera Garza's investigation into her own grief. It has inspired me to speak up as she has bravely done."
—SANDRA CISNEROS

LILIANA'S
INVINCIBLE
SUMMER

A Sister's Search for Justice

CRISTINA
RIVERA GARZA

HOGARTH

New York

Published in the United States by Hogarth, an imprint of Random House,
a division of Penguin Random House LLC, New York.

HOGARTH is a trademark of the Random House Group Limited,
and the H colophon is a trademark of Penguin Random House LLC.

Originally published in hardcover in the United States by Hogarth, an imprint
of Random House, a division of Penguin Random House LLC, in 2023.

This work, while originally written in English, is based on
and shares themes with "El invencible verano de Liliana"
by Cristina Rivera Garza, published in Spanish by
Literatura Random House, Barcelona, in 2021.

LIBRARY OF CONGRESS CATALOGING-
IN-PUBLICATION DATA
Names: Rivera Garza, Cristina.
Title: Liliana's invincible summer : a sister's search for justice /
Christina Rivera Garza. Other titles: Invencible verano de Liliana.
English Description: First edition. | New York : Hogarth, [2023]
Identifiers: LCCN 2022014200 (print) | LCCN 2022014201 (ebook) |
ISBN 9780593244111 (trade paperback) | ISBN 9780593244104 (ebook)
Subjects: LCSH: Rivera Garza, Liliana, 1969-1990. | Rivera Garza, Cristina,
1964—Family. | Intimate partner violence—Mexico. | Murder victims'
families—Mexico.
Classification: LCC PQ7298.28.I8982 Z4613 2021 (print) |
LCC PQ7298.28.I8982 (ebook) | DDC 362.88/20972—dc23/eng/20221028
LC record available at https://lccn.loc.gov/2022014200 LC ebook record
available at https://lccn.loc.gov/2022014201

Printed in the United States of America on acid-free paper

randomhousebooks.com

2 4 6 8 9 7 5 3

Book design by Jo Anne Metsch

In the midst of winter I found there was,
within me, an invincible summer.

—ALBERT CAMUS

CONTENTS

I

AZCAPOTZALCO

Time heals everything, except wounds.

—CHRIS MARKER, *Sans Soleil*

[here, under this branch, you can speak of love]

The tree is brimming with invisible birds. At first I think it must be an elm tree—it has the same sturdy and solitary trunk supporting the sprawling branches that I recognize from my childhood—but soon, just a couple days later, it is clear that it is an aspen, a foreign species transplanted long ago to this part of Mexico City, an area poor in native vegetation. We sit beneath it, right on the edge of a yellow curb. The sun slowly setting. Across the busy street and behind tall metal gates, gray factory towers stretch upward, and heavy power lines bend, barely horizontal, against the sky. Trailers drive by at great speed, as do taxis and cars. Bicycles. Of all the evening noises, the sound of birds is the most unexpected. I have the impression that if we move beyond the tree's shadow we will not be able to hear them anymore. *Here, under this branch, you can speak of love. // Beyond lies the law, the need, / the trail of force, the preserve of terror. / The fief of punishment. // Beyond here, no.* But we listen to them and in some absurd, perhaps unreasonable, way their repetitive and insistent singing triggers a calm that cannot erase disbelief. Do you think she will come? I ask Sorais as she lights a cigarette. The lawyer? Yes, she. I have never known what to call that movement, when lips pressed together stretch toward one side of the face, dismissing any illusion of symmetry. I'm sure we'll see her soon, she says in response, spitting out a strand of tobacco. In any case, it wouldn't hurt to wait another half hour. Or another hour. Looking at her sideways, hesitantly, I have to admit to myself that I mentioned the lawyer because I wanted to avoid asking her to wait with me. *Supplicate* is the verb. I did not want to beg. I did not want to beg you to wait here with me for a little longer because I don't know if I will be able to, Sorais. Because I don't know what animal I am unleashing deep within. We are now six hours and twenty minutes into a journey that started at noon, in what now seems to have been another city, another geological era, another planet.

[twenty-nine years, three months, two days]

We'd agreed to meet at noon at the place where I was staying. An old house turned into a boutique hotel. A white fence flanked by bougainvillea and vines. An old gravel passageway. Palm trees. Rose bushes. And while I wait for Sorais with some anticipation, I don't take my eyes off the city on the other side of the windows. It welcomes just about everyone, this city. It kills just about anyone too. Lavish and unhealthy at the same time, cumulative, overwhelming. Adjectives are never enough. When Sorais arrives at the house that is to be my home those few autumn days in Mexico City, I don't know if I will be able to.

There are two things I must do today, I tell her right away as we hug and exchange greetings. The aroma of soap in her hair. The moisture of her skin after a hot bath. Her voice, which I have known for years. Well let's go then, she answers immediately, without even asking for more details. It might take all day, I warn her. And it is then that she pauses, looking into my eyes. So where are we going? The intrigue in her voice betrays expectation, not suspicion. I am silent. Sometimes it takes a bit of silence for words to come together on the tip of the tongue and, once there, for them to jump, to take the unimaginable leap. This dive into unknown waters. To the Mexico City Attorney General's Office, near the downtown district. She keeps quiet for a moment now, paying close attention. About two weeks ago, I tell her, on another trip to the capital city, I met up with John Gibler, the journalist who helped me start the process of finding my sister's file. She looks down, and then I know for a fact that she knows. And understands. After a brief search in the newspaper archives, I continue, John found the news just as it was published in *La Prensa* twenty-nine years ago. He managed to contact Tomás Rojas Madrid, the journalist who wrote the four articles that documented the murder of a twenty-year-old architecture student in a surprisingly restrained tone, in language devoid of emotion or sensationalism, succinctly depicting the crime that had alarmed a neighborhood in Azcapotzalco on July 16, 1990. And I came, I continue explaining, to meet the two of them, the two journalists, at the Havana Café, that famed and crowded place, and walked with them to the building of the Mexico City Attorney General's Office. Because I wanted to file a petition there, I tell her. How does one even formulate such a letter? Where does one learn the protocols for requesting a document of this nature?

October 3, 2019. Mexico City.

C. Ernestina Godoy Ramos. Attorney General of Mexico City.

My name is Cristina Rivera Garza, and I am writing to you as a relative of LILIANA RIVERA GARZA, who was murdered on July 16, 1990, in Mexico City (Calle Mimosas 658, Colonia Pasteros, Azcapotzalco Delegation). I am writing to request a full copy of the case file that at the time corresponded to Public Ministry record no. 40/913 / 990-07.

If you need more information, please do not hesitate to contact me at the following address.

Best regards.

There is only a slim chance of recovering the file, I clarify again, after all these years. Twenty-nine, I added, twenty-nine years and three months and two days. I am silent again. Things are so difficult sometimes. But they are supposed to have an answer for me today, I say.

[the younger sister]

We decide to walk. The journey, according to Google, would not take us more than forty-four minutes on foot. And the day is spectacular. So we trek forward. One step after another. A word. Many more. If it weren't for the fact that we are pursuing the record of a murdered young woman, this could be mistaken for any random outing in a touristy city. Avenida Ámsterdam is a legendary street in La Condesa, a Porfirian neighborhood established in 1905 that still boasts its old art deco and art nouveau mansions, now sandwiched between apartment buildings with shiny windows and roof gardens. The neighborhood was also known as the Hippodrome because the avenue along which we walk this morning was, in its origins, the oval track where horses raced against each other. Desperately. It is easy to imagine them: the horseshoes against the loose dirt of the arena, the rattle of their gallop, their glistening skins, the upright manes. Their rosy gums. One after another, those horses. Running as if their life depended on it. Aren't we all? The air from the past lingers, crisp and sharp, full of uproar, against our nostrils while the canopy overhead prevents sunlight from passing through. Still, Avenida Ámsterdam remains a must-see. Elongated and paved with bricks, the path is a closed form, a kind of physical villanelle that thwarts the experience of continuity or the feeling of finitude. You always go around, endlessly, inside an oval, after all. You are always a horse running against the past.

The muffled echoes of English or French or Portuguese pass us by, ringing quietly on the sidewalks. But a street vendor surrounded by the pungent aroma of wild marigolds on one of the banks of the Parque México speaks Spanish. And so does the paper collector, singing his old-time tune while dragging a metal cart ever so slowly: papeles viejos, periódicos usados que venda. The construction workers who have borne the weight of the renovations that turned this neighborhood into an oasis for hipsters and young professionals speak languages that come from far away in the highlands or from shanty neighborhoods on the outskirts of the city. If I lived in Mexico I could not afford a home here. But I'm passing through. I take advantage of a research visit at the Universidad Nacional Autónoma de México (UNAM) to trace the file for investigation 40/913 / 990-07, which contains the arrest warrant issued against Ángel González Ramos for the murder of Liliana Rivera Garza, my sister. My younger sister.

My only sister.

[already exhausted, already fed up, already forever enraged]

It is easy to get used to the beauty of the space. Here, the city boasts its best features. Dogs on leather leashes. Strategically placed traffic circles and limestone fountains. Outdoor cafés. Poplars covered in golden light. We rush forward, and as our breath quickens, the words pour from our lips. There are so many stories we have to tell each other and catch up over. The words echo on the road that draws us from the freshly washed streets of La Condesa: we head toward Avenida Michoacán until we come across Calle Cacahuamilpa, where we turn left, then right into Avenida Yucatán and Eje 2 Sur. Did you hear about the professor accused of harassment who was banned from setting foot on the Iberoamericana campus? Almost immediately, we turn left and then right to find ourselves in Álvaro Obregón. Did you read about the Oaxaca Green Wave manifesto, where they blasted the organizing board of the local book fair as misogynous? A kilometer later, we dart left onto Avenida Cuauhtémoc and enter the Doctores neighborhood: from Dr. Velasco to Dr. Jiménez and, from there, on increasingly narrow streets full of poorly parked cars, to number 56 Calle General Gabriel Hernández. Have you seen *The Joker* yet? The pungent taco stands. The corner stores. The ramshackle balconies. Stray dogs. All these children walking on their own. Is that a hawk in the middle of the sky?

A couple of months ago, in early August, a squad of rightfully enraged feminists congregated in front of the Attorney General's Office, the same white building we are entering now. A teenager had just been raped by members of the local police while they were on patrol. What do we want? Justice. When do we want it? Now. The chants vary little around the world, rumbling from mouth to mouth, from fist to fist, against a common sky. Anthropologist Rita Segato has reminded us that behind the relentless war against women, which is being waged with equal ferocity inside homes and on public grounds, lies the "mandate of masculinity," which negatively affects women and men alike, albeit in different forms and with different lethal risks. Defined as men's perceived duty to dominate in order to belong to a brotherhood whose main aim is control over women's bodies, the "mandate of masculinity" helps us understand that while violence against women may appear to be sexual, it is, above all, a matter of power. The domination of female bodies brings a lesson with it: a pedagogy that promotes the normalization of cruelty, which in turn contributes to the perpetuation of the predatory system we know as patriarchy. Femicide is, in this context, a hate crime, one committed against women because they are women. Ten of them take place in Mexico every single day, leaving a trail of heartbreak pierced by impunity and flanked by indignation. While news of femicide has become customary over the years, this rape case sparked a new wave of national outrage. The protesters gathered behind the metal fences of the Attorney General's Office resolutely demanding an audience with the head of the institution and, when only her representative came down to meet them, assuring them that they were doing everything possible to pursue the case, one of the women—already exhausted, already fed up, already forever enraged—threw pink glitter at his head. The gesture, as spectacular as it was innocent, earned the feminist protests a new name: the glitter revolution. These grassroots movements have attracted more and more women, younger women, women who grew up in a city, and a country, that harasses them every step of every day, never leaving them alone or offering respite. Women always about to die. Women dying and yet alive. With handkerchiefs half covering their faces and tattoos on their forearms and shoulders, young as newborn planets, the women claimed the right to live peacefully and safely on this land stained with blood, torn by the spasm of earthquakes, and steeped in violence. They stood up right here, exactly where we stand today. Our feet on their footprints. Their footprints enveloping our feet. Many footprints. More feet. Our feet conforming to the invisible silhouettes of their steps. Their silhouettes opening up to accommodate the soles of our feet. We are them right now and we are others in the future at the same time. We are others, and we are the same as we always have been. Women in search of justice.

Exhausted women, yet close together. Fed up women, but bearers of a centuries-old patience. Already and forever enraged.

[0029882]

To enter the Attorney General's Office, you must pass through a security checkpoint, setting down your bags and jackets. Good afternoon. With your permission. Go ahead. We ought to dispose of the water bottles that Sorais bought toward the end of our trek. It is so very hot outside. Look at all this sweat. Later, much obliged, you have to stand in one of the six lines available just to learn which office to contact afterward. The bureaucrats' friendliness is overwhelming. Good afternoon. Please. May I bother you for your ID? I show the officer petition number 23971, addressed to Attorney Ernestina Godoy Ramos, bearing the stamp that indicates it was received on October 3, 2019, at 2:20 P.M. And he produces the record, imprinted with folio number 0029882, where it is noted that my original petition was transferred to three different jurisdictions. Put this red label on your blouse, he instructs us. A scarlet circle. A branding of sorts. My colleague will show you the way, he says. We take the elevator to the fourth floor and, from there, walk through crammed corridors barely covered by worn linoleum until we are ushered out of the building to reach the emergency stairs, an old metal structure that was once painted white. The creaking of footsteps. The feeling that everything is about to fall apart. There, inside of the building once again, turning to the right, to the end of the corridor, lies the Office of Management Control of the Office of the Attorney General.

The woman who works behind a small glass window stares at her computer screen and, without looking at us, assures us that she is listening. Her very long nails. Hair half black and half blond. One second, please. She enters the folio number into the system and something pops up on the screen that will then come out of the printer. For a few seconds I think that this is the file I am looking for, and my breathing stops short. Will this be the moment? Will I dare to read it all now? Sorais places a hand on my left shoulder. But the document, dated October 16, is just a piece of paper listing the three jurisdictions that may or may not have, or might have once had, the file I am seeking. Do I imagine things or is it true that the woman's eyes are saddened when she informs me, on the other side of her tiny window, as if captive herself, that it will be difficult for me to put my hands on such an old document? If it is not here, it may be in the Concentration Archive. And where is the Concentration Archive? There are many. It depends on the nature of the file. Suddenly, without thinking, I ask if it will be possible for me to reopen the case. Or open a new case? It is the first time I have thought of this possibility. She takes a deep breath. Looks at me again. I am not a lawyer, she says, but I do know that a person cannot be tried for the same crime twice. It is the law. But he was never tried, I say. She lowers her eyes. She stops herself from saying something. Go first to the General Directorate of Police and Criminal Statistics, she says instead. It's right in this building. Go back toward the stairs and turn right; they will be able to explain it to you over there.

[unusual]

The officer we need is in a meeting, but the woman behind the desk and the computer screen may be able to help us. Petition number? A case from 1990, you say? She remembers. Yes, she does. She discussed this petition with her boss a few days ago. The request remains clear in her mind because it is very unusual for someone to search for a document from this long ago. Do you know that? she asks. Know what? That it is even more unusual to actually find it. I turn to her very carefully, with some reserve, wondering if what I hear is a simple comment uttered in haste or if there is something pointed in that short sentence, an undercurrent of reproach. I can't help it. I have to ask myself: Why did it take me so long? So many things happen in thirty years. Death happens, above all. It doesn't stop happening. The deaths of thousands and thousands of women. Their corpses here, around us, barely touching the floor as they linger shoulder to shoulder with us. Behind our backs. In the folds of our hands, when they shake. At the very corners of our lips as we speak. Behind the knees, as they flex. They are here, next to the skin, ingrained in our grief. These are their faces on the posters that cover the lampposts, on the pages of the newspapers, in the reflections on the windows: the look they had before the crime, before revenge or jealousy, before love. Time crowds and contracts. Then it relaxes again. One year. Three years. Eleven years. Fifteen years. Twenty-one. Twenty-nine. I bow my head and look at the perfectly horizontal edge of the desk on which I slide very slowly, with all the parsimony in the world, my fingertip. I have to sigh, defeated. I lift my face again, my chin, my eyebrows. Mountains are said to move this slowly in deep time. I see her: her smooth skin, her straight hair, her very white teeth, the black eyeliner that frames those serene eyes. Have they been forced to take customer service workshops? Or do they know from experience that all of us arrive here heartbroken and guilt-ridden and angry? Her voice, even softer than her skin, instructs us to go down to the second floor, to the Office of the Deputy Attorney General for Decentralized Investigations. There they will be able to tell you something, she says.

[memorial]

Police. Lawyers. Women in high heels. Checkered-apron grandmothers. Victims. We stand shoulder to shoulder in the narrow elevator. Back on the second floor, to the right, awaits the green counter where another employee tells us to go a few steps farther until we reach another small window. In the official memorandum, folio number 0029882, shift / 300/14098/2019, it is established that: *A complete copy of the case file 40/913 / 990-07 is hereby requested. W / N Attached. Instructions of the Deputy Attorney General: It is sent for your attention and follow-up, so that it is resolved in accordance with the applicable law; you must mark a copy to this Deputy Attorney General Office of the attention provided to the present, referring to the corresponding shift number. Mtro. Joel Mendoza Ornelas, Prosecutor's Office Supervising Agent. October 17, 2019.* The employee lets us peek at the document but doesn't hand it to me. I'll do that, he says, as soon as you bring a copy of your official ID. He has uttered these words over and over again, relishing the disbelief and frustration they trigger. I have it right here with me, I say, as I unzip my backpack. Will you make the copy? Of course not, he smirks, can you imagine the number of people who come here on any given day. Go down the stairs and right outside the building, across the street, you will find a photocopier. On the way out we pass by a colorful poster with a date, OCTOBER 4, writ large. And next to it, glued to the wall, a thin, almost translucent sheet of onionskin paper featuring the memorial written in honor of Lesvy Berlin Rivera Osorio, a UNAM student murdered by her boyfriend on May 3, 2017.

Such a seemingly smooth phrase: "student murdered by her boyfriend." Lesvy Berlin Rivera Osorio. It took two years of tireless activism, two years in which Lesvy's mother insistently advocated for a rigorous legal investigation, to be able to write it in one breath. Still in pain, grieving for her daughter, Araceli Osorio Martínez took to the streets, joining many others in their demand for justice. She spoke to the media, often and strongly, denouncing slanderous depictions of her daughter's behavior. She was young. She drank beer every now and then. She liked to hang out with friends. She was sexually active. So what? Lesvy was no whore, no drunk, no junkie. And even if she were, even if she had been, would that justify her murder? How brave and relentless Araceli Osorio was! She soon contacted human rights organizations across Mexico and forced the attorney general to open a trial. Under the guidance of lawyer Sayuri Herrera, now in charge of the first femicide prosecution office in Mexico City, the predator was found guilty after a highly publicized two-year-long trial and sentenced to forty-five years in prison. Few believed him when he initially argued that Lesvy's death had been self-inflicted. To be more precise, only those used to sheepishly blaming the victim assumed that Lesvy had committed suicide. When the news began to circulate and readers realized that Lesvy had been found hanging from a phone booth on the university campus, the black wire around her neck, it was simply too hard to believe that Lesvy had taken her own life. The verdict, still fresh in the air, has run like a whiplash of electricity through my spine ever since. The news, which brought tears to my eyes, propels me directly into this place, this walk, this promise. Another world is possible, Liliana. Another love. We cross the landing, but I have to jerk Sorais by the elbow in the middle of the next run of stairs. Did you see that? About Lesvy? Yes, I did. Did you see the date? Sorais shakes her head from right to left. Which date? October 4 is the date my sister was born.

Lesvy and Liliana. The sound of the combined *l*'s forces me to put my tongue against my upper teeth, pushing the air around the sides of my mouth. A lateral consonant. Could they have been friends? Could they have partied together, their manes of hair up and down, shiny and wild, in a crowd dancing to cumbia sounds? Could they have run to help each other in the middle of the night in case of asphyxia, strangulation, sudden death? Alveolar lateral approximant consonant. Liliana. Lesvy. They *are*, I correct myself, substituting the present for the past. They are friends.

Everything on this day seems to be an encrypted message. Everything a small Pandora's box from which ghosts, specters, hallucinations arise. Daggers. When we reenter the building with a copy of my ID, a gaping mouth floating on my face, I walk resolutely to the window of the Office of the Deputy Attorney General for Decentralized Investigations, as if a miracle were about to happen. My eyes full of inexplicable hope. Now you have to go to Public Prosecutor's Office Agency number 22, in Azcapotzalco, the officer says nonchalantly, handing me the document and keeping a copy for his files at the same time. Is he rejoicing at our dismay? Is there a smirk dancing, barely concealed, behind his lack of expression? This is what comes next: we have to cross the entire city to know the rest. I have to warn you, he adds, a bit pensive, compassionate at last. Everyone goes out to eat at three in the afternoon. Are they gone for the day after that? They are expected to be back at 6:00 P.M. Are they? They are. We calculate the amount of time we have. If we hurry, we might be able to catch them right before lunchtime. But they would be hungry, for sure dejected, if we manage to get ahold of them before lunch. Instead of rushing, we prefer to do what they do. We choose to eat.

[a hand waving above the crowd]

The Attorney General's Office is near downtown Mexico City. A sixteen-minute walk will take us to El Cardenal, a restaurant located on the ground floor of a Hilton hotel, just across the Alameda Central and next to the great Palacio de Bellas Artes. Feverish activity sweeps across the crumbling sidewalks, where a steady stream of haggling customers draws the attention of blue-aproned employees who take care of business from behind glass counters, in front of shelves full of tin, plastic, and metal goods. There is so much noise that instead of walking side by side, we move in a single-file line that, at times, becomes a zigzag. Sorais walks ahead of me, saving me the trouble of wrestling with the incoming crowds, and when I look at her back, at the way she skillfully angles her elbows to move her way through rivers of people, I realize I have no idea what she thinks of all this. I've known her for years now, first as her mentor and later as her colleague and friend, but we have hardly ever talked about Liliana, much less about the circumstances of her death. We have examined, in utmost detail, books we've shared, films old and new, the maneuverings of politicians and scam artists. We've burst into laughter at the unlikeliest of hours, making fun of dubious men or unflinching women, going as far as imitating their movements and voices while sipping coffee or gulping glasses of wine. We've giggled together. Has she been able to glean through my half-formed sentences, the way I have tried so many times to articulate the words, weave the scenes, lace the characters and their intentions, just to give up at the last minute? Does she know, or else, does she imagine? The gap between us grows larger at times, so much so that I am afraid I'll lose sight of her at any moment. Is she here, leading the way, because of solidarity or out of pity? Are you here because you know, Sorais, or because you want to know? I am not so sure I'd make it through the rest of the day left to my own devices, bereft on the street, facing the past, which is always about to happen. It is right then and there that she turns, looking for me among the crowd. That big smile of hers, open as a cloud. Are you coming? she says. It is not a matter of knowledge, either producing or sharing it, I have to admit; it is this hand that, suddenly, abiding by its very own will, motions forward and upward attempting to reach yours. Ecstatic. Under the reddish reflection of the traffic light, people talk about summer. The one that already was, the one to come. Other words are lost between the hunger and midday miasma. Sometimes everything in life, even the body, seems real.

[gastric juices]

Can you enjoy life while you are in pain? The question, which is not new, arises over and over again during that eternity that is mourning. Much is said about guilt, but little about shame. Guilt may usher in a healthy suspicion, even a rational hesitation, about pleasure, joy, company. Shame, on the other hand, is a door firmly locked. Few activities require as much energy, as much attention to detail, as self-hate. Millimetric. Exhausting. All-consuming. Right after Liliana's death, when years were piling on top of each other and it was impossible to even pronounce her name, it became increasingly important to abandon any pursuit that could interrupt the ceaseless dance of shame and pain. This recurring ceremony. A choreography we learned by heart. Something almost religious. It is never a conscious decision, but it is brutal. Now, as we go into the restaurant, when we are at the table and the food arrives, that old reprimand resurfaces. Do you have the right to taste this fresh cheese, this pumpkin flower, this tree chili sauce? Can you really afford the pleasure of this dry noodle, this roasted octopus, this very cold mineral water? Do you deserve the trust of this friend across the table, so willing to follow you blindly in this journey? Food, as usual, fills the mouth and gets stuck in the throat, but unlike twenty-nine years ago, I have now learned to chew each bite thoroughly and, between words, have managed to discipline the maxilla, the pharynx, the esophagus. I now know how to wait for gastric juices to degrade food little by little, conscientiously, until the chyme is formed. I even burp, albeit demurely. This is eating. This is making the decision to keep looking for you.

[place of anthills]

There is no way to get to Azcapotzalco on foot. Instead of taking public transportation, we request an Uber. We want to be on time. We want to be there, at Agency 22, Azcapotzalco Territory 1, before six in the evening when everyone is expected to be back from lunch. On our drive, the city looks grayer. Perhaps it is the natural change of light as the day prepares for sunset, or perhaps it is the pollution that weighs on the sky or the reflection of the construction sites as we move away from the historical downtown district. Maybe it's just sorrow. It has been a while since I last saw the buildings surrounding the Plaza de las Tres Culturas in Tlatelolco, where a student massacre took place in 1968. As French youth protested the ravages of capitalism, imperialism, and consumerism on the streets of Paris, Mexican students organized by the thousands to fight against an increasingly authoritarian regime, but they lost. Their words and passion versus the bayonets of the state. Their outrage. Their hope. Azcapotzalco comes next, one of the sixteen municipalities of Mexico City, "a place of anthills," in Nahuatl. According to legend, after the creation of the Fifth Sun, Quetzalcóatl's mission was to remake the human species. To do so, he had to enter Mictlán, the realm of the dead, and recover, one by one, the bones of the men and women who had perished. Small and disciplined, marching forth as an army, the ants not only guided Quetzalcóatl to Mictlán and, once there, helped him load the bones of the dead, but they also brought back the grains of corn without which life, new life, would have been impossible.

Just like the past, fear comes in blurry images. Memory is an old photograph muddled by recurring, millimetric friction against many others in a long-forgotten pile. The entire composition descends in one piece: the ants, which once crossed the border between life and death, slip through the skin now, linking the outside and the inside, history and event, myth and injury. A puncture. A crack. As we get physically closer to the dossier that contains the police reports of my sister's death, the ants climb the inner face of the body's organs and, laboring against tissues and mucous membranes, advance steadily until they reach the most intimate crevices, the rifts. Collectors on the surface, predators under the ground. The ants have already colonized every corner of the planet and yet, clearly unsatisfied, they now travel through the lymphatic system, the large intestine, the very fine network of veins and arteries, the hidden side of the tongue. I have to shake them off on the back seat, where I sit paralyzed by fear. I have to force myself to stretch my fingers or jiggle my foot. I have to close my eyes. And then, I must open them up again. A blink. There are 130 million years of history on the backs of these ants but everything happens in a blink. Time contracts. Time decomposes itself. Some 130 million years ago a wasp became an ant and, thanks to the expansion of flowering plants, the ants survived. Time elongates itself. Some eighty million years ago an ant was trapped within amber and the fossil of *Sphecomyrma freyi* came into view. Time thins out. In 1966, a team of scientists led by E. O. Wilson identified the scraps under the controlled light of a laboratory. *Hymenopterans, mimetics, symphites,* the words amble away and cross the border of Mictlán. Here they go, one after another, words and ants, carrying the bones of the dead on the protective shells of their exoskeletons.

Perhaps we are entering Mictlán, or perhaps we are leaving Mictlán. How do we know for sure, Sorais?

While the Tepanec people dominated the fertile Valley of Mexico, and until they were defeated by the fearsome Triple Alliance of the Aztecs in 1428, Azcapotzalco was a site of true power. It is hard to believe that this public prosecutor's agency full of poorly dressed officers and bony bureaucrats, this building eaten away by neglect and budget cuts from which agents leave in a hurry to examine crime scenes and identify corpses, or where, stricken, the families of the deceased arrive looking for information, was once the command center of an empire.

[oh jeez]

We stop in front of a policewoman who guards the entrance, and she directs us to the counter where yet another woman must tell us where to go. When I let her read the document that has brought us to Azcapotzalco, she shakes her head, thoughtfully. Are you Liliana? she asks me. I am taken aback but cannot stop considering the question in all its seriousness. Am I? Could I ever be? I gaze at her, pensive. No, she is her sister, Sorais says. The policewoman apologizes. She reads again. Oh jeez, she says. And there it is, that look; I still can't figure out if it is pure compassion or a performance of it, learned in some customer service manual. We need to see Prosecutor Martha Patricia Zaragoza Villarruel, but Prosecutor Martha Patricia Zaragoza Villarruel has not arrived yet. I am about to faint or cry. We have come from the other end of the city, we say. I have waited twenty-nine years for this. But her secretary is here, she interrupts, sparing us the frustration. The tears. She can help you. We go upstairs where two men are laying new mosaics on the concrete floor. There are rows of old plastic seats against the walls, and some metal desks painted in yellow and brown tones. If I did not know that this was a government office in full swing, it would be easy to mistake it for a makeshift refuge in a war zone. So many things happen in thirty years. Death happens. Death never ceases to happen. A woman with perfectly delineated green eyes greets us at the entrance of a narrow corridor that leads to an office we cannot make out. When she enters the folio number into the system, a new document pops up. It is not here, she informs us matter-of-factly. The case was handled by Agency 40, Azcapotzalco Territory 3.

[Azcapotzalco Territory]

Lic. Arlette Irazábal San Miguel
Public Prosecutor's Office Supervising Agent
Agency in Charge at AZ-3
PRESENT

Based on the provisions of articles 21 of the Political Constitution of the United Mexican States; 59 and 60 of the Regulation of the Organic Law of the Attorney General of Mexico City and 27 sections III and IV of Agreement A /003/99 issued by the holder of this Institution, Shift 300/1827/2019, signed by Mtro. Joel Mendoza Ornelas, Agent of the Public Prosecutor's Office in the Decentralized Preliminary Investigations Sub-Prosecutor's Office, as well as folio 0029882, signed by Lic. Rigoberto Ávila Ordóñez, Private Secretary of the Attorney

General's Office, through which he remits, promotion signed by the C Cristina Rivera Garza, by means of which she requests a complete copy of preliminary investigation number 40/913 / 990-07.

Therefore, I instruct you to agree on what is in accordance with the law and to duly notify the promoter.

Without another particular for the moment receive a cordial greeting.

Sincerely
The District Attorney.

[Are they real?]

We have to go farther north. Irazábal's office is located on Avenida de las Culturas and Eje 5 Norte. This is the area where the 170 buildings of the El Rosario Housing Complex are located. You can't miss it, the secretary says, writing down the complete address on a wrinkled piece of paper. Can you give me a copy of the document? I ask her. I expect her to roll her eyes, annoyed, but instead she gets up from her desk. Give me a moment, I'll be right back with it, she says. I want to have all the documents from this day. All the documents of all the days that await me in the future. A hoarder of bad news. The windows on the second floor open out to a park of stunted trees and broken benches. There, among those ruins, she emerges for the first time during this journey. An apparition. Her hair. A flight of doves hovering above her long stride. That attitude of heading into eternity. I'm about to say her name. I am about to say: Liliana. And to smile.

But we have to continue.

Outside, the gray of the cinder block walls, smeared with cement, spreads up to the sky. There are no ecological reserves in the 2,723 blocks that make up the neighborhood. There are no wild indigenous species in the fifty-four parks of Azcapotzalco, only willow trees and transplanted pines. The only body of water that runs through this area of the city, the Los Remedios River, carries industrial waste or garbage. The corpses of so many women have sunk there, only to reemerge later downriver, silently floating around old factories and urban wastelands. The few green areas include Parque Tezozómoc, Parque Alameda Norte, next to the Ferrería metro station, Plaza Hidalgo, and the campus of the Universidad Autónoma Metropolitana (UAM), which opened in 1974. This is Liliana's territory. This was all touched by her eyes. The birds that greet us as soon as we arrive at Agency 40 are her birds. Where do they come from amid all this desolation? From which faraway unknown site have they been transplanted? How do they survive?

Are they real?

[records don't live forever]

A man hunched over his keyboard informs us, without raising his eyes, that Ms. Arlette is not there but that she is expected back. Maybe at 7:30 tonight. Maybe later. Maybe eventually. She is in a meeting at a high school nearby. Do we wait? I ask Sorais with my hopes high. Sure, she says. In the waiting room, a few rows of orange plastic seats. Promotional posters. Desks with Formica tops. This is Agency 40. Will you come out with me to have a puff? Sorais asks. I haven't done that for years. How do you feel? she asks as we flex our legs and sit on the curb. Aging adolescents. Women not bound by notions of decorum.

The smoke mingles with the light of the evening, which is slowly decaying. A woman appears out of the blue and, after climbing the curb, walks behind us to throw something away in a large trash can. Be careful, she says. You might get a bug on you sitting there. What kind of bug? I ask. An earwig, for example. I have no idea what earwigs do, but instinctively I run my right hand behind my back and tuck my blouse tight. Then, suddenly, as if she teleported herself, she's next to two policemen who stand by the parking entrance to Agency 40. The woman lights her cigarette and, like Sorais, turns her face upward, toward the unsheathed sky, pressing her lips and expelling smoke. Carbon monoxide. Ozone. Sulfur dioxide. Farther back stand the factories whose numerous incandescent lights have just been turned on. The last shift. And, above it all, that messy and blurred thing that is the night sky. Here, under the foliage of the tree and the song of invisible birds, we are protected. Here we can speak of love. Here, in the territory that surrounds the agency, my sister passed away.

I stand corrected: She was killed here.

According to the arrest warrant, he killed her here.

On the morning of July 16, 1990, two or three policemen left this agency for Calle Mimosas 658, in the Pasteros neighborhood. An emergency call. A community in suspense. Tomás Rojas Madrid, the journalist who covered the case, might have opened this very door on his way to work. The forensic reports and photographs and the witness statements arrived here first. Here, at some point, preliminary inquiry 40/913 / 990-07 passed from hand to hand. Here, enough documents were gathered for a judge to issue the arrest warrant against Ángel González Ramos, who ran away and was never caught. Who remains at large.

Maybe I was here twenty-nine years ago.

One of Ms. Irazábal's assistants walks by and, taking pity on us, tells us to join her inside, at her desk. The lawyer, her boss, does not have the dossier we are looking for, she explains with infinite patience. The lawyer, her boss, is the head of the Cold Case Unit. If they sent you here it is because someone believes that there's a chance that a dossier from that long ago could have been kept here. A chance, I hear. Look at this, she continues, pointing at her computer screen, didactic and desperate at the same time. She enters a password and then the number of the case file. The system no longer recognizes it, see? We see. When I arrived here, she explains, about eleven years ago, they changed the entire operational system. And I'm sure it had been changed before then too. But some files have to be preserved, don't they? I ask, believing that all documents will eventually find a place in the dead archives of the state. Some go to the Concentration Archive, she agrees, nodding intently, but, even there, there is a time limit. They cannot stay there forever. She looks into my eyes. Do not believe for a minute that records live forever. I don't blink even as I stop breathing. I barely move as an army of ants creeps up inside my limbs, leaving a burning trail in their wake. My body begins to freeze over as it dawns on me that, without this file, the institutional trace of my sister's life will be lost forever. Without this file I am after, her experience on earth will be as good as nothing. Her memory, erased. In the future, I tell myself as I try to escape this moment, I will say that this is when I realized that I must write, I must replace this file I may never find. There is no other option. In the future I will say, this is the split second in which I understood how writing defies the state.

Wait for the lawyer if you want her to explain it to you, the assistant says, exhausted.

[a rapist in your path]

Femicide was not officially recognized in Mexico until June 14, 2012, when the federal penal code incorporated it as a crime: "Article 325: The crime of femicide is committed by someone who deprives a woman of her life because of her gender." Before that date, femicides were called crimes of passion. The victims were loose women, wayward girls, women without fear of God. They were called, why does she have to dress like this? They were called, women have to respect themselves first. She must have done something to end up in this mess. It was her parents' fault. She made a poor decision. They were called, she deserved it. The lack of language is overwhelming. The lack of language handcuffs us, suffocates us, strangles us, shoots us, skins us, cuts us off, condemns us. When the feminist group Las Tesis performed "A Rapist in Your Path" on the International Day for the Elimination of Violence against Women in 2019, in the center of Santiago, Chile, the piece resonated with so many around the world. *And it was not my fault / or where I was / or how I dressed*. Such pure, devastating words. It was a language already in use, a language that various groups of activists, and various groups of survivors had put to work in courts and in squares, in bustling marches and around dining room tables, but it had rarely reverberated like it did this winter of 2019. So forceful. Sharp as a knife. Overwhelmingly true. *Patriarchy is a judge / who judges us for being born / and our punishment / is the violence you already see*.

Do you know that the first time I called the district attorney's office to request an audience, they asked me what I was looking for? Sorais smokes with unwavering dedication. There is certain sensuality to the way she holds the cigarette between her fingers, and then in the way she brings it closer to her face and places it with such delicacy between her lips. Taken aback, suddenly frozen, I did not know how to answer, you know? I stammered. I hesitated. I am looking for her file, I said. The smoke in the air. The scent of something very old between our bodies. Just that? The voice on the other side of the phone insisted, puzzled. *It is femicide. / Impunity for my killer. / It is the disappearance. / It is rape.* Right then and there I realized, in the course of that phone call, how little I was asking for. How little that was: a file. No, I said, speaking hurriedly now as I was afraid he'd hang up on me. No. I'm looking for something else. *The rapist is you.* The figures formed by tobacco smoke rise and, little by little, dissolve into the air. I want to find the murderer and I want him to pay for his crime. I fell silent again. I swallowed hard. I seek justice, I finally said. And I repeated it again, echoing so many other voices. I repeat it once more, more firmly this time, with absolute clarity. *The oppressing state is a male rapist.* I seek justice. *And it wasn't her fault / or where she was / or how she dressed.* I seek justice for my sister. *The rapist is you.*

Sometimes it takes twenty-nine years to say it out loud, to say it out loud in a phone call with a lawyer at the General Attorney's Office: I seek justice. Sometimes it takes an eternity to return to Azcapotzalco and sit under the sheltering foliage of a tree as you listen, trembling with fear, full of disbelief, to the improbable song of some birds.

[umbilical cord]

It's already completely dark when we decide it's time to go home. Empty-handed. There is hardly anyone in Agency 40, Azcapotzalco Territory 3, now, but the police guarding the entrance accompany us to the sidewalk to wait for the Uber we requested. It's pure caution, he tells us when we turn to look at him with some suspicion. You should not wait here alone. Alone? We look at each other, exchanging knowing glances, but we are so tired that we let

the comment go unheeded. The driver, this time, is a woman. It's going to take a while, she announces, as she looks at the map on her phone. Traffic is hell at this hour. And you're going to the other end of the city, she says, either annoyed or regretful. It seems that traffic is always like this, I say, glancing at the swarm of taillights in front of us. Yes, she agrees, correcting herself, taking a deep breath. Traffic is always a devilish thing. Cars crawl along, drivers using the brake and accelerator almost simultaneously. Although the traffic lights work, green and amber and red in the middle of the sky, the intersections turn into instant traffic jams. The sound of a horn. Two. Many more. The driver, distressed and dejected, suddenly places her forehead on the steering wheel. She cannot bear this any longer. It has been such a difficult day.

Here you go, says Sorais. And she hands her a piece of candy. Don't worry. We will get out of all this soon. Thank you. I'm not usually like this. I usually put up with a lot, she says in a shattered voice. But today. Sorais and I glimpse at each other, faint smiles on our faces. She takes advantage of another driver's distraction to join the only lane that is moving forward. The brake. The accelerator. The raindrops that fall on the windshield are totally out of place in October, but they spread wide and foreign as if it were summer. The brake.

Files also die, I mumble, defeated.

As everything stands still, suspended in this knot of rain and stalled cars and cracked pavement, I try to locate the sky. Anger is a lot like resignation. Impotence very much like fright. This is just the beginning, Sorais says, sitting on the edge of her seat and placing her right arm around the front seatback. She wants to see me face-to-face. She wants to confront me. We reached the land of the anthills. Now we have to dig, like underground predators. The driver takes increasingly narrow roads to escape the traffic, but she has less and less of a clue where she is or how she can avoid the traffic jams that appear on her new route. Desolate, motionless, her eyes in the rearview mirror tell us all we need to know about despair. Files may die, Sorais says. But they all leave a lingering trace. They have to. There is no other way around. You're a historian; you know better. She nods as she speaks, her cheekbones slightly blushed with fervor. Her conviction moves me. Even if it is not true, even if files, just like people, are forcibly disappeared, with nothing to be found in their wake, her conviction shakes me to the core, and I suddenly know what is next. I know I have to hire a lawyer to help me track down the dossier. And while the lawyer carries out the process, guiding my requests for documents and records through the intricate legal system, fielding their explanations for why these records are missing, I have to rebuild the archive. While gazing out of the car windows, trying to locate the sky above Mexico City, it dawns on me that I have to produce the documents, the reports, the testimonies, the interviews, the evidence that the state could not, replacing the institutional archive with our archive, our own repository of touch and breath, voice, proximity, affect. I have to bring into being not only memory, but the bearers of memory itself. I glance at Sorais, suddenly ready for what's to come. If that dossier slips away, I say aloud for the first time, there will be no official trace of Liliana's life on earth. If that dossier disappears, the possibility of locating and arresting the murderer, bringing him to justice, will also disappear. Forever. There must be a trial. There must be a sentence.

She looks at me, unflinching.

There must be justice.

Take care, says the driver when we reach our destination. You too, we tell her. Here we are, motionless, with our hands in our pockets. Tousled hair. Withered skin. We have gone through the

city like soldiers through a battlefield. We have traveled through
time. We have lost everything, and we have been saved. All at
once. Although we are not hungry, we also have no desire to say
goodbye just yet. Without a word, we start walking beneath the
trees, looking for a restaurant. We don't have a reservation, so we
accept the first available table at the first place that will take us.
And the table turns out to be in the back, very close to the path
that leads hasty and anxious waiters to the kitchen. It's going to
take a while, Sorais says, repeating the phrase with which the
Azcapotzalco driver greeted us. Before ordering some appetizers
and glasses of sparkling water, I see him. You won't believe this, I
immediately tell Sorais who, facing me, cannot look at the entrance. Don't turn around. I bow my head and look down, but I
still watch the man in the blue suit and shiny tie approach our
table. Who? she insists, full of curiosity. When he sees me, when
he recognizes me, he quickly turns around and collides with the
woman holding his hand. She does not understand what's happening and, instead of retracing her steps, she continues heading
toward the available chairs at our table. He, now with his back to
me, jerks her by the elbow toward the exit. Remember when we
were talking about the professor accused of sexual harassment
who is no longer allowed to set foot on the Iberoamericana campus? Sorais opens her eyes. Really? She bursts into laughter. I
can't believe it, she says. If you turn to your left, you will see him.
He and his companion were given a table next to the entrance
door. Sorais finally turns her head and—after catching a glimpse
of them, after verifying that they are here, the professor accused
of harassment sitting next to a young girl at a fashionable restaurant, after confirming that nothing has happened to him, that
nothing ever happens to men accused of gender violence, men
accused of macro- and microaggression, of unimaginable brutality

against the bodies of girls and young women and the elderly, can go on with their lives as if nothing has ever happened—she returns her head to its original position. I really need a smoke, she says. If I didn't see it, I would think it was just my imagination. Or a sick joke. Or a mediocre lie. But you're looking at it, I tell her. I'm looking at it, she nods. We don't have to agree again, we don't have to say a word, but we raise the glasses of mineral water at the same time. We are going to topple it, we say, echoing so many women's voices. Patriarchy will not fall on its own; we have to tear it down. Together, we say.

And our glasses clink.

[October 4]

We are in the afterward, which is long. A day after visiting the Mexico City Attorney General's Office to try to get copies of preliminary investigation 40/913 / 990-07, I go to the cemetery with my parents. It is October 4. By now, Liliana has spent many more years underground, her bones cloaked by the fertile soil of a volcano, than on the surface of the earth. It would have been her fifty-first birthday. It is her fifty-first birthday. Libra with an ascendant in Capricorn. A rooster, in the Chinese zodiac. Here are the three of us, still invited to the feast of her life and her memory. We bring a hoe with us to weed out her grave and a couple of buckets to carry water. The tombstone is small and rectangular in shape, her name and the dates of her birth and death engraved in golden letters. No epigraph. No decorations. We have not forgotten to bring flowers, buying them as we have for twenty-nine years, from the same vendor. Out there, beyond the boundaries of the cemetery, we might pass for normal people. On the other side of the rusted iron gate, we walk and eat, greet friends, celebrate triumphs, offer condolences, attend classes or parties. Lives unfolded out there, apparently unscathed: careers, books, trips, birthdays, children. But in here, softly brushed by this wind that first rips the peaks of the volcano and later touches, meditatively, the interior of our lungs with its cold wings, here we are pure sorrow. It is a lie that time passes. Time is stuck. There is an inert body here, stuck between the hinges and bolts of time, suspending its rhythm and sequence. We have not grown. We will never grow. Our wrinkles are artificial, contrived indications of the lives that we could have lived but that have gone astray. The cavities, the fragile bones, the gray hair, the numb joints: mere impersonations that hide the repetition, the redundancy, the refrain. We are locked in a bubble of guilt and shame, asking ourselves over and over again: what did we not see? This is the echo. Sunlight is always spectacular in the fall. Why couldn't we protect her? The whisper of the wind through the oyamels. The clarity of the pines.

My father does not relinquish the hoe and, even though he is eighty-four years old, he removes the weeds all by himself, bending down to pluck the most stubborn grass or to undo the clods with his own rough hands when nothing else succeeds. He is soon out of breath. He sweats copiously. And, while he toils over her grave, shedding some discreet tears in silence, I wonder how many times a day he remembers Liliana, how many times he recalls the amount of money that officer from the Attorney General's Office demanded from him, some thirty years ago, to continue the investigation of Liliana's femicide. The required bribe. How many times a day does he blame himself for not having enough funds back then? How often the profane words, the crude words, the open-jawed beasts of words with which the police commanders and agents referred to Liliana's body, to Liliana's life, to Liliana's death, resonate in his ears? How many times a day does he murmur the word *justice*? You are never more defenseless than when you are rendered speechless. Who, in that summer of 1990, could have said, with their head held high, with the strength conferred by the conviction of being right and truthful, *It was not her fault, nor did it matter where she was or how she dressed*? Who, in a world where the word *femicide* did not exist, the term *intimate terrorism* did not exist, could have said what I now say without the slightest doubt: the only difference between my sister and me is that I never came across a murderer?

The only difference between you and her.

In a world such as this, staying silent was a way of tucking yourself in, Liliana. A clumsy and egregious way to protect you. We lowered our voices and secluded ourselves, with you inside, so as not to expose you to slander, ghastly curiosity, the ambivalent looks of compassion. We lowered our voices and walked with foggy footsteps, shrinking our presence as we passed, trying to vanish or to become the ghosts we already were. How do you avoid the attacks, the scathing, the sideways glances of those predisposed to blaming? How do you explain, even to the well-intentioned, what would have been obvious, in plain sight, had we lived in a more just world? We were trying to dodge the harassment, the condemnation against you, and against us, who were by your side, holding our hands together. We were so utterly lonesome, Liliana. We had never felt so orphaned, so adrift, so far from humanity. We were alone, more isolated than ever in a city that came upon us with the powerful jaws of machismo: if you hadn't let her go to Mexico City, if she had stayed at home, if you hadn't given her so much freedom, if you had taught her how to distinguish between a good man and a bad one. We did not know what to do. Faced with the unimaginable, we did not know what to do. Faced with the inconceivable, we did not know what to do. So we shut up. And we shrouded you in our silence, resigned to impunity, to corruption, to the lack of justice. Alone and defeated. In pieces. As dead as you, we were. As airless as you are. And while this unfolded, as we crawled under the shadows of the passing days, dead women multiplied in our midst. The blood of so many rained all over Mexico as a misnamed war, the so-called War on Drugs, devastated entire villages and cities, clearing the path for further plundering and pillaging, for more death. We lost count of them, didn't we? More and more women, young and old, from working-class backgrounds and from reputable neighborhoods, fell under the blow of violence. Their bodies a mere extension of the lethal math of the state. The dreams and cells of so many, their laughter, their teeth: it all went away. And the murderers continued to flee, fugitives from laws that did not exist and from prisons that were for everyone except them, they who had always enjoyed the benefit of the doubt, the anticipated apology, and the support of those who blame the victim without so much as a flinch and, even now, after so many years, still question the girl's decision, the girl's lack of judgment, the girl's tremendous mistake. But the day finally arrived and, together with others, thanks to the strength of others, we were able to conceive, even fathom, that we too deserve justice. That you deserved justice. That you, among all too many, ought to have justice. That we could fight, aloud and with others, to bring you here, to the language of justice.

We cleaned her grave a few weeks ago and look at it, all overgrown again, my father says. Nothing is what it used to be, he insists, but he does not give up. He tires, it is true; he is short of breath, indeed; but he does not give up. My mother, who sits on the right-hand side of the grave while absentmindedly brushing the grass, only manages to sigh from time to time. She looks up at the sky and she sighs. Occasionally, as if they were pieces of conversations that occur somewhere else, or from another time, some words manage to escape the silence that surrounds us. *Look. Water. Summit. Dwelling. Destiny. Happiness.* I have never known what we say to Liliana during these visits. But I am sure that we, each of us in our own way, talk to her. I'm sure she answers back. For the first time I am not ashamed to be here by your side. For the first time in these many years I know I can pronounce your name without falling to the ground, knees thudding. There are others. There are so many other names. An echo and many more. And, there is this: the embrace that always welcomed us inside your body, sister of mine. This is the air of your full name: Liliana Rivera Garza. Yourself.

II

THIS SKY, ANNOYINGLY BLUE

Oh, I'm burning! I wish I were out of doors—
I wish I were a girl again, half savage and hardy,
and free; and laughing at injuries, not maddening
under them!

—EMILY BRONTË, *Wuthering Heights*

[writing and secrecy]

Childhood ends with a kiss. The dream is not hundreds of years old and the fleshy mouth does not belong to prince charming, but that pure expectation that is childhood finally comes to an end with a kiss. Lips on lips. Teeth. Saliva. Shortness of breath. Eyes open. Childhood ends with the inauguration of secrecy. *I will never forget January 22, 1982. It was just a fantastic day. Nor April 28. Not May 20. My first kiss on November 31, 1982, between 2:30 and 3:00 P.M.* Liliana had written extensively before this kiss. She had penned innumerable sentences on small graph paper for her eyes only, sent a good number of long letters written on sheets torn from her notebooks, delivered birthday cards and Christmas cards and Valentine cards filled with doodles and drawings, thoughtful messages, which she signed with an elaborate rendition of her name. She had inscribed, surreptitiously, entire lines in her classmates' notebooks, which they would find only hours later or days later, a burst of laughter as they tried to pinpoint when or where she had done it, what was the window of opportunity she had taken advantage of, how she had managed to evade detection. Winding letter-size sheets of paper around the cylinder of the Lettera 33, the mechanical typewriter we shared, she had also typed lengthy descriptions of the ever-so-slow days brimming with nothing but mirrors, silence, repetition. Liliana committed words to paper to express her feelings and points of view as much as to connect with others. She knew well, albeit instinctively, that writing was a distance-demolishing technology. She craved closeness, camaraderie, trust. Now, the secrecy surrounding the first kiss confirmed that writing could, in addition, offer her some control over experiences that were to remain all her own. Writing was a refuge or a spacecraft, it did not matter which, as long as it could take her deep into herself. And writing did. It delivered. From now on, Liliana wrote as much about daily life as, increasingly, about things she could not, or preferred not to, enunciate aloud, matters that she could have talked about but chose to keep to herself, and that silent activity quickly became her main occupation. She practiced it every day.

Liliana made sure she never forgot that glorious November 31, 1982. The name of the boy or the location of the event, on the other hand, remained unclear. But the fact alone mattered. The event in and of itself mattered: the skin had reached its own limit and, exhilarated and curious, moving ahead without looking back, it had leaped out. *My first kiss.* This is your hand, Liliana, slowly waving to bid farewell to what is behind you: the eruption of the Chichonal volcano, a new devaluation of the peso, the local release of *E.T.*, the worldwide success of *Thriller*. At this point, Liliana is now trekking forward, but she is, at the same time, glancing back at her life, and taking it with her into the future, for every single note, even the smallest piece of paper, ends up in her cardboard box. Abiding by a logic all her own, Liliana hoards her writing, and she does it methodically and voraciously. The torn piece of a paper napkin that bore a verse. A creased note, folded a thousand times, where her friends jotted their own version of an exquisite corpse. The letters and the drafts of the letters, all revised and corrected. The bus tickets and the movie tickets, inscribed. Liliana is stepping out of her childhood and, simultaneously, inaugurating her archive. She is unforgetting as she skips lightly, confidently, down the path. She wrote before, but after that kiss, writing would become the record that, by being external to her, by laying itself voluntarily or involuntarily before the eyes of others, gave shape to secrecy. Its material being.

Adolescence is the very name of the archive.

[cardboard boxes]

They were always there, bulky and lined up next to each other, on the top shelf of the closet. Seven cardboard boxes and about three or four wooden crates painted in lavender. Liliana's possessions. We picked them up from her small apartment in Azcapotzalco just a few days after the funeral. What do you do with the possessions of the dead? How do you account for the touch they preserve, their smell, the infinitesimal particles that cling to fabric or chipped wood? Once in Toluca, at my parents' house, we organized her books and notebooks, blueprints, posters, dolls, clothes, shoes, and placed them in boxes that were carefully labeled in capital letters. As if we were going to forget. As if there was the slightest possibility of mistaking them for something else. Then, trying to give an external order to the chaos that churned inside us all, we carried them one by one to a closet shelf that had once accommodated empty suitcases or winter quilts. The boxes stood there, unblinking. They stared at us when we were looking for an old coat or a pair of shoes we had not worn in years. Their gaze brushed the backs of our necks, sliding down our spines, vertebra by vertebra. When my parents moved out of the home they had once shared with her, the boxes found a place on the top shelf of a closet in a new house that, just a couple of kilometers farther west, promised if not a new start, at least a change of scenery. A truce. No one had opened the boxes for thirty years. For thirty years they had remained there, in sight, but not within reach.

And now, after so long, you finally feel ready to face not just the tragedy, but the knowledge of the tragedy. What unleashes the sensation? How can you be sure that this is the right time to ask questions and, above all, that you are finally ready to hear the answers? I do not know. What I do know is that once I filed that first petition at the Attorney General's Office, I could no longer stop. Sleepless nights and sudden tearful outbursts multiplied through the fall. But *crying* is such a subdued word, a mere decoy. Something intelligible. What was happening there, in that house surrounded by oaks and magnolias, their branches looking in through the windows, took place elsewhere altogether. I was at home in Houston, but I walked, simultaneously, on the outskirts of time. Grieving, which over the years had become a solitary ceremony I attended in silence, with a poise learned in the rigorous school of defeat and shame, forced its way outward, howling and wailing. The presence of the wind. The might of a thousand ghosts. Every time I felt the pressure spreading through my chest and something akin to a moan peeked out from between the vocal cords, I removed myself from the present and opened the door to her room again. Hand on knob. Speckles of dust floating within a slant of light. Her books. The posters she saw every morning when she was a child. What is to become of me, she wondered in one of the letters she once wrote. The notebooks. Her pencils and brushes. The skirts she wore, the swimsuits. And the question, piercing the past and rupturing the present: Who am I now? I had a sister and then, all of a sudden, I had none. We were two and then, swiftly, there was only one of us. What kind of orphan are you when rendered sisterless? I was in Houston, but I dwelled somewhere else, a place unintelligible even to myself.

A couple of days after Liliana's funeral, when relatives and friends had already vanished into their daily routines, away from us, I cried alone at home, in her room, in a way I imagine animals or rocks do. A high-pitched scream, paradoxically quiet. A shrilling sound slipping through the furniture, leaving a clean path in the floor dust as it tried to find, desperately perhaps, its way out. A roar from outer space or from within my own depths. Whatever it was, it took over the room, then the house, and then the overcast sky. No one heard it, yet it ripped the air in two. It rained those days. Abundantly. The sound came from an unknown world and communicated, similarly, with worlds yet to be born. There it was, the slow, squeaking friction between dissimilar materials. Something with battered edges and a stench. Something shapeless. You have to hold your abdomen and curl into a fetal position on the floor. You have to hide your face. You have to beg. Above all, you must beg.

Time stands still.

Here it was, all of it, intact. A wave, unsurmountable. The past as never the past.

And, much like thirty years ago, suddenly there were nights in Houston when I was awakened by the certainty that this time, yet again, I would not be able to. The certainty that pain and shame and guilt would keep the door of truth tightly shut.

If asked, I'd have to say I don't know. One day, you wake up and the world as it is, as it appears in front of your eyes, has become suddenly untenable. Or one night, still sweating and out of breath after a nightmare, you realize there is no way you can go on. There is a door, the door of no return, and one day you know you have to place your hand on the knob, slightly twist it to the right, and open it. And walk through it. You know it for sure; your bones know it, the tips of your hair know it, your chewed fingernails. I sifted through the few notes I had from that time and began asking questions among the members of my family who lived nearby. I visited aunts, I attended quinceañeras that I had so far managed to avoid; I made phone calls. Cousins my age, who had been close to Liliana, answered in monosyllables; younger relatives chattered away, to no end. They would all look down at some point, embarrassed. Sorry, they said. I don't remember anything else. Some shed tears. I soon realized, it was so clear, that we knew very little. A naïve girl, prey to the daily abuse of a manipulator. A woman perhaps too free. A disciplined swimmer. A confused young woman ready to try everything. A good and docile youngster, exceptionally blind to danger. A customary liar. An outstanding student. An all too innocent teenager. A friend for life. A woman full of love. A sloppy kid. Someone with a past. The pictures painted by these stories, and even by my own memory, multiplied exponentially, contradicting each other without so much as a blush. The outcome, however, was the same: thirty years of silence. The fear of falling to pieces or the fear of not being able to endure the pain or the fear of dying out of grief or the fear of shame, unleashed shame, shame in all colors and textures, shame in the form of guilt and vice versa, had turned us all into accomplices. We were all there, exchanging glances as statues in a forsaken museum, while the cardboard boxes looked at us from afar. Unblinking. Will I be able to open them up this time and face the presentness of all objects, their very hearts?

[telling it like it is]

What distinguishes domestic violence, especially intimate partner homicide, from any other type of crime is love, says Rachel Louise Snyder in *No Visible Bruises*. No other act of extreme violence feeds on an ideology that is so universal. Who in their right mind would raise her hand against romantic love? The hundreds of thousands of women murdered by their partners could answer that question easily. Or could they? Just like the rest of us, women in danger need a language capable of identifying risk factors and moments of extreme danger before they can answer this deceptively simple question. Often, this language has been lacking. In a country like Mexico, where, up until recently, even popular music unabashedly praised men who murdered women in fits of jealousy or at the slightest provocation, generating that language has been a heroic struggle whose triumphs, however small, belong to activists determined to question patriarchy's violent everyday operations. Every little victory counts. Take catcalling, for example. For years, the whistling, the hissing, the jeering of men on the streets was generally perceived as an innocent act, an intrinsic feature of public life through which men celebrated women's beauty. It was, in any case, an experience women of all ages had to deal with on a regular basis. It took generations of feminists to denounce these actions as everyday instances of public harassment. Telling it like it is. It takes time and rage and collective effort to forge a new vocabulary, concepts able to render the world anew. Labor harassment. Discrimination. Sexual violence. *The rapist is you.* Removing the veil that hides the violence afflicting and killing hundreds of thousands of women inside and outside their homes has not been easy. It takes a village to create a language precise enough, powerful enough, widespread enough to alert women of the menacing hand, the prescient whiff, of intimate partner violence.

The investigations of Jacquelyn Campbell, a nurse from Michigan who specialized in domestic violence cases, led to the adoption of the first Danger Assessment tool in the United States. Based on her own experience caring for numerous patients, Campbell developed test questions to help assess—and when appropriate, diagnose—the level of danger faced by women who came to emergency rooms with bruises, broken bones, or strangulation marks. Believing that these were incidents that belonged to the private lives of their patients, doctors had previously refrained from asking further questions about how they got hurt, leaving women unprotected. The test developed by Campbell allowed doctors and nurses to treat violence against women as a matter of public health and granted these patients, and women more broadly, a way to identify the severity of their situation.

Campbell drew up a list of twenty-two risk factors for domestic violence, including substance use, possession of firearms, and evidence of extreme jealousy. Death threats, strangulation, or forced sex. Isolation from friends and family, suicide threats by the predator, and stalking were also telltale signs. A whole catalog of abuse. A cartography of violence that we did not see. And that we now see. If Liliana had had access to this medical evaluation in the early summer of 1990, perhaps she would have believed what was for her unbelievable: that a man who claimed to love her dearly, even vehemently, was capable of taking her life. She would have had a way to confirm what she sensed but what required a leap of cognition to admit: that the man she loved, or had loved, was a real threat. Love—this love—was a matter of life and death. In her letters and college notebooks Liliana recorded, almost in passing, instances of extreme jealousy, his suicide threats, and stalking. But, had there been more?

Where homicidal violence is generally understood as a kind of outburst that suddenly overcomes an individual who would otherwise be rational and unaggressive, Campbell argued that "the single biggest risk for domestic homicide . . . is the prior incidence of domestic violence." Few kill their partners on the first try. Statistics around the world corroborate what Campbell told

Snyder in an interview included in *No Visible Bruises:* "Levels of dangerousness operated on a specific timeline. Dangerousness spiked when a victim attempted to leave an abuser, and it stayed very high for three months, then dipped only slightly for the next nine months. After a year, the dangerousness dropped off precipitously."

Could the traces of the growing danger that Liliana faced be there, inside those cardboard boxes so motionless and discreet on the top shelf of the closet? Would everything we were able to see, and especially what we didn't see, be there, numb and crippled, inside a box?

[handwriting]

For graphology lovers, handwritten letters are a privileged passageway into the soul. Hidden aspects of the scribe's personality, desires otherwise concealed, or long-lasting obsessions, may be drawn from the size of the letters, the shakiness or regularity of the lines, the spacing between words, the connection, or lack thereof, of uppercase and lowercase letters, and the lifting of the pen or pencil from paper. Perhaps that is why the manuscripts of famous writers have followers as devoted as they are addicted: as if readers of private letters or diaries could stumble upon something scandalous or shameful, something unique, that would be undetectable in printed books. The truth is that learning to write by hand, like everything else that takes place in a classroom, is often the result of rigid methods included in a wide range of study programs implemented by teachers with humble salaries. Social gymnastics. We all learned to take the pencil between our thumb and index finger, and to flex our elbows and bend our backs so that, little by little, with different types of pressure, the letters that we scribbled over and over in double-lined notebooks emerged. We all partook of the exercises that Cy Twombly has turned into works of art: a horizontal spiral, poorly traced, on lines of an almost blue, almost red color. Students of my generation were taught to write in cursive, with entire lines of connected words often slanting slightly to the right. My sister's generation moved away from cursive, as many found it hard to read, and learned instead to write in block script: the words she wrote consisted of disjointed letters, each one its own discrete unit. Letters like islands. Sentences as archipelagos. The result in both cases was less a unique or highly idiosyncratic handwriting, the hallmark of the author's unrepeatable personality, and more a penmanship that betrayed the generation as well as the regional or class origins of the scribe.

Liliana's handwriting was always stunning.

Liliana spent hours writing and rewriting letters on sheets torn from notebooks, usually a French-ruled notebook with plastic spiral binding. Sometimes she sent these messages out; and sometimes she hung on to them. Sometimes she did both: mailing the original and keeping a copy in her files. She also wrote notes to herself, often in the third person singular, in which she developed intricate dialogues with a Liliana that was, at the same time, a different person. She used pencils, colored pencils, ballpoint pens. On certain occasions she opted for the brown, almost burgundy, ink of a fountain pen. She also typed some of her letters on sheets of kraft paper that came from the university offices where our mother worked, or on letter-size sheets of paper originally intended to type fair copies that, due to some mistake or typo, were otherwise destined for the trash bin. She wrote in the spur of the moment, with a linguistic courage that did not evade the casual joke or fortuitous rambling. And she wrote during quiet times, when tiredness or boredom led her to scribble the names of friends in alphabetical order or endless to-do lists. She wrote daily and in moments of celebration. She wrote rough drafts that were later tidied up in fair copies. She checked her own writing over and over again, obsessively. She would transcribe entire notes or letters of her own, frequently with minimal revisions, until the wording was to her liking and then, only then, would she let it go. Her relationship to those texts was one of expression—more than once she emphasized her need to relieve herself through this exercise—but also one of critical inquiry: what she wrote, even what was meant solely for her eyes, embodied formal standards that far exceeded the mere task of individual confession, challenging conventional notions of the literary. It was not uncommon for her to question, for example, the accepted order of the letter by jokingly starting her missive with a postscript and proceed backward from there. She also transcribed profusely and incessantly. Poems. Book quotes. Whole paragraphs. Liliana was the true writer of the family, by a long way.

While her handwriting through her middle and high school years was sophisticated and polished, her years as an architecture student sharpened her awareness about materiality in all its forms, writing included. The penmanship she used while in Azcapotzalco, when she was already a university student, conveyed a newfound sense of personal style. Something nontransferable. Inimitable. The regular shape of each letter, and especially the vertical aspiration of her words, came because of an ever more meticulous control over all aspects of writing. Her personal idiosyncrasies emerged from a handwriting that was both elegant and unusual, but also from the way she folded the paper on which she wrote. Her letters were origami bombs that literally exploded in the hands of her readers, thus increasing the shared experience of mystery and complicity, joy and mischievousness. Opening her letters even now, thirty years later, is a careful operation. Once they are liberated from the straitjacket of envelopes or the pressed pages of books or notebooks, it is necessary to approach the paper with great care, letting it hang by one of its corners, allowing it to unfold little by little, at its own pace and will. Eventually, the missive leaves behind the illusion of three-dimensionality and conforms back, grudgingly, to its two-dimensional condition.

For Liliana the writer, nothing was left to chance. The selection of the texture and size of the paper was elaborated upon in the writing itself. So was the choice of colors, both in paper and ink. The size of the letters she formed, the position of the sentences above or below the lines, in the corner or in the center of the page. And let us not forget the strategic incorporation of doodles, drawings, and stickers. A letter from Liliana was an invitation to enter a vast and complex personal world, a bit childish, a bit bizarre. Fun. It was the world of someone increasingly in control of her own materials and, at the same time, it was the world of someone aware that connectedness and engagement were the ultimate, true goals of writing.

Liliana wrote assiduously until the last day of her life. Long, planned letters or scribbled notes in the margins of her lecture notes. Poems transcribed cleanly and carefully, over and over again. Song lyrics. The last time she picked up her purple-ink ballpoint pen was on July 15, 1990, at 10:30 A.M. Eighteen hours later, according to her death certificate, Liliana stopped breathing.

[*Solanum tuberosum*]

In the beginning, there was the potato. It was cotton that lured my grandparents north, all the way to the U.S.–Mexico border, but potatoes propelled my nuclear family into the highlands of central Mexico. My father had become an agronomist engineer at a private university in Monterrey and, after working for a couple of years at a company in Delicias, Chihuahua, he was still looking for a way back to the classroom. So he applied to a graduate program at the Universidad Autónoma Chapingo and, when he was admitted, my mother agreed: we would venture south, leaving all that was familiar—the weather, the food, their friends, the accents—for a chance to improve our lives. He became a geneticist. A plant breeder. And he was offered two jobs once he graduated, one in Ensenada, Baja California, and the other one in Toluca, in the State of Mexico. Ensenada was a long way from Tamaulipas, in northeastern Mexico, where we returned to visit family during the summers and where we used to spend the Christmas holidays, so they didn't give it much thought. A new move. More goodbyes. A new arrangement of objects and routines. We arrived in Toluca, the highest city in the country, in the middle of the rainy season, just in time for the fall semester. Liliana was four years old and was still very, some said overly, attached to my mother. My father signed his first employment contract as a plant-breeding researcher on July 16, 1974, exactly sixteen years before my sister's death.

Potatoes are herbaceous plants from the genus *Solanum* and the *Solanaceae* family. When my father felt like stirring scandal among researchers who visited the facilities of the National Institute for Agricultural Research, he mentioned carelessly, almost in passing, that the true origins of potatoes were to be found in the foothills of the nearby Nevado de Toluca and not in the Andes. The provocation never failed. Encouraged by the lavish meals my mother served and, later, by the alcohol with which they paired the after-dinner conversation, researchers spent a good amount of time debating the absurdity of his comment. It didn't matter if they came from Peru or Saint Petersburg or Wageningen or Munich, if they were men or women, if they spoke Spanish well. Laughter barely concealed their animosity as they provided scientific evidence to contradict my father's claim. They brought up historical data. They made references to field observations. Liliana and I watched them through a crack in the doorway. We made a habit of imitating their intense gesturing and their various accents. We put pencils in our mouths as if we were smoking. We crossed our legs and threw our hands into the air at the same time, mimicking their movements. Their laughter was our laughter. Making fun of others in secret, developing our own pantomime of sarcasm, made us more than sisters: we were accomplices.

We spent many weekends in the muggy greenhouses where my father carried out his studies on late blight, the fungus that, among other misdeeds, had the dubious honor of bringing an end to the potato crops in Ireland, causing the legendary nineteenth-century potato famine, which, in turn, drove more than a million migrants into the United States. We spent countless afternoons testing the thin potato chips that came out of my father's experiments in our own kitchen: taste, sweetness, texture, color, size. Which one did you like the best? We spent innumerable days going up and down the slopes of the volcano, splashing through streams of icy water and losing our breath on steep paths, all to glimpse the white and lilac flowers of wild potatoes, whose genes my father used to produce new species immune to late blight. We ate potatoes. We breathed potatoes. The potato was our god. In the surroundings of the volcano, we spent hours collecting pieces of dry wood or leaves or broken twigs to light a bonfire without having to resort to lighter fluid, as my mother had taught us. We spent days reading the dramatic highland skies: altocumulus, cumulonimbus, cirrostratus.

When we lived in Chapingo, in graduate student housing on the university's campus, we ate local food that was once unimaginable for the border migrants we had been: mushrooms, huitlacoche, pápalo, tlacoyos, blue corn, pulque. To that long list, Toluca added green chorizo, quelites, wild mushrooms, romeritos, marrow soup, tacos de obispo, milk cream Mexican sandwiches. A rigid diet, which prevented us from eating sugar or street food, accentuated the exoticism of all these dishes. Once, one of the laborers at the research facility invited our family to a barbecue on the slopes of the Nevado. Jerónimo had been a Cabañista guerrilla, an armed movement of landless peasants that had threatened the modernizing agenda of the state in the 1970s, before fleeing to Guerrero and settling on the shores of Toluca. For the barbeque, he brought a very young goat delicately wrapped in cheesecloth. He lit the fire with expert hands, stacking his tinder at the center of a ring made of rocks, and set up a wooden frame that allowed the meat to rotate above the flames while his daughters ate the chocolates and marshmallows we had contributed to the feast. The smell took us aback. The image: two families from so far away gathered on the slopes of a sacred mountain around a bonfire. The adults talked in low voices, endlessly. Soothing words, words that attached themselves to the incandescent charcoals only to flee with the slightest gust of wind. Their words hung momentarily from the branches of the oyamels and fluttered up the mountain little by little, until they plunged into the waters of the Laguna del Sol and the Laguna de la Luna in the crater of the volcano. Words floated around, barely disturbing the surface of the water. Words swam, calmly stroking forward. Alternating arms. Words breathed in and out, creating a slow-paced cadence that moved along the millimetric rotation of the earth. This is what a conversation was. The talk faded afterward, like sunlight, little by little, becoming thinner and then vanishing away. It was cold by then, but as we drove back home, in a silence that neither of us dared break, we kept the flavor of the baby goat that an ex-guerrilla roasted on the slopes of a sleeping volcano on the tip of our lips, right on the creases of memory. It was the closest thing we got to a welcome.

There is an old photo of my father as a teenager, on a horse by
the side of a cotton field. His back, erect; the bridle, deftly tangled
in his hands. He is about to smile, but at the last second, he de-
cides not to: more a gesture of caution than of shyness. A strange
conviction, which could well pass for serenity, glimmers through
his fifteen-year-old gaze. Perhaps it is necessary to see that image
to understand the words *far away*, the adverb *outside,* the phrase
I am my own refuge. Liliana and I didn't need to see the photo to
know that we were not from here—and here was everywhere we
happened to be. What we heard over meals, right before going to
school, after we were tucked into our beds at night, was that every
door was an exit. Searching for it was our daily task. If it did not
already exist, we had to carve it out. We came from elsewhere or
from far beyond: that was an instruction. I once slammed the door
after a family row at dinner. My mother waited for my return and,
very calmly, with the kitchen already sparklingly clean, informed
me that this was what other people did when they got angry. We
did not. We descended from people who had overcome everything: poverty, illiteracy, the decline of cotton. Our people, from
whom we descended, had even survived the influenza epidemic
of 1918. We, and she said this very candidly, were alive by pure
chance, and that chance in itself, its very miracle, was our re-
demption. Let others despair. Let others slam doors when they
couldn't utilize their intelligence or their powers of observation or
their patience. Let others waste their time and waste their talents,
because we, who came from so far away, we who were free, we
who would overcome everything, had important things to do. Understood? My mother's voice, intimidating in its calmness, did not
admit any reluctance. Hesitation, even the hint of it, would have
meant betrayal. We were a volatile sovereign republic of four in-
habitants, requiring so little from the outside world. That was our

strength, the secret to our method. It would not have occurred to anyone at the time that someone besides us four could be part of that union.

When we arrived in Toluca, we had already moved through a good portion of the national territory, from the northeast to the center, but little had prepared us for the cold demeanor and stern hierarchy of an industrial city that measured itself mostly in terms of material goods or income. We complained about Toluca for years: the climate, the boredom, its narrow-mindedness, its mediocrity. *Toluca, which means unfortunately.* Although we adored its clouds and never let much time go by without visiting the volcano's crater, we resisted Toluca every day, inch by inch. It was clear that we were just passing through, especially the two daughters. If it weren't for the swimming lessons our parents enrolled us in, there was little that this conservative, overly sedentary city, with strictly delineated places for men and women, could offer these two girls who were clearly going places.

I, who was just shy of ten years old when we arrived, escaped as soon as I could without making friends. I avoided putting down roots at all costs; but Liliana lived her childhood there, as well as her adolescence. Liliana grew up under the shelter of that annoyingly blue sky.

[friends forever]

The girls go to the bathroom together and exchange secrets. A silly giggle in their wake, this restless cloud of fireflies as they tread on, attracting the gaze of others. There they go in their school uniforms or, over the weekend, in the jeans and fitted T-shirts that reveal the slight bulge of their breasts. They still wear white socks and leather shoes with rubber soles. Their long hair, tied with colored ribbons, arranged in stiff ponytails. They don't paint their nails or use eyeliner yet, but soon they will stop running around the school grounds without rhyme or reason. They will be taught propriety. Decency. Femininity. Until then, they observe each other with great care, measuring each other, feeling each other out, betraying each other. There is no criticism harsher than the ones that come from their lips. They love each other too; no, they adore each other. Perhaps there are no more ardent love letters in the world than those exchanged between teenage girls.

A good portion of Liliana's archive consists of letters from her girlfriends. They are not only the most numerous, but also the ones that are written with the greatest care. A letter from a girlfriend was not only a piece of paper studded with words: the medium was as important as the message and, for this reason, each letter came decorated with colored borders, glitter, various stickers—among which Hello Kitty reigned supreme—different inks, letters drafted and redrafted, and even dried flowers or herbs. More than a letter, each was a small sample of postal art.

In a society where landlines were still a luxury item that parents oversaw with stern zeal, phone calls were not safe. Telegrams were absolutely out of the question. But writing letters was simple: they just had to put aside a couple of pages from a notebook, or buy, if necessary, a good sheet of cotton or colored paper with stylized margins and find an envelope. If an envelope was not readily available, it was enough to fold the chosen paper in some intricate design and then seal it with adhesive tape or a colorful label. Then, the letter could be delivered personally to its addressee, hand to hand, in between classes; or it could be left, as if by chance, inside a backpack or in between the pages of a book. Courting surprise.

Liliana often traveled to the U.S.–Mexico border, where she visited cousins and made new friends. Close relationships mattered much to her, and her letters traveled distances both great and small. She received letters from Poblado Anáhuac as early as 1983, for example, and not only from girls her age—Adela Orozco, Patricia Castillo, Amelia Rivera, Leticia Hernández—but also from older aunts and neighbors who became fond of her. And Liliana answered them all, punctually, cultivating their affection. She also had long correspondences with friends she met in swimming competitions, as was the case with Rodolfo López González, who began to write to her from Morelia, Michoacán, and did not stop doing so even after his move to Inglewood, California, as he was struggling to adapt to his new city. Time, there is lots of time, physical time and emotional time, in that loving accumulation of papers and envelopes. The time of girls in bloom.

"I want you to know that there is no one in the world who understands me like you do," Liliana and her friends wrote to each other quite frequently. And although they did mention an uncompromising mother or an authoritarian father from time to time, they didn't really elaborate. They did not talk about siblings either. Any mention of lewd relatives or street harassment was completely missing from these letters. Family life hardly worried them. Nor did school or exams distress them: references to teachers were scant and fleeting. Every now and then they wished each other good luck in tests, but nothing more. They used the letters to apologize, and they did so profusely, for a number of transgressions: for some gesture or phrase that, out of context, could have been misinterpreted; for having been in the possession of information that they should have shared earlier, but had not; for some rumor that they now had the opportunity to confirm as false; for talking to some girl on the opposite team. Offering and accepting

apologies was a difficult art sustained through labyrinthine protocols they knew by heart. Teenage girls were thin-skinned: a bad
word could unleash a flood of tears; a look out of place could cause
a wound that would only heal, if it could at all, over time. In the
end, if all was well, the girlfriends swore their eternal love for one
another. Lilianita, they called my sister quite often. Dearest
friend. My true and only friend. Lylyhanna. They thanked each
other for their understanding and promised that nothing would
destroy their friendship. They swore their friendship would carry
on through thick and thin until the end of time.

But the girls wrote letters mostly to talk about love and, more
specifically, about the love they felt for boys. Since no one fully
understood them, they claimed, they shared secrets they could
not tell anyone else. Together, they groped their way into new territory: love was the other name for desire. While the adults around
them assumed their daughters lacked libido or sexuality, or trusted
that, if they possessed them, they would be able to tame them,
especially in families attached to the rigid principles of the Catho-
lic Church, the girls gradually entered the yet unknown reality of
the body. Hormones did their work. And so did the imagination.
In long letters, based on meticulous descriptions, which did not
eschew humor, their predicaments emerged one by one: the boy
she fancied was going out with another girl; the one she did not
like was way too persistent; the boy she had broken up with would
not take no for an answer. The one she liked had moved to another city; a boy from another class had sent his wingman to let
her know he wanted to go out with her; the one she liked had
brushed lips with her; the one she didn't like kept sending little
letters on waxed paper. Was that normal? Had that ever happened
to her too? What would her advice be? The letters were a way of
moving forward together, protecting each other as they left be-

hind the solid ground of obedience and docility and childhood. Through this hidden communication, thinly disguised as innocence, they warned each other of ongoing dangers: they named the uptight, arrogant boys who were best avoided, and clearly identified the cheaters, the callous, or the simply rude. They were aware, and made sure others were aware too, of the boys who wanted to go all the way.

Moving to a different school or to the next grade scared them. The changes forced them to question who they were, who they were going to be. "Why? Why does it have to be this way?" Yazmín wondered as the end of middle school approached. "I thought I didn't mind leaving this ridiculous educational institution, but it turns out I do. I care a lot, but not about Raúl, Oscar, Marcela, Claudia or Alejandra and Cecilia, they can do whatever they want. But . . . you, Liliana, strong and fragile at the same time . . . What will become of my life? What will become of yours? What will become of us? Will life continue with its relentless race, a race whose only finish line is death? Yes, this life, which always unnecessarily turns into death. What is the use then of desire, ideals, goals, even the future, if you already know that death looms at the end, and the only thing it produces is pain? Liliana, I don't want to part with you. I love you very much!"

Yazmín was the author too of one of the darkest missives Liliana received, in April 1984, when she was fourteen years old: "From over there, from far away, from when the races were born and the first man emerged, came this mixture of bestiality and tenderness. This man is the conqueror, thirsty for gold and glory, who raped each country, just to abandon it later, sad and defeated. Each child is the true product of the love or lack of love of his parents. And when a child is borne out of that bestiality and that sadness, from the bloody spoils of the victor and from the outrageous defeat of the conquered, he has to be hard and soft, cruel and holy, and he has to cry with a waltz his mother's sorrow, and to avenge the outrage committed by his father when he begot him."

An unsigned letter, written in pencil on the red lines on a leaf torn from a small block, announced ominously in anonymous handwriting: "Liliana: If you were to lack those you enlighten, what would your happiness be? I admire you, that gentle eye of yours that can contemplate even excessive happiness without envy. Your gaze is pure and your mouth does not conceal your repugnance. You are changing now, you have become a girl, you are awake. What are you going to do among those who remain asleep? You lived in isolation as in the sea, and the sea carried you: Do you really want to jump to land? Do you want to drag your body onto this land once more? Do you love men? Man is too imperfect for you. A man's love would kill you. Don't go to the men! Stay in the forest. Go with the beasts, over the men. Why, like me, don't you want to be a bear among bears, a bird among birds?"

[I hate when they love me like this]

Liliana wrote Ángel González Ramos's name for the first time on June 10, 1984, a Sunday. It must have been a cloudy evening, the early summer rain pattering on the roof. She was probably lying on her queen-size bed, her feet covered with thick woolen socks. A teenage girl's room: the soft pale blue gingham bedspread, the eyelet dust ruffle around the bed, the delicate pillow shams. On the wall, right above a simple bedframe, the posters of Che Guevara and Marilyn Monroe looking at each other sideways. The Golden Gate Bridge to their right, a seagull perennially perched in the sky. Just slacking off, as she'd say of herself at times. Lazy. Simply unmotivated. If she had leaned out the window, she could have felt the icy air rushing down from the volcano on her face. And she would have seen the snow, gentle and spectacular, on top of the sacred mountain. Instead, she remained in her room, day-dreaming of this robust, solicitous guy she had recently met at the Juan Bosco Gym, a private establishment that mostly attracted professional or wannabe weightlifters before exercising became mainstream. Following the advice of her swimming coach, Liliana had joined the gym when she was about to graduate from middle school in order to strengthen her legs and arms before plunging into the water. Ángel took a fancy to her almost immediately, ask-ing for her name, phone number, and address. But Liliana was slow to react. If she liked him, she kept it to herself for a while. If she felt flattered, she did not betray her true feelings. She told her friend Carla, who went with her every afternoon, the two of them exercising together until they were both out of breath, that Ángel was such a bother. He doesn't take no for an answer, she said roll-ing her eyes, paying no heed to his lurking presence. Ángel took Liliana's response as a challenge and stepped up his efforts. He arrived early, ready to greet her by the door, and stayed at the gym, lifting weights or chatting with the owner, as long as he could. He usually left a prepaid sports drink or a couple of smoothies at the counter for the two friends. On one occasion, he invited Carla into his car to ask her whether Liliana fancied him. Has she said anything to you? He was curious. Carla did not want to be rude but did not want to lie either. She has not mentioned you, she said, unblinking. C'mon, Carla, help me out, he said then, jerking at her elbow, only half-jokingly. Carla looked at him sternly, con-sidering his request: he looked much older than her friend, al-most an adult in any case, outside of their circle of friends from school or the swim team. What was she doing in his car, anyway? You just have to tell her that I am a nice guy, he insisted. Girls listen to their girlfriends, right? I cannot do that, she said. Why not? Because I don't know you, she replied. But you know me now, he contended. You've been knocking back the smoothies I leave for you at the desk, haven't you? Carla opened the door and dashed back to the swimming pool.

Guess what, Lili? she said.

180684

I am not writing with my pen today because I don't have it with me. I let Ángel borrow it. I like him. I like him very much. And I don't think it sounds corny to say that I really really like him. I came to love him just because of SILLY STUFF. Lily.

After three years at a middle school in a well-established neighborhood of Toluca, Liliana enrolled at High School No. 5, Ángel María Garibay, located on one of the city's outer edges, on land formerly devoted to agriculture and animal husbandry. Hills and plains strewn with greenery in the summer gave way to the golden luster of the fields after the harvests. A color cycle. Toluca's old downtown district was far away, as was the industrial corridor that connected this city of investors and factory workers to Mexico City. Metepec, an indigenous town with a long-lasting pottery tradition, remained far to the west. The austere buildings of the public high school that corresponded to our family's new home were built on a no-man's-land, on fringes that no one dared to call the suburbs. Spurred on by the success of Residencial San Carlos, a new kind of residential community that brought together politicians, businessmen, and drug lords alike in mansions protected by tall walls, real estate agents sold land to housing complexes for the nascent middle class. With no urban regulation involved other than speculation and maximum profit, the outskirts of Metepec became, in the mid-1980s, that liminal zone between agricultural development and urban deployment that expressed itself in the halls of Liliana's high school: children of peasants and businessmen—fieldworkers and boys with some economic power but no lineage—all attended an unbecoming campus, built in a rush, often sharing space with stray cows and flocks of sheep. Liliana was just about to turn fifteen years old when she first set foot on campus. One of the first people she ran into was Ángel.

When she finished her first semester of high school, with grades she was proud of and even boasted about a little, Liliana confirmed their courtship in a typewritten letter addressed to Leticia Hernández Garza, a cousin of about the same age with whom she maintained an intermittent but constant correspondence throughout her life:

Leticia:

I don't think you have any problems worth dying for, so I'm not even going to ask, OK?

The problem is I'm not dying for anything either, and if it were so, I wouldn't have to write to you, but as I'm already on vacation and I'm so lazy right now, I decided to write to a cousin who never (I say so!) answers me... YOU.

I thought about visiting you for summer break, but since I have the state double A (AA) swimming competition in two weeks, I have to train and... tough luck! What am I going to do:

but do not think for a moment you have been spared...I MIGHT DROP BY, (but not on you)!

Guess what? Well, your cousin Liliana is very studious, she got good grades in her filthy first year of high school; by the way, I already found out that you took your entrance exam, and that you are afraid you did not pass it (that's the last straw). I really think you would pass with flying colors...(I am sure of it).

Do you remember when I was a total flirt? Well, that crazy fever has passed, now I just do it a little tiny bit. Since I started high school, and after what happened with my so-called friends in middle school, I have only had (I don't like the term in use: boyfriends) three best friends. Blas (do you remember him?), La chíchara (César), and Ángel, that's exactly his name, neither more nor less! Oh! Oh! By the way, there were these two naughty boys truly obsessed, one of them got already over it, but the other one is still clingy. DANG.

Ah! There is this other guy (I say so) from Morelia, he came with his team to the competition, AND THAT'S IT! He is fifteen years old and has competed at the national league level, and I will see him in October (I think), well his name is Juan Carlos Tellez. I'M TIRED OF TALKING ABOUT LITTLE FOOLS.

You may wonder why your ugly little cousin named Lilianita writes on a typewriter, and the answer is that my hand-writiiing (with three iii's) has gone sloppy (I don't type very

well either, but please take into account that I'm lying on my
bed with the typewriter on my belly while watching TV).

   Do you know something? I AM TIRED (better say) I GOT
TIRED ... that means I'm going to rest, and indeed (I say), and I
can't rest if I'm writing ... that's why I'm going to stop writing ...
and that means:

GOODBYE.
LILIANITA (MEANING MYSELF).

P.S. Be careful with the folding.

One semester later, toward the end of June 1985, Liliana wrote
three messages addressed to Ángel: the first, on Friday the twenty-
eighth, at 9:37 P.M., to tell him that now she felt calm and that she
wanted to dream about him; the second, on Saturday the twenty-
ninth, written at 8:32 P.M. immediately after hanging up the
phone, to thank him for the trust he placed in her, and to let him
know that she had just started another letter to him; and the third,
a very short message, written on a green piece of paper that time
has almost faded, to say:

   You made me laugh a lot and I love you more for it.

These are the typical short notes, written in the heat of the
moment, with which the lovers convince themselves of what they
are feeling. The eruption of feeling not yet coded, barely struggling to enter the narrative of romantic love. Many lovers have
scribbled those kinds of notes, and many more will, but Liliana
kept them all. That was the difference. Her difference. The urge
to write and the urge to archive appeared at the same time. That's
why it is possible to discern that, in the height of summer, just a

couple of months later, in August, while Liliana was making plans for her summer vacation, the situation with Ángel had taken an abrupt turn.

In a small notebook with a white Hello Kitty on the cover— *Visiting my uncle's farm is what I like best / saying hello to the animals out in the field*—which she used as a diary while spending three weeks at the border in our parents' town, Ángel ceased to be the cause of laughter and tranquility. On the contrary, and for reasons that Liliana never fully mentioned, Ángel now only triggered annoyance and contempt.

300785

I liked José Luis Gómez more than ever yesterday and today. I had a very funny dream. I hope I remember it forever. I know I will. I just want to note down the following keywords: a copper red rug, spiral staircase, THAT THING, poverty, THAT THING, persecution, NO. Well, I am not so sure.

050885

Isabel and I have already agreed on when we are going to go on vacation. She wants to leave as soon as possible and I do too, so we won't get bored here. We are leaving tomorrow afternoon at 5 p.m. I hope I have time to go to the IMSS. I'm dying to see José Luis. Hopefully he will show up, and if he doesn't I'll kill myself (well, not really). By the way, Ángel was calling me and all I wanted to do was curse him out. I am (ALREADY) fed up with him. Hopefully over there (in El Poblado) they won't make me feel as bad as they usually do.

060885

We are leaving tomorrow! (What a relief). Correction:
Wednesday.

I went swimming and talked with Beto about what
happened with Marín, Pancho, and César. I think we were to
blame, so we held a meeting with those of us who participated in the regional competition. I think we reached a compro-
mise, but things cannot go back to the way they were. For his
part, our coach Julio promised that he would try to change. I
met with José Luis and we were playing together — him,
Fontana, and Oscar. I think all three fancy me... and I like all
three! Oh! Oh! By the way, one of the divers (GERARDO)
likes me, and I like him a lot, because nothing ever happens
with José Luis after all. Ángel just called me once again and I
think I was very uptight with him, but no remorse about it.

Querétaro 080885

We just arrived from Toluca, we left there at 2:30. It's been an
uneventful trip, I hope it remains this way.

It is approximately eight o'clock in the morning. I am at the bus
station in Matamoros. The bus that goes to El Poblado just
broke down. WHAT BAD LUCK!

We came from Querétaro in a Tres Estrellas de Querétaro, bus
227, the seats were awful (right across from the bathroom).
We arrived in San Luis Potosí at 9:00 and left at 9:30; we
arrived in Ciudad Victoria at 2:30 and I don't know what time
we left, I guess at 3:00. We arrived here at around 6:40.
Everything OK, except for this, waiting.

It's about eleven o'clock. And I am here already. We finally took the nine o'clock bus, although we almost missed it. The family welcomed me all right, but it depresses me so much to see the same things.

090885

I just woke up, everyone is asleep except for my aunt Tome. I think three weeks is just too much for my state of mind. It's only 6:52 a.m., and it's already extremely hot. AND HOW THE HEAT IRRITATES ME!

180885, Saturday

Today I woke up later than yesterday. I did not sleep well. I don't know what I was thinking. I didn't do anything special (nothing special ever happens here). There is one of those ridiculous balls today, one of the many weddings. I hope everyone goes so I get some time alone (more?).

I have thought of José Luis, of my José Luis. I don't need to say what I thought.

Hopefully Gerardo remembers me. I was too hard on Ángel. He is to blame for loving me the way he loves me...It's their fault and I hate when they love me like this.

Yesterday I ran about 2 kilometers at night. It felt OK.

The ability of language to disclose and conceal at the same time. Window and curtain. Telescope and fog. There is something that walks, voluminous and transparent, between the block letters of that first mention of Ángel of June 1984 and the references that appear a year later, in August of 1985. Something has undoubtedly happened. Something Liliana does not name explicitly, but that is hinted at more by its effects than by its origins. There is a way of loving, she says, that bugs her, that annoys her, from which she flees, and against which she fights. It is a way of loving that, in addition, she does not recognize as her own. It's their fault. They are to blame. It is their responsibility, especially Ángel's responsibility. Without fear, almost instantly, Liliana reacts quite firmly to that something that shocks and bothers her, that which has taken laughing away only to bring repugnance: she calls herself uptight and tough, but she says she has no regrets. What happened then, what prompted such a radical switch and strong response, however, remains invisible in the archive. Unnamed, perhaps unnameable, Liliana decided not to speak, or could not speak. Or had no words to speak of it.

[the apple lover]

210686

Adrián:

I hung up the phone about 10 minutes ago (I was talking to you) and went to watch TV. I was sitting quietly (eating) and an advertisement for engineers popped up on the screen (as if by magic). "This is the most common image (of something) for engineers for whatever it is...etc." Then I really wanted to write a letter for you (you are Adrián). So, I got up, stopped eating (in that order), went to my room (which is a total mess), tried to clear my bed (without success), took out a notebook of graph paper (there is nothing I like more than you and graph paper), I looked for a pen (just in case, not to bother

the chickens' pen, I'll say ball-point-pen), and I started to write.
OOOOH! AND THAT'S IT. No more, no less. And here I am:

END (THE END) OF THE CHRONICLE OF HOW LILIANITA
    WRITES A LETTER TO ADRIÁN (Leonce, Valencia,
    Francisco, Pancho, Paco, etc.).
START OF LILIANITAS LETTER TO ADRIÁN: HELLO! (just
    the greeting).
THE TEXT OF THE LETTER IN ITSELF (or "out" of self, it is
    the same):
I love you very much (and I will "always" beat you).
THE END OF THE LETTER IN ITSELF OR OUT OF ITSELF:
BYE. Crocodile tears / well, (yes! Indeed, for you!) (Eeeh! You
    really bought it, SMUG YOU!)
Well, (again, because I strayed, took another path, changed
    the subject, etc.).
SO LONG (hopefully "long" is short):
END OF THE END OF THE LETTER:
Endly…

START OF THE P.S. (POSTSCRIPT, YOU FOOL!)
P.S.
POSTSCRIPT BODY: Be aware that I change over time (time
is an arrow).
MESSAGE FROM THE P.S. *:
* Note (look it up): The P.S. is mute.

COMMENTS:
  1. I don't know how Marilyn can laugh all the time (ever since
     I bought her).
  2. The horses were very thirsty (they drink water nonstop).

3. Not a single car passes through the Golden Gate Bridge (rare indeed).

4. The feathered friends (what property!) of the posters do not tire of flying.

5. Che is very discreet (he always looks at Marilyn out of the corner of his eye).

6. Liliana Rivera Garza. Lover of apples, happiness, and many other things. Adrián's girlfriend (BAH!). Student (ha ha ha) in the fourth semester of high school. Do you know her? No? Ah! Well, she digs laughing, but never alone; she likes to laugh with her friends, and she just loves to make them feel good (although she messes up sometimes). Mother of four children (Juan and Adriana Rendón, Liliana Beltrán and Oscar Robles), planning the adoption of a fifth one (Salvador Diliz). Divorced (from Juan Blas). Thin, straight hair. Not prone to take care of her gentle little self. An honest clown (from the Atayde Hermanos circus). She does not have a friend-friend, but she sure can trust several people (Adrián, Xóchitl, Arturo). Dreams of being a sailor, of walking around the world, of daring to learn many things, of being accepted, loved. Can't you find her? Well, she dislikes hot milk, and she is not herself when she gets angry (I mean, excuse me, when she eats pork, shellfish and fish). She once dreamed of being a guitar player, then she thought she would be a painter, and for most of her 16 years she has dreamed of becoming a professional swimmer, but... there is always something in the way. There are some things that prevent her from doing it (THEY DO NOT MATTER). She fell in love at 16, it seems that it all happened between April and May of 1986 (it does not matter with whom). She will never forget her first love (what a

joke). There are some people crazy about her, but none are as talkative as Adrián (that's why she keeps thinking about him 24/7). Lately, she has noticed that Gaby (yes, Gaby) is drifting away from her little by little every day, but she also thinks that Gaby is right because Lily spends so much time playing games and (how can I say it?). Well, I don't know how to say it (with Chava, Arturo, Fontana, etc.). What's more, she has come to think that she was rude to Adrián just for being with them all the time (but they amuse her greatly). You have to understand her… (she is very innocent […]).

[fantasy]

Well, here I am, trying to write something that frees me from everything I have inside, that frees me from myself … well, I don't know. "The love that you give me is like a gray day … things are like that, a cheater, a woman." That's what I can hear from outside … funny, right? Well, it makes me laugh, laughs and smiles, yes: little friends, your friend Bozo the clown will give you _____ just by calling the phone ///////// and telling us what is the capital of Solitudelandia, until then the I will delight you with my song +++++++++++, good morning, LLLLLLLiiiiTTTllleee FrrrrrrrrlEHDSSSSSSSSSSSSSSSSSSS!

What a clownish thing to say, right?) () (). Things are weird, well, they become weird the moment I want to feel I am outside everything, and I decide to see everything weirdly. Yes, look: if I am inside of everything, it all seems normal, but what happens if I am not? … who knows? I want

to spend some time talking about each of the people who at
a given moment... at a given moment, what? Well, I don't
know. I just turned to the window and looked at the blue sky,
blue like the blue of the Fantasy colors pens that I owned as
a child (the lightest blue, of course, the celestial blue). Yes, I
started using them when I was a little girl, when I no longer
wanted simple color pencils, but markers too, also Fantasy,
and so my parents bought some markers because they
thought they could be useful (the markers were useful for
everyone except for me). I have owned several small boxes,
no more than three. Well, those were all the colors I've ever
used. Now I have the leftover pens, and colors of the sun,
sorry, the light, the sunlight, and with those, as with the
ones from before, I paint everything I want. I would now like
to paint Gabriela in yellow, Oscar in many colors, all the
rainbow for him, it would be beautiful, right? Caro in green,
Jazmín in violet, Fontana in blue, Adrián in brown, Aída in
red, Xochitl in white, César in purple, Martha Mendiola in
black, Manuel in wine color (and I love to drink it, drink
it, drink it), Julio in pink, Oscar in rainbow, Oscar in rainbow,
Chava in bottle green, Tocho in beige, Arturo in royal blue,
Oscar in rainbow.

[keeping quiet about some things]

"Respectable" sir (ha ha ha):

You have called me a liar and... I don't know, I'm not sure said
designation offends me or rather flatters me, since I know
that indeed, I'm a liar, although I don't think I like that word

very much (why didn't you look for another one?). Well, well, there is no time for that right now, is there? We were we… we were saying I am a "liar" (with an option to another name). Ah, I will tell you that it amuses me. You can invent an infinite number of things and feel them for real, why not? (all you need to do is try) and mess with people afterward (…) No, no, I'm not talking about anything specific, but it's just cool to know what other people truly think while they can only make guesses about me, about what remains exclusively mine (that's why it was given to me in the first place).

Well, I don't know, I feel like any José Luis right now, and I feel sorry (in my soul) to say, as I always tell him, that all those lies contain an infinite amount of truth, you just need to look for it, but… as I believe I've noticed that this respectable sir likes everything digested, well, tough luck.

I want to ask you one (or several) questions: what will become of this poor world if we don't keep quiet about certain things? What if everything, and I mean everything, was spelled out in the open? No mystery? How boring, right?

The fact is that this, your gentle servant, is one thing some days and something else other days, do you get it? And I do not call it fickleness (which would be an equally terrifying defect) but relativity (which comes naturally to thinking beings [or at least a being that tries to think]).

As always, "it's a matter of approaches, thinking positively"…(OK?)

You know, there is this person who I think knows me more than I know myself, and that puts me at such a disadvantage, because I love her, because this person knows what's up with me, and I can't do anything…it can't be helped. And that person, a he or a she, it doesn't matter, never asked me any questions. This person just discovered me, I don't know if consciously, but there you have it!

I think that's the only way to be sure that you will always have someone close by: little by little, like a rough draft, and then you can work things out, thoughts, feelings, and actions. Never all at once, because otherwise there is no longer a mystery, there is no longer a why. And...what exactly would be the point then, do you see what I mean?

[this annoyingly blue sky]

I am a seeker. I want to try new things; maybe more pain and loneliness, but I think it would be worth it. I know there is more than these four walls and this sky, annoyingly blue. How can you love so much without really loving?

MILENA

                              MILENA   milena

M I L E N A

                                        MILEna

mi-le-na

[you don't know how to love]

We got into fights, like all sisters. I hated that, as a child, Liliana would follow me from room to room when I wanted to be alone.

Don't bother me, I would say. I am thinking. It maddened her that since our mother took us to school at the same time, but dropped me first, my reluctance, my inability to get up early or my lack of consideration for her time always turned into a delay that jeopardized her punctuality. And she cared about punctuality. She despised my messy room, how ungainly my outfits were, my utter lack of grooming. I hated her stuffed animals, Hello Kitty's invasion of the house, her sense of fashion. When girls started using hairspray to lift the wave-shaped fringe over their foreheads, Liliana used it. And I scoffed. Corny. Consumerist. Feminine. She listened to pop music, becoming a fan of female teen bands such as Flans, which I, who had become a radical sociology student at UNAM, loathed. A silent but indisputable border placed me on our father's side, among other things because I bore a close physical resemblance to him, and Liliana on our mother's side. The similarity between them, which went unnoticed at the time, is evident in family photos: both are tall, with very long legs and thick, straight hair, bushy eyebrows, large eyes. Full lips. My sister was always a stunning woman.

The single biggest discussion we had was about love. The date is uncertain, but the place clearly bursts into memory: there we are, Liliana and I inside a car parked in front of Morelos Market. It's Toluca again. Toluca, which means gray rain, which means sad birds, which means unfortunately. Toluca and its damn blue sky. It must be a winter day because the light, crisp and very thin, cuts the shadows of the trees with great precision on the sidewalks. My mother steps out to buy something and I, who just had a ferocious argument with her, shift in the passenger seat with my fists clenched. I hate her, I say. Between my teeth. I hate her.

I remember Liliana saying, very calmly, now that our mother cannot hear her: what happens, Cristina, is that you don't know how to love. The phrase takes me by surprise. I spent a lot of time thinking about love those days. Since I got to university, I had done nothing but mull over class struggle and love. Love hinders me, drives me crazy, suffocates me. I hate love. When my female friends share their love stories, enraptured by the minutiae of the encounter and the seeming inescapability of the affair, I can only read submission into them, lack of freedom, professional failure. Many say they want to travel the world, achieve something of significance, but they end up falling in love and, later, getting pregnant, and soon their lives are behind them. Soon they are behind themselves. Someone must stop love. Someone must turn love away. In those days I spent much of my time writing against love. Not manifestos or essays, but stories. Short stories. There is a female character, a young woman who calls herself Xian, who desperately flees, with little chance of success, from men and women who promise her love. Love is this, inventing lies and believing them thoroughly, she says. Xian perseveres across the pages, refusing to leave my stories. Soon, I have three, then four. Then more. I still don't know that I am writing my first book when Liliana, from the seat of the car, assures me that I do not know how to love.

There is something in the way she says it, as though she knows something that I, her older sister, have failed to grasp. So intelligent, and so dumb. So close-minded. So selfish. Is there wisdom beyond her age in her words? Is that what people call resignation? She is not trying to convince me; she is not passing judgment on me. What pours out of her lips is just a statement of fact. You don't know how to love, dearest sister. And do you? I am tempted to ask, but befuddlement and rage, and mostly fear, blind me, forcing me to shut my mouth. I know the answer. I know the answer by heart.

I never doubted Liliana's love. Better yet: I never doubted that Liliana loved me. I was suspicious of everyone else: boyfriends, friends, relatives, even my parents. I assumed that the relatives who cut me out of their lives because of my atheism did not love me. And it mattered little to me. Those who were disgusted by my lifestyle in the city, which they called rakish and which I defined as free, did not love me. And they mattered little. I assumed that the boyfriends who drifted away or the girlfriends who, without explanation, stopped talking to me, did not love me. And I couldn't care less. I came to believe that my parents' insistence in curtailing a freedom they had instilled in me was also proof of their utter lack of affection. I doubted them all. But I always felt protected in the world because I knew, I was absolutely certain, that whatever happened, at the end of it all, Liliana would always love me.

I believed blindly, absolutely, honestly, in her capacity to love.

[what if you knew what would become of me?]

This is the last page of my notebook, well, the first one from back to front, you know what I mean? Depending on how you look at it because "it is a matter of thinking young, it is a matter of thinking positively, a matter of focus." Don't you like that advertisement? Ah, well I do… (so what?) (Well nothing).

I am in such a (completely) lazy mood, and I am very sleepy too, and when you suffer from those two conditions "but nevertheless" you also have an aversion to sleep during wake hours, there is this very big shock and, do you know what happens? Well, in addition to sleepiness and laziness, a very funny foolishness crops up (that is happening to me right now) so much so that you even feel like sitting down, or lying down or kneeling just about anywhere. And then it just so happens that you inevitably start thinking, and thinking, and you turn to look at the clock on the wall, and you think that your mother is going to arrive soon, and that you have to pay your school tuition bill, and that today you did not see Ángel, and you don't feel like training. You also think that you no longer want to train because when you are not in a quiet environment it is impossible for you to develop your concentration and full physical potential, and you think that your exams are almost here, and above all you worry, but your worry is not big enough for you to get up, grab your notebook, and study, right?

Well, something similar happens when you're like this, because it's something exactly like that, huh? And if you don't know how to express what you are thinking, then something happens that seems very strange to you, it is something like wondering if you really are the one who is writing, as if . . . AND SUDDENLY! (as if by magic) you remember a dream (I don't know when I had it) and as soon as it arrives it just goes away and you forget it. And you are even more sleepy now, and more. And, ouch, your back itches, you scratch with fury because it bothers you that you can't scratch comfortably, jeez, and you wonder why they put so much chlorine in the pool? It makes my skin so very dry! And dryness is not the worst, but what dry skin gives off: itching. So, you keep on thinking about the swimming pool, and the chlorine, which in addition to the itching leaves a characteristic smell of the so-called substance, whose chemical symbol is Cl. And then you remember your chemistry class and something else as a result but it is nauseating, and you prefer to leave it in peace. Peace. Damn. What if there was peace? What if there were no people starving in the world? What if there was justice? What if people really appreciated other people for who they are and not for what they look like or their image? What if I fell asleep? What if you knew what would become of me? But I am sleepy, and I am tired of looking and looking for affection, understanding, tranquility, and I am also tired of finding it all, and I am tired of feeling bad because I look for things, I find them, and then they don't fill me, they don't satisfy me. Maybe it's because I look for them in too crude a way (or too refined). Well, I don't know, but that's how it is and I'm sleepy, and I'm still sleepy, and I'm sinking into my dream. And oh! Oh, what? Well, nothing, nothing happens right now, in this moment, small, pretty, silly, very little moment.

And then you close your eyes, and you imagine seeing something really beautiful, flowers, many, many, green and blue-green flowers, flowers all over you, at your feet, and everywhere, and with that thought you fall asleep, and your mom finally arrives and wakes you up. And you get angry, and you think that you have seen (at least in the last five years) many people get old, and it hurts to think that you would be considered old when reaching that certain age that people have imposed on us as a limit to youth. So sad!

And your whole body hurts. And then you think that it is because you started to do something at last, and that's it!

III

WE GO LIKE SHE-DEVILS,
WE GO LIKE BITCHES

[You know what I mean?]

21051987

Lety:

Things should appear in order, but this time I say that things should be a mess. So:

> Goodbye, greetings to all
> Liliana.

I was looking at some photos from what feels like two centuries ago and I immediately thought of writing to you. We were so very young, I mean, younger, and since I want to avoid overeating, I set out to do something that would keep me busy (at least for ten minutes).

We have grown up, and that has me in awe. Did you feel how you grew up? Except for my period, and the development of my innocent little body from where I was 6, or 7, or 13 years old, I have no other proof of the changes I have undergone. Darn!

When are you visiting, huh?

How are you doing in your high school? You enrolled in the concentration in Humanities, as far as I know. I'm in Physics-Mathematics, or its equivalent, which I understand it would be Exact Sciences over there. Or something like that. I'm taking very interesting classes: geometry, drawing, calculus, physics, and all those things that I really enjoy.

Have you changed, Lety? Do you think in a different way

now? You might think that I am traumatized by the idea of change, but it seems that it has just dawned on me.

How are you? Hi, how's it going? I am fine but with lots of work.

You know? Things have happened, I do not know if it's lots of things or just a few, but they are momentous. Anyway, they set the tone for the surge of another person in oneself... I didn't think that there would be situations that spoil what one has thought for years, but it seems that there are.

You know what I mean?

Exactly, that's what it's about.

This is just a little note from someone who loves you very much, and not just because we are cousins, and not even because of chance, simply because it is you.

Answer me please.
Liliana.

[vehemence]

The university strike turned the world upside down at the beginning of 1987. I had finished my coursework for my bachelor's degree, but I was still in the process of writing a two-hundred-page thesis on women's involvement in the urban popular movements of Mexico City, based on a field study that we had carried out in the Belvedere neighborhood, a squatter settlement south of the city. I was, in addition, teaching an introductory course as a teacher's assistant on my campus, and had also landed a couple of classes at the Universidad Autónoma del Estado de México (UAEM)—the public university located in Toluca—where I had enrolled, rather reluctantly, in a master's degree program. I no longer lived in the spacious bedroom, with floor-to-ceiling windows, that my parents had paid for during my years as a university student, and I was living hand to mouth between tattered little holes in the slums of the city, couch surfing in friends' living rooms, and failed attempts to live in communes. I did not have any money, but enjoyed a freedom that mostly meant I had finally escaped my parents' grip. I traveled by bus to Toluca regularly, but mostly just to teach my sociology classes at the Faculty of Political Sciences. I often went straight back to Mexico City and very rarely stopped by the family home that, as the years went by, I found increasingly suffocating.

It was during that time that I learned about Ángel.

Liliana and I were not in the habit of sharing intimate secrets. Very early in our lives we somehow arrived at a tacit agreement to avoid the topics of sexuality and love. We talked a lot about the books I brought with me—books that I did not buy myself but that my anarchist friends "expropriated" from the different bookstores and shops of the city. We talked about the vinyl records I brought home, which I bought mostly on sale, with my teacher discount, at the UNAM store. Jaime López and Rodrigo González. *Sessions with Emilia.* Eugenia León. We talked about politics, about how difficult it was to change a world we both found unbearable, about corrupt politicians and white unions, about wars fought in distant lands, about the poverty that I witnessed in the settlements in the fringes of Mexico City. We talked about women most frequently, how my feminist views let me see how my father limited my mother's life, for example, or how women were de facto second-class citizens, without proper rights and generally treated as minors. Liliana heard me defining myself as a feminist, unabashedly and more than once. We talked, in the most somber moments, about the possibility that at that very instant the radiation that had escaped Chernobyl more than a year ago was coming through the window. Can you imagine? We went on and on about the trips we wanted to take. Africa. San Francisco. The Himalayas. We'll always have Paris. We obsessed about freedom: the freedom to love, the freedom to enjoy our bodies, the freedom to go from one place to another. *Who cares what I do,* sang Alaska y Dinarama. And we both knew the tune by heart. The sacred right to do as we pleased.

I always thought that the stocky white guy with blondish hair and hazel eyes who came to look for her so often was something temporary. The typical boyfriend from back home that Liliana would forget or get rid of once she truly began her life in some faculty of UNAM or UAM in Mexico City.

Ángel never came inside our family home because no one who was not part of our sovereign republic of four came into our home. It was less a matter of prudishness or morals and more the daily confirmation of a fact: there are four of us. We will be four. But we all took notice when he arrived on his racing bike or in a souped-up Renault car that memory sometimes paints red and sometimes black. And we caught a glimpse of him waiting outside, patiently, lovingly, either near the front yard of the house or by the park across the street. We laughed at him, high-heartedly. We told her: your driver has just arrived, when his car approached our home. We told her: send him for some bread, get him to do some errands for us. Bemused and a little annoyed by all this, Liliana laughed through it. C'mon, behave, don't be like this, she'd say without much conviction. The few times I heard him speak, it was clear that he had a speech impediment because he dragged out his *r*'s more than he should. Either that, or he was a spoiled child. Or an idiot. Or both. He was a güero in a land of brown-skinned people, and that gave him an edge. Short but beefy, he could pass easily as a handsome, bull-necked young man with those gym-trained arms and shoulders. T-shirts tight to the torso. A black leather jacket. He looked like trouble. He worked for his family's auto parts business at Avenida Pino Suárez Sur 2006, in the Juárez neighborhood. A busy road. His family home consisted of a series of dark rooms he shared with his widowed mother, Irma Ramos, his sister, Verónica Beatriz González Ramos, a single mother who had recently given birth to Jonathan Efrén, and two younger sisters who came and went very much at will. There was a two-year age gap between Liliana and Ángel, but they lived in completely different worlds.

In the first letter Liliana wrote in 1987, on the first day of the year, she mentioned she was on a diet and that she planned to look thinner by February. She also announced to her unnamed addressee, although it surely was someone who lived in Poblado Anáhuac, she had a new haircut and "fluffed her straight hair with a perm." She was quite pleased with the result, she wrote. And that simple joy, a general state of well-being and satisfaction, led her to elaborate on the minuscule affairs of her everyday life: a younger cousin spent a few days at home and she felt good with "a fake sister," her ability to prepare French toast, the absence of spectacular events in her life. She stopped when she ran out of things to say, which occurred right at the lower limit of the graph paper where she scribbled her signature. She was serene, albeit a bit bored: a sky with no storms in sight.

It is clear from the archives that they began dating early in 1987 because at the time of the first major breakup, on July 26, 1987, Liliana mentioned that if it had taken two years for Ángel to win her over, and if they had already been together for six months, she expected that forgetting him will take her less time. How did he ease himself back into her life? Up until then, Ángel had been one of many suitors—young men who had tried, unsuccessfully, to retain her attention. She dated Adrián Leonce Valencia, one of her swimming coaches, for a little while, but he moved to Mexico City and, although he continued sending letters, the relationship quickly faded. She had been drawn to swimmers and divers on her swim team, but nothing serious came of it. She knew when her elongated body charmed a boy's gaze, and rejoiced in the attention. She knew when they flirted with her, and she flirted back when she felt like it, adventurous, full of curiosity, ready to leap from the grip of childhood. She was aware she was fancied, desired even. That February 14, 1987, Ángel sent her a huge red card and a bouquet of flowers. In capital letters, without punctuation marks, in a sloppy line that makes reading difficult, he addressed her as Lilianita, using a diminutive that became the rule in their interactions, and said:

WELL YOU KNOW THAT HOWEVER IT IS HOW-
EVER IT SHOULD BE SAID OR WRITTEN IT WILL
ALWAYS BE THE SAME WHEN I SAY OR WRITE
HOW I FEEL FOR YOU. I LOVE YOU SO
MUUUUUUCH!

The little card that accompanied the bouquet of flowers that he bought at the Crystal Flower Shop, Villada No. 314, with telephone 3-36-63, added, misspelling included: ON THIS DAY I SHOULD HABE WRITTEN. FOR SOMEONE SPECIAL. BUT BETTER YET. FOR SOMEONE VERY SPECIAL. ÁNGEL.

The Valentine's Day card is a strange artifact in and of itself. Its design a double-edged sword. The matte front of the card, crammed with lines of bright red hearts, boasts a question that ends, however, in an exclamation mark: "Valentine, do you know who loves you very much!" The suspense is part of the surprise: you have to open the card to find out the answer inside. A solitary YO surrounded by exclamation marks leaps out at you right then. I, not love. I, not a name. I above all. Far below, in subdued type, the generic phrase in generic font: Happy Valentine's Day. Did Liliana notice this? Barely concealed in a Hallmark card, ready to jump at her, Ángel's "I" rushed out from the card to hit Liliana's eyes. His "I," not his love, was both the medium and the message. As he bombarded her with flowers and chocolate boxes, rides between school and home, and a relentless attention she described as his vehemence, was a sixteen-year-old girl equipped to identify the menacing grip of control? Liliana and Ángel soon became the *it* couple at high school, both of them good-looking and daring. Unusual. Picture this: the tall and graceful girl hand in hand with the hulky guy who drove noisy state-of-the-art motorcycles through town, now lingering, carelessly, apparently free, on the outskirts of campus while smoking cigarettes and sipping beer. She must have felt special. He must have felt accomplished. Was there, in her world, in ours, a language capable of identifying the early warning signs of what was to come?

By May, Liliana harbored some doubts, and a general unease, which she interchangeably called nerves and hysteria, tainted her letters. In *Gaslight*, the 1940 British psychological thriller directed by Thorold Dickinson, a man willing to do whatever it takes to get away with murder and robbery convinces his wife that she is losing her sanity. Unaware that her husband enters the attic from the house next door, she notices both footsteps and the dimming of the gaslights, which he adamantly denies, claiming instead she is irrational. Luckily, a clever detective unveils the

deception in time, but real life often lacks that timely interven-
tion. Liliana's increasing use of words such as *hysteria* or *hysteri-
cal* to describe herself gave out the same flickering shine as those
dimming gaslights in her letters. She often wondered whether
Ángel had already tired of her, while simultaneously rejecting an
idea that seemed just plain inconceivable.

I don't think love, vehemence, and understanding can disappear so soon, can they? Yes, I know things may come to an
end in the blink of an eye, or at least that there may be a
moment when disappointment surfaces just so, and destroys
everything in its path, right? Just a moment. In a moment. What
will time be? I still can't quite grasp what that is. Time. It can
be measured, I know, but what is time?

The word *vehemence*. This is the first time it appeared in Liliana's vocabulary. And it would not be the last one.

A letter from Ángel, written on May 22, at 12:30 P.M., brought her
some relief. Ángel apologized to her, admitted he was a fool, a
selfish man, and explained to her that he had been dealing with
"council meetings," "legal proceedings," and people who "are
screwing me up because I am not jumping through their hoops."
Right there, in lines of capital letters that, again, did not include
any punctuation, Ángel stated, in a somewhat convoluted way,
that those problems that negatively affected him caused him "a
neuronal congestion that makes me not want to explain it to you."
"Forgive me," he added, "but I didn't feel like talking about
politics today. I don't know how to start a conversation like that.
Please, do not think that I'll always be this way. I promise you I
will no longer cause you any more discomfort or problems. I will

leave that, but do understand that, at times, one does it for other reasons. I don't think that political talk is worth getting angry about OK. Ángel."

"I will leave that," he says, trying to make amends and appease Liliana. *That,* handwritten notes would later reveal, was not in place of a town or an addiction but a person. Her name was Araceli. He was promising Liliana he was going to break up for good with Araceli, a former girlfriend he at times went back to because of "other reasons."

The situation did not improve. And it finally burst into many pieces on July 26, at 9:45 P.M.

Dear Ángel:

I would like to write so many things...you know? Anyway, I was already afraid of it. You haven't been able to forget her, to forget Araceli. I feel so extremely sad. Yes, sad is the word; not even humiliated. It was silly of me to think it was possible, feeling like you could do it. Why, Ángel? Why do things have to be this way? I do not disapprove of anything, no one can command over our feelings, our doubts.

Verónica didn't have to tell me, why did I have to find out from your sister? Why didn't you tell me? I would have understood, really. Why? Why didn't you say anything when I asked you directly? !!

I am not as weak as I may seem. Naïve, yes. I fell in love with you, yeah. The first time I've loved this way. Now I'm alone.

Why haven't I found what I'm looking for? Perhaps what I want is too perfect, perhaps too sublime, too simple or clean.

But no, I'm not going to give up. I'm going to keep looking (maybe later...) Not now. I still love you too much.

What are you talking to her about? Are you kissing her, are you touching her? How. At this very moment!!!

First all these things with my family, now this. Are there any honest people left in this world?

Well, I love you anyway...It took me 2 years to do it, it might take me less time to stop doing it. Hopefully.

                                                    With love.
                                                    Liliana.

"Wherever you decide to go, my support will continue as long as you do not give up, because there is no responsibility more atrocious or more sacred than that which forces us to be ourselves."

                                                            L.

P.S. I didn't deserve it, I know I TRULY DIDN'T!

Liliana kept on adding and deleting paragraphs, typing and retyping the letter, until two days later she emerged with a fair copy of it:

Dear Ángel:

I am truly confused (more than anything), sad and humiliated... Can you forget things so easily? Can you forget them?...I can't. I don't know whether fortunately or unfortunately, but I am one of those rare 17-year-old girls who has some values, you know...honesty, for example, and all those strange things attached to it. And I'm not talking about morals or prudishness, I am basically referring to what enables us to love others and oneself...love, yes...simple love, not only selfish love for a single person, but for everything around, for everyone...Maybe I'm an idiot, but I firmly believe that I am right.

Things pass by in front of you (or if you prefer, behind) and, if you are interested, you take them, otherwise the best and most sensible course of action is to let them go...I cannot understand, I simply cannot, why you took me just to do this afterward...why didn't you just let me slide by? Did I deserve it? I know I didn't. Oh! I have had so many thoughts, my brain is in chaos.

I do not censure that you remembered or even loved another person, not that. In feelings, in doubts...it is pretty hard to control that, but what I cannot conceive, what seems so dirty to me, entirely reprehensible in fact, is that you did not talk to me, that you never told me...You cannot say that I shouldn't ask questions about this, that these are things of no concern to me, because I have the right to know, indeed, our 6 months together (or were there two years?), 6 months full of words, 6 months full of so many things, grant me the right to know.

Why, Ángel? If I didn't ask you for your loving words, if I didn't beg for your attention, why did you give them to me?... Why with so much vehemence? I never imagined you were like this, and even now it is difficult for me to believe so. I never thought of you as a bad person. I know you are short-tempered, aggressive, stubborn, and even a bit foolish, but a bad person? My god (well, not my god, no, because I don't have one), no.

Did you think me too weak to understand, too fragile? It may seem like it, but I'm not weak, I'm not. I have fallen to pieces in the past and I have gotten up again. I am not saying that my life is a Greek tragedy because it is not, but I think my parents have educated me to be better, not to let myself be defeated, to create and to learn...

Well, after my big rant, I can only tell you that if it took me a year to fall in love with you, I hope that forgetting you will take me less time.

I know that, sooner or later, I will find what I am looking for.

I suppose you will not want to answer this letter, much less look for me, and given the circumstances, I will find a way to send your things to "your" home.

Yours (for some time).
Liliana.

P.S. Why did I have to find out from Verónica? It was so humiliating.
P.S. to the P.S. I KNOW I DON'T DESERVE THINGS LIKE THIS!!!!
THIS IS UNFAIR!!!
(in just a few words)
Toluca, Méx., one Monday of july 1987.

[the first July of the rest of our lives]

Tuesday july 28, 1987

I thought that this month would pass like any other, like any other month of my life, and like the july of any year, but it is certainly not the case. This year I will start college (I hope), and all that that entails cannot go unnoticed. This july I graduated from high school, barely so, but I did it nonetheless. This july I am in crisis. This july I am so utterly sad, it is so ugly to see that all things end, that not even the things that are most our own can be eternal. I am not trying to imply that sadness is an unpleasant state, no. I think that I have come to like my sadness, even my loneliness has grown on me...I don't know what else to say, but I have so much desire to write: to write what I think, to write what I dream, to write about the gray sky and the misery of people...Write.

I got caught in a downpour yesterday and was soaking wet immediately. I couldn't resist doing it. Sure, I felt horribly frozen afterward, but I didn't mind, not even when I got a cold, with all its discomforts. I felt very well, in fact, somewhat clean (and not because I had not bathed before). I felt solitude closer than ever, right on the skin. The difference that exists between my self and the whole world was so real.

[entrance exam]

During Ángel and Liliana's first major breakup, I was at a point in my life where I just wanted to be free. I was working at the time, but above all I lived in total freedom. I attended packed demonstrations in downtown Mexico City and then wild parties where expropriated bottles of whiskey, homemade marijuana brownies, and red-and-black flags hanging from the windows were the norm. After dancing, after taking their clothes off, men and women in the crowd ended up singing "The Internationale" loudly, their left hands across their chests. Eyes closed. I knew it by heart and sang with gusto. I smoked and wrote. I wrote and smoked. I moved from place to place, taking only the heavy Lettera 33 typewriter and a pile of blank pages with me. Xian—that figure of my literary imagination—would not leave me alone.

Xian did, in her own way, what I dared not do. Or was it the other way around? I couldn't travel to Africa or Timbuktu, but I could take a train and get far enough away. I did it a couple of times, on a whim. Without backpacks. Penniless. Once I went to the desert with a taciturn boy who claimed to love me; other times, like that summer, the trip took unexpected turns, stopping, for example, on the coast of Guerrero in the south of Mexico. In between places, framed by arresting views of the countryside, fueled by adrenaline, we managed to write a manifesto in unison: We are not in love. I had met this fellow traveler a night before leaving, starting a conversation that lasted for entire days. We asked for money at crowded bus stations with which we later purchased the cheapest tickets available, we stowed away in old train cars, we hitchhiked in trucks loaded with oranges. We read, aloud and in full, the complete poems of Ezra Pound. We stole ham and blue jeans and fine chocolates, which we then exchanged for regular food in local diners. We saw a whole cycle of German cinema in Guanajuato for free. We ate grilled baby goat in Monterrey. We breathed in the sea breeze in Tampico. We threw our hands up, waving goodbye to the children on the road from the train's caboose. An overcast city, devoid of soul, waited for us back home. *If I had illusions / if there were crazy passions, reasons / there would be no need / to spend hours / drinking canteens / of this gray loneliness.* And that monstrous, sprawling city that had brought us together by chance soon tore us apart. I lived for a while in a cousin's apartment, in a bedroom that, he told me with glittering eyes, was haunted by the ghost of a murdered girl. A short time later, I found a large bedroom, with glossy wooden floors, in the rough neighborhood of Buenos Aires, almost in front of the Medical Center, very close to the French cemetery.

My room was on the second floor of a shady building, whose ominous entrance bore the colorful prints of urban graffiti. My window overlooked a narrow alleyway, from which you could hear the voices of drifters or crooks selling stolen car parts or cocaine. Or illegal commodities brought from the United States. Or pot.

This is where I lived when Liliana came to Mexico City to take her entrance exam for the Universidad Autónoma Metropolitana on September 21, 1987. Due to student strikes, UAM had to reschedule both the exam date and the start of classes that fall. Liliana stayed with me the night before and, very early in the morning, left the apartment to catch the metro. I saw her leave through the living room window. Her long stride. Her straight hair swaying from right to left through the rarefied morning air. A beautiful girl in the big city. When, a couple of weeks later, she found her name on the acceptance list, we learned that the architecture degree was offered at the Azcapotzalco campus. And I started looking, through my acquaintances at the university, for a place she could rent close to campus.

"When I grow up I want to be a guitar player," she once wrote in some of her teenage notes. She also wanted to be a painter and had taken drawing, watercolor, and woodcut classes from time to time. She thought hard about becoming a swimmer, but she soon understood that her times, while good for state competitions, were not stellar enough to compete in national tournaments, much less in international ones. She once considered studying genetics, like our father. Something to do with inheritance, she said. But the classes in drawing, calculus, and geometry at her high school had convinced her that she could be a good architect. She had taken the entrance exam too, at UAEM, the local public university, and passed it. But when the news arrived that she had been admitted at UAM, she did not hesitate. She would go to Mexico City as I once did.

In a brief note that Ángel wrote to Liliana on October 30, on a yellow page of a Scribe notebook, when Liliana was already preparing to move out of Toluca and into her adult life, he told her that he was having a pretty bad time. He apologized again. He regretted "not being able or not having been able to pass the entrance exam" and announced, with an objectivity that seemed forced, that he was preparing his documents to get a passport and leave. "If I manage to go," he added, "I will hurry and come back as soon as possible, ready to take the exam again." The optimism did not last long. His enduring frustration was palpable as he complained about how he would feel "when I cannot have you near me and I have to toe the line. All that makes me sick out of my mind. Forgive me." Although he did not specify the destination of his trip, the mention of official documents suggested that he would go abroad, most likely to the United States.

[receive the affection of your father]

Uppsala 12 / X / 87

Liliana:

Happy birthday and happy non-birthdays too! Wishing you all the best in everything you undertake, especially your final exams comping up. I was preparing for an exam when you were born—that was a very beautiful moment. Your birth. I went to the hospital to see you when you were born, you were

such a chubby, adorable baby. Your mom has taken good care
of you.

    Thanks for everything.

Your father who loves you very much
Antonio Rivera Peña

Uppsala 8.X.87

Lili:

First, I want to congratulate you for having passed the exam at
the University of Mexico City and at the same time I want to
ask you for some additional information about the campus, the
program, and your plans. Now we are going to see each other
only over the weekends, and we'll sorely miss the communica-
tion of daily life. This separation from both of you saddens me
so, you who were just little girls not too long ago. But the evolu-
tion of life is such, and we have to prepare ourselves for the
future, but this does not change how much it pains me not see-
ing you every day, and not seeing your mother now. I really
wish this would all end soon. I think the relationship between
you and Cristina is the logical result of a series of circum-
stances and sharing a common university environment will im-
prove the communication between you two. It gives me such a
great satisfaction to know you girls are sisters and friends at
the same time. I wish you the best in the world, and take good
care of yourself.

    On the other hand, Cristina did stir trouble (specifically
with the extended family). Distance is the best answer in this
case, since things will not be fixed with a simple "excuse me"
and some tears, or with people trying to make peace at any

cost. That is a matter that concerns solely our family and we will decide what to do. There are so many good things in life worth our attention and time, and you have such an ample life ahead of you. Tread with confidence. Don't hesitate. Your father. Antonio Rivera Peña.

Uppsala on October 20, 1987

Hello Lili!

How is everything? I hope all is well. Lili, please, take good care of yourself in that Mexico City and try to understand the Chilango people so that they won't make things difficult for you. How I wish I were in Mexico, now more than ever, but the situation is quite different (because I am doing this doctorate at the wrong time). Things are going well, but I am paying such a high price with this time away from all of you, precisely because I am unable to see you and support you more closely. At times this whole thing becomes overwhelming, and I want to reconsider my original plans. How I wish I could rush things, but publishing my articles does not depend entirely on me, the verdicts of the advisors and the reviewers have to be taken into consideration.

Lili, now that you and Cristina are in Mexico City, take good care of your diet, especially Cristina, I don't know what the best and most balanced diet will be, but what I know is that a larger variety of natural foods keep people energetic and awake, preventing exhaustion and counteracting too the atmosphere of the city. You have so much to do in the future. I would love it if your mother could live with both of you for a while in Mexico City, making the transition more gradual for you, and not as fast as you are doing it now. You are starting a period of more independence, in which everything or almost everything will depend exclusively on you, but a direct support from your mother is always better, I think. We should have done this with Cristina throughout her time at the university, however, she responded as a strong woman (although I sometimes see her as very weak). The good thing about life is that it fortunately offers us the opportunity to support our loved ones, which is one of the things that I like to do the most, and I will continue to do it with her and with you.

I am so happy you are liking the university (I don't remember where it is located) and, regarding the demanding classes and the intensity of the work, well, that is what gives an institution its prestige. Naturally, graduates from those centers remember that good things come with a price, a steep one at times. It is true that there will be moments of despair or loneliness, it is even possible that things will not go the way you want, but all that will be rewarded in what you achieve, which will in turn give you the courage to continue with more determination than before. Good things don't come on their own, of course, you have to provoke them, you have to work hard for them. The strength of a person is not determined by physical force; real strength involves mental power and will above all. Will is what makes you move ahead, based on concepts and principles that have been acquired throughout life. There will be many choices in life and you have my full support in what you have chosen to study.

I tell my colleagues here in Uppsala that I receive letters from a younger girl and from an older girl. When I tell them your ages they can't help but laugh a little. I often forget you both are not girls anymore. Some days I write more than others. I have to leave three papers ready for publication before

going back to Mexico. I was in Copenhagen consulting mate-
rial, and may have to go to England, but this is a tentative plan
for now, related to wild potato issues. Receive the affection of
your father. Antonio Rivera Peña.

[like bitches, like she-devils]

I submitted the manuscript for "The War Doesn't Matter" to the San Luis Potosí National Short Story Award with more courage than hope. I had participated in a couple of literary workshops at the university, but I was expelled from the second one for having upset the instructor, contradicting his ideas about Octavio Paz. I kept writing just because; because it was my automatic reaction to the period in which economic crises, currency devaluations, the total abscence of freedom and democracy, international wars, made life impossible, nearly undesirable. I kept writing, just as Liliana did, because there was no other way.

A very fragile plotline kept Xian's tales, which were discrete units in themselves, somewhat intertwined, forming a kind of faltering, brittle novel, always about to unravel. That was more or less my vision of Mexico City back then. I felt trapped in a network of holes that, paradoxically, offered no way out. Xian drank too much, ran too much, lied too much, failed too much. Her relationships with men and women were equivocal, tinged with rather opaque affections, sad passions that lingered and then vanished as did the exhaust fumes from cars or the vapors of alcohol. Everything ended up being lost in the city she inhabited, especially her will to live.

In one of the stories, a man kidnaps Xian because he wants to know the whereabouts of Julia, the red-haired anarchist whose location constitutes the central enigma of the book from its very start. Did you also fall in love with her, dirty old man? the girl asks sarcastically before receiving a loud slap. Otherwise, the kidnapper is patient. He lets her loose in a spacious white apartment where she does nothing but plunge into the warm water of a porcelain bathtub, where she sits with her memories. And she mostly remembers Julia. The way she met her, thanks to a scheme concocted and carried out on the spot. The way Julia believed that complicity, rather than truth, was what genuinely mattered in this world. Give me a name, call me whatever you want, she dared Xian during her first whirlwind tour of the city. And Xian rapidly baptized her as Terri, because the woman was, indeed, terrible. Unemployed, with rather capricious connections to underground radical organizations, the girls spent their days traveling in rickety trains, nosing around crumbling neighborhoods, or sitting on the steps of decrepit buildings. It is right then and there that a black dog comes by, humble yet menacing, with a gaping maw. Terri is not afraid to pet her. It's the devil, she tells her friend. How do you know? It is obvious, look at her: either she is looking for an owner or is ready to tear people apart. Like you, Xian says. And like you, my dear little friend. We go like bitches, we go like little she-devils, with our loneliness in tow.

Now, all these years later, I wonder if I ever had that conversation with my sister in the gloomy building in the Buenos Aires neighborhood. Did we have a chance to discuss our own loneliness as we briefly coexisted and then grew apart in Mexico City? Were we still talking, as we once did, about love?

The book, in any case, won the award. In November of that same year, I traveled to San Luis Potosí to receive a diploma engraved in gold letters and a check that, along with some meager savings, paid for the airfare that brought me to the United States in the early summer of 1988. When, two years later, the book launch was held at El Cuervo, a bar in the center of the Coyoacán district in the south of the city, Liliana was not there.

Liliana lived, however, inside the book's pages.

Liliana was always there.

[it hurts to be away]

Uppsala, April 14, 1988

Hello Lili.

My little baby girl:

I got your last letter earlier than the next one, in other words, the one you wrote on March 15 arrived on April 13, and the one from March 23 on April 5. It came along with a letter from your mom, so I feel very happy these days. Receiving letters every week keeps me alive. It feels really good inside. So, I will comment on them according to the dates in which you wrote them, not the dates I received them. But first let me tell you a little about how things are going around here, on this side of the pond (the Atlantic). I have already submitted my first work for publication and now I just have to wait for the decision, there is no alternative, either they will accept it or not. In the meantime, I'm working on the next ones. Fortunately, I now know enough English, which is not yet perfect only acceptable, to write my drafts, but they have to go through revisions by people in Languages, and the Umerus, my advisors, also have to review them. Their English is very good and they have good ideas too, I grant them that. My plan now is to advance things as much as possible, which means trying to conclude my work before I go to Mexico in June, so that I only have to come back to Sweden for the PhD defense in September. As you will soon see, plans rarely come out as intended with this PhD business. The weather in Sweden is improving. There are more sunny days. The sun usually rises at 5:30, with the sunset at 8 in the evening. These are longer days indeed, which is definitely better than winter, although the temperature is still between 0° and 10° Celsius.

Well, April 30 is coming. Congratulations to you on Children's Day. Be very careful when driving, if you can, please, get your driver's license, it is always better; otherwise I strongly advise that your mother go with you when you drive. College life is like that, live and enjoy your student life. What worries me is that whole business of moving to a new house, meeting new people, people we don't know anything about. Take good care of yourself in that city of Mexico. How I wish I were there to support you in whatever you need. Remember to always establish the bases of coexistence with your new friends from the very beginning, so as to avoid any misunderstandings later. And eat well, don't forget the stomach problems you had when you were a child. It hurts me to be away from you. I am trying my best to hurry things up and return earlier. It's been many months now and I want to see you grow up and talk about things, everything: successes, problems, joys, sadness, studies, how you are progressing. Now that I've been here for so long I really don't know if it's worth it. I want to get this degree, but the price I am paying in being away from you is so very high. By the way, it has never crossed my mind to treat you and Cristina differently, and I'm sure your mom doesn't either. So, get that out of your mind. Each individual has their very particular characteristics, which it is natural, but the most important thing is to know yourself well, and do everything possible to understand others.

I think that all of us in our family, we understand each other, so go ahead. It is clear to me that you now spend most of your time away from home, but remember that it is these slightly difficult moments that forge a person's character, making her stronger and preparing her for life in the future. You know your principles, you have my full support, life is earned with courage, persistence, a lot of will and work. Being a student is one of the most beautiful stages in life. Remember that you have your parents and a sister who love you very much, very much. And more. Your father, Antonio Rivera Peña.

IV

WINTER

It's winter that makes people who they are.

—YOKO TAWADA, *The Naked Eye*

[Harrisburg Trail]

One may not know the truth for many years, but once you want to know, you want to know everything immediately. A strange rush, as if I were still about to save her, ran through the nervous energy of those days after my visit to the Attorney General's Office in Mexico City. I was teaching a graduate seminar in Houston that fall. Despite the humidity and the high temperatures, despite the relentless sunlight, I walked from home to campus on a regular basis—a forty-minute journey that allowed me to process my thoughts. All the university students bore her face, and seeing her face there, on those other shoulders, under those shiny heads of hair, brought me to tears. There were also the nightmares. I often dreamed that she was being murdered and, upon waking up gasping for breath, sweat running down my neck and torso and a heavy pressure right in the middle of my chest, I realized that reality was worse: Liliana was not mine to lose. Liliana had been thirty years deep below ground.

We spent Christmas 2019 at our Houston home. My parents arrived well in advance of the holiday, ready to enjoy those days of visiting relatives, forgetting about strict diets and telling stories already shared a thousand times. We soon fell into a long-established routine: taking a walk every morning along the Harrisburg Trail, a path originally intended for bicycles that lies about seven blocks from the house. The journey took about fifty minutes at my father's slow pace. Although spirited and strong for an eighty-four-year-old man, he didn't mind sitting down for a while on one of the wooden benches along the path, while my mother and I made it to the end of the track and returned to meet him at his resting spot. One very sunny day, a day when the birds were making an unusual fuss among the oak branches, a day of maddened squirrels and loose dogs, I told them very carefully, taking my time to enunciate each word clearly, that I was trying to retrieve Liliana's file. The world stopped for a moment. A whirlwind shook the branches of the oak trees and a string of dry leaves landed on our hair. The scent of grapefruit trees had never been more pungent. A flight of doves. Something was about to happen in the depths of winter. Exhausted, a thousand times defeated, my father said: I'll do whatever I can to help you. My mother opened her eyes, suddenly full of silent tears, and said: justice must be done.

We decided not to do anything elaborate for New Year's dinner: we bought flour and corn tortillas, and meat prepared with achiote and pineapple from a family shop where traditional Mexican food is sold. We placed gold-colored base plates on the table, linen napkins, and took out the best china to eat our humble but delicious tacos al pastor. I put the white flower arrangement that I had bought weeks ago, when it was just a handful of bulbs buried in a wooden box, at the end of the table. Next to the blooming flowers, I placed a photograph of Liliana. We had never done anything like this before. But it felt right. She had always partaken of our festivities, our solitary family suppers, the many times we ate alone, but this winter it was not enough. Knowing she was there was not enough. I wanted to see her. I wanted her to see us looking at her. This is your rightful place, Lili. The portrait is in a small cherry-colored wooden frame with a discreet old-gold trim. Her hair bathed in the stinging light of the highland winter. A pure luminous flash through time, her hair. She's wearing the antique gold-rimmed glasses I chose for her at a flea market in Mexico City: little ovals whose narrow sides bore an intricate carved design; a dark green flannel shirt falling off her shoulders. Her lips, about to open, less to articulate a word and more just to breathe. Liliana looks straight into the camera, somewhat taken aback. I have for years read desolation in those eyes. Confusion. Reproach. But this night, this New Year's Eve, looking at her out of the corner of my eye as we dined, I believed she was gazing at us differently.

We talked about her in complete sentences for the first time in ages. Contrary to what I expected, none of us burst into tears, knees crumbling, falling to pieces. The scenes appeared one after another, unhurried. A smile here. A sigh there. Lili as a child, chasing me from room to room at our home in Delicias, Chihuahua. Liliana, swimming. The first day Liliana attended kindergarten. Lili in the children's hospital, suffering from a kidney infection. Her inimitable smile. The way she loved. The way she lavished each one of us with the luxury of her affection. At twelve o'clock we placed, one by one, the twelve traditional grapes in our mouths. I could hear our shared silent wish as we swallowed them. Then we raised our flutes and toasted. As we hugged each other, when it was no longer possible to hide our tears, it occurred to me that this was something else that I never did with Liliana: drinking bubbles.

The next day, in the middle of a nearly deserted Harrisburg Trail, a lone cyclist crossed our path. Without warning, without so much as a greeting, he extended his hand to me. He looked straight into my eyes, indicating that I should take the envelope he was offering. I hesitated for a moment. Anthrax, I thought. What other types of deadly poison are transmitted in sealed envelopes? In the end, I took it because I wanted to teach my morning paranoia a lesson. By the time I took out the card and found two bills inside, one twenty and the other five dollars, the cyclist had already vanished. I never knew why, among the few walkers of the first day of the New Year, that young rider with withered skin and lean hands chose me. But I thanked him. I said: Thank you, Liliana. How could we not think that everything was now related, in one way or another, to you?

I sensed her hand behind the invitation that I had accepted, some six months earlier, to teach an intensive course at UNAM Casa Azul at the beginning of 2020. I sensed her hand in the ease with which Saúl arranged for us two to meet in Mexico City on January 9, 2020. Living in grief is this: never being alone. Invisible but evident in many ways, the presence of the dead accompanies us in the tiny interstices of the days. Over the shoulder, inside the folds of our voice, within the echo of each step. Above the windows, on the edge of the horizon, among the shadows of the trees. They are always there, and here, with and inside us, shrouding us with their warmth, protecting us from the open. This is our waking work: acknowledging their presence, saying yes to that presence. There are always other eyes seeing what I see, and imagining that other angle, imagining what these senses that are not mine could make out through my own senses is, all things considered, the best definition of love I know.

Grief is the end of loneliness.

[Mimosas 658]

Three months prior, I had walked with my friend Sorais through the streets of La Condesa, reaching the offices of the public prosecutor in Azcapotzalco later in the evening. This time Saúl Hernández-Vargas, my husband, would join me as I crossed the border of Mictlán, back into the land of the anthills. It was late at night when Saúl arrived at my hotel, and we went out to look for something to eat almost immediately. The area, usually bustling, was still and strangely silent. Just when we were about to give up, we found a Japanese restaurant. When did the city turn into this? The couple next to us spoke English, but they were not from the United States. There was a rowdy group of Germans. All of them, even those who spoke a Chilango Spanish, were very white, their light-brown heads of hair suspended in the air. All so young too. Whining about everything, including the food, did its job: it relaxed us and made us laugh. On our way back, even before we went to bed, too exhausted to even talk, we observed the sky of Mexico City through the windowpanes. Somewhere in that darkness pierced by electric lights there were stars.

Before going to Azcapotzalco, we arranged to meet a lawyer, Héctor Pérez Rivera, at his office of the Association for a Culture of Human Rights. I had contacted him in October, thanks to the recommendation of a friend, and hired him over the phone to take charge of locating Liliana's case file through the intricate twists and turns of justice, which so often become the infinite twists and turns of impunity. Given our continuous bureaucratic failures, we had decided to file a complaint with Human Rights in mid-December just before the staff of the Mexico City Attorney General's Office left for the holidays. If all goes well, we should have an answer soon, Héctor Pérez Rivera had promised. Saúl watched him carefully when he arrived late, alluding as always to the demonic traffic in the city, although adding the detail that he had a flat tire on his bicycle. Héctor, who at first seemed to be in a hurry, patiently answered the questions we posed over and over again. Finding a thirty-year-old file could prove difficult, but it was not an impossible task. Rulings from the 1990s did not include the charge of femicide, and the documents I was able to gather and send to him labeled the case as a homicide, not first-degree murder, which should have been the case insofar as the crime involved both treachery and an intimate relationship. He would be responsible for all official communications with the justice system and, on the side, he'd do some research in different courts and public prosecutors' offices. We shook hands when we said goodbye, kissing each other's cheeks, as is customary. We are going to find it, we said in unison before closing the door. A wave of optimism came over us and propelled us into the streets.

This time we decided to take public transportation to get to Mimosas 658, in the Pasteros neighborhood, where Liliana lived as a UAM student. The ride lasted a little over half an hour. I need to see the campus she attended, I had told Saúl one morning in Houston. The place where she lived. The streets she walked on. The stores where she bought bread or cigarettes. The little food stalls where she ate. Her metro station. Her bus stop. I need to leave flowers for her in all those places, I said. And there we found ourselves that dry, sunny morning, on the worn stairs of a metro station where Liliana, surely, had placed her feet many times. We were again in territory Azcapotzalco.

Her apartment stood only a couple of blocks from the metro. We trekked straight on Calle Ahuehuetes, a wide street with a tree-lined median, and we turned right onto Mimosas. It was now, as it had been then, a working-class neighborhood with one-story brick houses and plenty of mom-and-pop stores and bakeries. A populous neighborhood, but not a violent one. Years ago, José Manuel Álvarez, a colleague of mine, had heard that I was looking for a safe place for my sister, who had just been admitted to UAM Azcapotzalco, and offered to rent her a small apartment below his own family home. The apartment had the basics: a living room, a dining area, a bedroom, a bathroom, a kitchen. The caveat: they used the bedroom as a storage space, and Liliana would have to make do with sleeping in the dining area. The real perk was its location: Liliana could get to UAM campus in about fifteen minutes, using a fairly quick combination of metro and bus. José Manuel was married and had a couple of young children. There were no other tenants around. I thought Liliana would be safe here.

Streets are living entities that evolve over time. The numbering of the houses was new and did not coincide with the 658 we were seeking. I had been there a few times, but memory betrayed me. We knocked on several doors to no avail, before we asked a mail carrier who directed our attention to the burnt-red building next door, which bore two sets of numbers, 658 and 92A. We pressed the buzzer and placed our ears close to the intercom. A woman's voice greeted us, cautiously. It was difficult to explain what we were doing there: I am the sister of a young woman who was murdered here thirty years ago. Could you let me in? I did not say that, exactly, but I implied it in a long, convoluted story that became more and more complicated as the minutes passed. Moments later, the girl emerged, leaning out without opening the security door all the way. Yes, she had heard something. Yes, she had an idea of what had happened. What? we asked her. She couldn't tell us. Instead, she told us that her boss was not there, and we would need his permission to get in. I gave her my business card through the narrow opening before she closed the gate to make some phone calls. It didn't take long for her to reopen the metal door to inform us that her boss was about to return. That we could wait for him, if we wanted. How long? Half an hour. We smiled at her. We had already waited an eternity.

We spent those minutes walking around. We browsed the market, which was only a block away. We queued at the tortillería. We sniffed at the taco stands. We stopped at an auto parts store, taken aback by the coincidence. Surely that tall apartment building with the large windows wasn't here back then, Saúl said, and I agreed. We were leaning on a car next to Liliana's old house when we saw a gray-haired man hurriedly coming out of the building next door and, without thinking, I ran after him. I gave him the same hasty, somewhat tangled explanation. Do you remember something like it? He refused to shake my hand, albeit kindly, but stopped anyway right after he had left the sidewalk and set foot on the pavement. Saúl joined us promptly and held my right hand. Streets change, it is true, but they are not forgetful. Yes, the man said, lowering his voice, as if about to share a secret. That girl was so pretty. She was such a good person too, he said. She used to buy bread here every morning, at my dad's bakery, on her way to class. I looked back at a water store he pointed out, and he clarified: my dad fell ill and got rid of the bakery. That's why I am here, to see him. He is so terribly sick, he said, shaking his head. And then he said: she was a college student, right?

Do you remember what happened? I managed to ask him. He fell silent again, uncomfortable. He squinted, and then squashed some imaginary insect with the toe of his shoe. He pretended to turn away, twisting his waist ever so slightly, but his feet remained rooted in the street. It was her boyfriend, right? We saw him around here quite often. He had a black car and, sometimes, he came on a red motorcycle. A good-looking guy. I must have been twelve years old back then. We learned about it from the newspaper. Didn't the police come? It was so many years ago. Please, forgive me. I have not thought about this in a long, long time. All that comes to mind is that she was such a good person. She greeted everyone, always. She even greeted us kids playing soccer on the street. How sad it all was. When I offered him my card and told him my name, I asked him for his. Excuse me again, he replied, sincerely sorry. But so much has happened around here. Kidnappings, you know. The killings. You no longer give your name out so easily.

The owner of the building behind the metal gate at Mimosas 658, a slim engineer with a calm voice and friendly manner, was not long in coming. We did not have to offer much explanation before he let us inside. It is always strange to move through the spaces where our dead dwelled. That slight tremor at the very base of the hypodermis: a vibration made of pure flesh that, once in the ears, turns into a shivering noise. A buzz. The uncompromising march of the ants through the nervous system and, later on, through the body's circulatory system. And the pressure on the chest. We moved very carefully, as if everything around us were made of ancient glass. This was sacred territory.

Architect Fernando Pérez Vega, one of Liliana's close friends during her years at UAM, drew from memory the plan of an apartment that, very soon, became a regular hangout. Since it was not far from campus, Liliana's classmates gathered here to do homework and, once the quarter was over, it was here that they partied and celebrated. Beers, some cheap rum, lots of cigarettes. It was here that they stayed up late, listening to music, always careful of the volume because the Álvarez family, who lived on the second floor directly above Liliana's place, was sensitive to noise. Some of her closest friends slept over at times. It was very basic, with just the bare essentials. As agreed, Liliana left the bedroom-storage untouched and placed her mattress directly on the ground in the dining area. To make up for the lack of a closet, she brushed some lavender paint over simple wooden crates, stacking her clothes and shoes on them. Over time, she acquired a small bookshelf, where she put her most beloved books, tin boxes stuffed with little pieces of paper and secret messages, small wooden boxes with some bracelets and earrings in them, pencil holders. Eventually, she filled the walls with posters. Her drawing board, which took up almost the entire living room, was nestled next to the louver windows. She owned a stool, maybe a couple of chairs. And nothing more. She seldom used the kitchen, which was large and dark, with a concrete countertop, interrupted only by a stainless-steel sink and the four burners of a gas stove. A small metal and opaque-glass door opened onto a tiny interior patio barely illuminated by the natural light that poured in from above. She had a few plates and a collection of unmatched glassware. She had some brittle mugs for coffee; and plenty of ashtrays, where the butts of the many Raleigh cigarettes she smoked with devotion, with pleasure, finally rested. The window of the tiny bathroom, which had just enough space for a shower and a toilet, also opened onto the small interior patio. A young girl, who helped the Álvarez family with housework, slept during the week in a room adjacent to the bedroom-storage, whose entrance led to the common courtyard, then directly to the front gate.

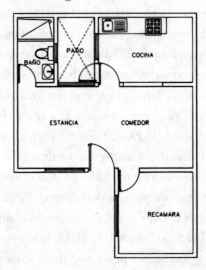

My aunt Santos, who to this day has a well-earned reputation as a visionary and natural healer in her neighborhood in Houston, said that she dreamed of Liliana the night she was murdered. She could clearly see the layout of this house, which she had never been to. She said she walked slowly down an exterior corridor, which connected the main gate to the apartment's front door through a courtyard and from there, through a slatted glass shutter, she could see Liliana, her arms and legs shaking as if unable to wake up, or as if asking for help. My aunt opened her eyes before she could help her.

The owner of the property and the two secretaries let us roam at will through what was now the office of a construction company. He had bought it five years ago from José Manuel Álvarez. And what have you changed since you bought it? Saúl asked him, looking around the building and discreetly placing his hands on the walls. Everything is more or less how it was, he said without hesitation, the structure remains as I found it. I have only renovated or completed the unfinished areas of the property. Like the floors above, right? I said. Like the floors above, he confirmed. He did not object to our taking photographs. But when I asked him if he knew about the tragedy that had taken place here, he denied it. The secretary who had previously said she was aware of the story fell silent.

[living hearts don't forget dead hearts]

The UAM system was inaugurated in early 1974, in direct response to the pressure exerted by the student movement of 1968, especially after the brutal repression of October 2 when between 150 and 200 students were massacred by the government of Gus-

tavo Díaz Ordaz. With five campuses distributed in the sprawling
urban area of Mexico City—Cuajimalpa, Xochimilco, Iztapalapa,
Lerma, and Azcapotzalco—these public universities not only addressed the increased demand that came with the city's rapid
growth, but also presented itself as a novel, avant-garde alternative to the established but more conventional institutions of higher
education. They used a quarter system and, instead of awarding
grades based on individual classes, they adopted a pedagogical
method that favored interdisciplinary teaching and teamwork. If
moving to Mexico City would have always involved a radical
change in landscape, speed, and lifestyle for Liliana, transitioning
from a traditional high school, where cows and sheep often wan-
dered the halls, to a generously-sized campus with a cutting-edge
pedagogy would have been a drastic but welcome change for her.
Liliana must have been happy here, I said as soon as I set foot on
the bustling walkway that led to the central library.

It took us no more than twenty minutes to get from the apartment on Calle Mimosas to the orange doors of the university campus: first the metro, and then in a pesero that waited right outside
the UAM station. We shared the narrow space of the vehicle with
students carrying long rolled-up architectural plans, young people
with earbuds, old ladies with children in tow. We got off where
everyone got off. We had to write our names in a red-covered
entrance record to get in, scribbling the time of our arrival. A
talkative employee described to us in great detail how to get to the
architecture department. The buzz of students coming and going
filled the air. Uproar. Laughter. The din of bodies close together.
The smoke from many cigarettes. There were paintings demanding the impossible and posters announcing film cycles or the visit
of an international speaker on the walls. There was, above all, en-

ergy. A nervous vivacity, very supple, tangled and untangled from the trunks of the trees at high speed and scattered, then, around the public sculptures, passed through the windows, under the doors, between the stalls where loose cigarettes were sold, electrifying the environment completely. Liliana had been here, and was here now. Her body, hurriedly passing us by. The smoke of her cigarette. The subtle echo of her shoes. What turns on in our brains when we become utterly convinced, convinced against any evidence, that what we lost long ago will suddenly appear in front of us?

The architecture building emerged like a charm behind the dining rooms. A modest photographic exhibition and a couple of tables with books for sale welcomed us at the entrance. There were students everywhere. Groups of young men and women with heavy heads of hair and blue jeans chatted placidly or engaged in passionate discussions, bursting into laughter from time to time. Look, Saúl said. We were able to peek into the empty classrooms: the winter light shone through the large windows, illuminating the many wooden drawing boards arranged in rows. LIVING HEARTS DO NOT FORGET DEAD HEARTS, said the letters on the mural that decorated the stairwell with large colorful flowers and images of the Ayotzinapa students, who had been forcibly disappeared in September 2014 in the state of Guerrero, unleashing national and international uproar. The architecture department was in the university, but also in the world, engaging symbolically, and critically, with state violence. We listened to the murmurs and observed, in the movement of the bodies, her body in motion—alive among them.

A taciturn young man smoked a cigarette alone, his forearms leaning on the concrete wall of the bridge that linked the second floor of the building to the next. When we passed him, he turned to look at us out of the corner of his eye, as if he had known us for years. A sorrowful smile hung from his lips. Glancing over the campus below, the unguarded fields, the expanse of plazas and halls, it was easy to feel openness and freedom. The buildings embodied the pedagogy and spirit of an institution that, at least officially, strove for, and actually embodied, change. Ángel must have been terrified here, I told Saúl. Anyone obsessed with control would be scared by a campus as open as this, I continued, as we walked down the stairs. The winter light pierced the air and fell on the leaves of the trees, triggering luminous flashes that lent the atmosphere an unreal quality. Time stopped and exploded simultaneously, multiplying on the spot. There was Liliana, in another winter, with the light of the same sun stinging her skin. There she was, running, trying to get to class on time. That was her, examining the ends of her hair while leaning on the stone wall of one of the patios. Her voice, I could hear her voice everywhere. The echo of her laughter.

A colleague put me in touch with the man in charge of academic records at UAM. While issues of privacy prevented us from seeing Liliana's transcripts, we did learn that her GPA was above average. We went to yet another office, to officially request her records. Not having access to a computer, I wrote the letter out by hand, even made a copy of it, and submitted it immediately. What I would like to do, I told Rocío Padilla, who was in charge of the newly created Office of Gender Equality, is a commemoration. She had received us in her office immediately, without an appointment. Her serene, expressionless face could not conceal the swift mechanisms of her mind at work. I would like to create a space at UAM Azcapotzalco where my sister's presence, her passage through these classrooms, through these corridors, through these gardens, is honored. And the presence, I added, of other murdered girls. The presence of any young woman who has survived, or has not survived, gender violence. I would like, I was going to continue, but Padilla stopped me: Let's think together about how to do it. Let's work together on this one.

V

THERE GOES
A FREE WOMAN

[Laura Rosales]

How could I not remember her? She was the first person I spoke to the very first day I was in college! She was already in the classroom when I got there: her striking long hair, so straight and shiny, her open smile, and those long arms and legs. She was so tall. So feminine without a drop of makeup. Liliana was very beautiful but acted as if she was unaware of it or, if she knew it, she didn't attach much importance to it. Her sense of humor was even more striking than her looks: she made fun of everyone and of no one in particular; her sarcasm was so fine, so subtle, so sharp. I soon realized she was special.

I came from Magdalena Contreras CEBETYS, a technical education system for working-class people that UNAM did not officially recognize at that time, so I had no choice but to apply for admission at UAM. And even though I wanted to become an architect, people suggested that I avoid the architecture program, because it was very competitive, and that I seek admission in the industrial design program instead, which few people were interested in back then. I followed their advice, and when I received my acceptance letter in late October 1987, I was elated.

We became friends rather quickly. We shared classes and worked together in the same group. We talked endlessly, in the cafeteria, in the halls in between buildings, in the meeting areas right outside the library, often bursting into laughter and criticizing everyone. Liliana spent a lot of time in the stacks of the library. She did most of her homework there, but she also devoured novels by Agatha Christie one after another. She was always reading something: novels, poetry, stories. She carried *La Jornada*, the leftist newspaper, or at least it seemed to us to be on the left at the time, with her every day. She was a nerd, no doubt. A very nice and outspoken and friendly nerd.

I moved out of my family home and lived in an aunt's house in the Clavería neighborhood, close enough to the university, and one day I invited her to have lunch with us. They all adored Lili, and we could have talked for hours, but she had to leave early because in those first days at UAM she lived in what she described as a very rough, almost dangerous, neighborhood on the city's periphery. She didn't like it at all, and I have no idea how she got there. Not too long after that, though, she rented a large house on Avenida de las Granjas, closer to the university, where she took up very little space. Later on, she moved to the apartment in Mimosas, where I visited her from time to time.

Liliana was very motherly; she treated her friends as if they were her own children, protecting them, guiding them, even feeding them. But she was a wicked mother at that. When I came to visit, for example, she would open the empty refrigerator and mischievously, with great fanfare, grace me with the sight of a lonely beer bottle. We usually went out to buy groceries at a nearby market and, once back, she would say: sit down, Laura, I'm going to prepare the best French toast you've ever tasted in your whole damn life. She said quite the same about cans of tuna or oranges. A light and festive air surrounded her. Everything was momentous, massive, earth-shattering when you were by her side. She gave off the impression that she thoroughly enjoyed being alive. It didn't take long for me to realize that Liliana was a noble girl, very devoted to her studies and, especially, to her friends. When Liliana loved you, she loved you wholeheartedly, sincerely, accepting you as you were. No questions asked.

I sometimes stayed overnight at her Mimosas apartment without telling my family, because I did not have what she clearly reveled in: freedom, an independence that she was proud of, a sense of autonomy. She received a monthly allowance from her parents and, although they visited her from time to time, and she went back to Toluca most weekends, she owned her days and nights. Although we were all broke students, Liliana was well-off in my eyes: she had enough money to buy the materials our professors asked for, and to eat wherever she wanted, and even to buy the newspaper every day. She was disciplined with her expenses, though. Despite the apparent chaos to her life, there was an order beneath it all. Sometimes I would watch her walk through the hallways and I would say to myself: there goes a free woman. I had great admiration for her intelligence and strength. She was alone in Mexico City, but she faced everything without whining, and with a lot of curiosity. She resented loneliness, but never said a word about danger. I was not that free or brave. And I was proud to be her friend.

We became full-fledged citizens together, voting for the first time in the elections of July 6, 1988, when we all believed that Cuauhtémoc Cárdenas, a popular candidate for leftists, would unseat the archaic Institutional Revolutionary Party (PRI), at least in Mexico City. We felt very important as we cast our ballots. When the computer system crashed and corruption resulted in more of the same, the electoral fraud genuinely disappointed us, and so we went out and protested together. It was the first time for both of us. I don't know how we managed to get hold of them, but soon we both held banners proudly over our heads. We joined the chanting: What do we want? Democracy. When do we want it? Now. We supported Cárdenas, of course, like many young people of our generation. We were just these young women, barely eighteen years old, and we demanded the impossible.

[Raúl Espino Madrigal]

Did you attend middle school in Toluca? I timidly asked her the day I finally summoned the courage to approach her. Her enormous, luminous smile disarmed me. Her sonorous laughter. Yes, Raúl Espino Madrigal, she said, surprising me. I had no idea she knew my full name, but she explained right away that she remembered my brother Javier from the days they trained together on the same swim team. I had admired her from afar ever since we shared classes in the first quarter, but it was not until we were in the Operative class together, in the third quarter, that I dared speak to her. It must have been around 1988. Graphic design? I asked her after a long, awkward silence. She smiled again, noticing I was deathly nervous. How dare you ask that? she said, feigning offense. I am an architecture major, of course, a real profession, she added, only half-jokingly. This would become a theme between us: she belittling graphic design, and I defending a profession I love even now.

All new students in the Division of Arts and Design at UAM took the same general education classes in our first three quarters, the Common Core part of our training. If we managed a passing grade, then we moved on to our majors: architecture, and industrial or graphic design. It was then, during that transition, that I realized I was falling in love with Liliana. We said hi and even talked a bit when we ran into each other on campus, but it was not enough. I wanted to get to know her better; I wanted to spend time with her. I daydreamed of Liliana often and came up with endless schemes to meet her "by chance." But nothing seemed to work. Since we both went back to our parents' houses in Toluca over the weekends, I suggested that we ride the bus together, but she demurred. I invited her to the movies, but she claimed she did not have time. Then, after countless rejections, it finally happened. Yes, Liliana said.

It was a Sunday. She came back from Toluca earlier than usual and met me at the metro station. We hadn't picked a place to eat, so Liliana suggested that we grab some groceries and cook something simple in her apartment. I was absolutely delighted. It was way more than I expected: I was not only going to spend half a day with her, but I'd be at her place, close to her stuff, her knick-knacks, within her realm. I didn't really believe it until we opened the door of a small apartment, a bit cold and damp, that she had made cozy by adding color and posters, and her drawing board. I was living in my aunt's home, in a comfortable middle-class neighborhood in the south, and here she was, a true amazon, living by herself in a rough area of the city. I was full of awe and admiration for her. With the groceries we bought at the market, we threw together something basic, like tuna with vegetables. We'd also bought a can of peaches for dessert. I distinctly remember how she opened the can and dipped her fingers in the syrup to pluck out the first peach. I followed her lead, sheepishly charmed by her gesture. I loved the simplicity and spontaneity, even the sweetness, of the moment.

We planned to go to the movies after lunch. We wanted to see *Mississippi Burning*, which had just been released in theaters, so we took the metro all the way to the cinemas at Plaza Universidad, a shopping center in the south of the city. It was fun to see the contrast between the families and the couples, and us, walking side by side, at the mall. After the movie, we went for ice cream and, as we chatted, I tried to talk a bit about "us." It's been such a great day, I said. I really enjoyed being with you. Liliana looked at me quizzically, paying close attention to my words without saying anything, and let me continue. I told her that I thought she was very intelligent and then, out of the blue, suddenly emboldened, I told her that I *liked* liked her. I could learn a lot from you, I said, echoing a phrase from a corny love song by Emmanuel, a pop singer who was a big deal in those days. She took it quite well. It also happens to me that I think quite a bit about you, she said, making a tricky play on lyrics by Joan Manuel Serrat, a Catalan singer who was way more sophisticated and cool than the one I had quoted. I made a silly comment about our differences. She smiled, looking at me as though she were far away, peeking in from a place where I couldn't reach her. But she seemed serene rather than flattered, vaguely interested. I thought it was a great start.

[Laura Rosales]

Lili invited me to spend a weekend with her in Toluca and I happily accepted. We got to her home and, since no one was there, we walked to her boyfriend's house. His name was Ángel. I did not meet him then, nor did I even catch a glimpse of him because Liliana went into his house very quickly, just to fetch the keys to an old white Beetle that we'd use to drive around. I am going to take you to a magical place the likes of which you have never seen before, she declared as we got into the car. A cautious excitement spread over me. We drove past the city, on a two-lane country road flanked by weeping willows. Almoloya de Juárez. A sacred spring behind a colonial church. There were kids bathing in the medicinal waters of a stream. A few women washed clothes by hand, their heads covered by rebozos. Get ready, she said. Keep an open mind. We placed our hands on the iron fence surrounding the spring and stretched our necks downward. Colorful fish slipped calmly through the algae. A bunch of golden coins looked back at us from the bottom of the water: amulets of so many wishes from the past. Heavy clouds rested, tremulous, on the surface of the still water. I did not know where I was for a moment. It felt like I was down below, amid that aquatic forest, running hand in hand with Lili. Look closely, she said, breaking the spell. If you pay attention, you will see a line on the water. What do you mean a line on the water? I asked, incredulous. It took me a long time to distinguish what she also described as a tiny long hair that divided the dirty water from the clean water in the spring. When I finally saw it, we laughed. It was, as she had promised, a magical moment. I experienced those quite often with her.

Lili was either just learning how to drive, or she wasn't used to the car, because the old VW Beetle stalled several times on our way back. But we made it back safely and returned the car in one piece. We walked to her home from there, and then took the bus back to Mexico City. I spotted that same white Beetle a few times in the university parking lot, or from the pesero when I was on my way to or from campus. I assumed that the guy driving it was the Ángel I had not said hello to in Toluca.

[Ana Ocadiz]

Can I try your custard? she asked me one day out of the blue. We were at the cafeteria, sitting across from each other and, although we were eating together, Lili had been distracted throughout the meal. We had seen each other around campus and even talked from time to time, but we weren't close enough to eat from each other's plates. I was a bit surprised by her request, but also pleased.

Yes, I said, be my guest. She then proceeded to stick her index finger directly into the custard, and licked it with obvious pleasure. The audacity. The whole scene left me shivering. No one had ever done anything like it in front of me, and no one ever has since, but the joy that overcame me right at that moment was strong and new. Something completely undecipherable. Lili looked at me self-consciously after that, as though she were expecting some form of judgment. As I sat there, looking straight into her eyes, she remained silent. I must have smiled because she looked suddenly relieved, as if some strange weight had been taken from her shoulders. As if she had been released from some disturbing burden. We burst out laughing.

We did that quite a lot together: burst into laughter. We laughed at ourselves, and we laughed at the world. We made fun of our professors, of certain songs, of some of our classmates, of the soap operas on Channel 2. In fact, we began watching soap operas just for the strange pleasure of making fun of them. It was our own little thing, something we didn't share with anyone else. Her irony was endless. Her sense of humor. She had a very different outlook on life—she read a lot, and that made her different. She was intelligent, even bright. Luminous, I should say. We clicked. Back then, I lived in Lago de Guadalupe, a district far away from pretty much everything, and I often stayed at her place, which was just minutes away from campus. It was like an endless pajama party: we gossiped, we did homework, we commented on the state of the world. We complained. And we laughed.

Liliana sticking her finger in that vanilla custard at the cafeteria in our third or fourth quarter at UAM. I go back to that memory quite often, to that riddle. I look through the windowpanes of time and all I see are these two girls laughing their hearts out as they break free from convention. They glide over the thin ice of seriousness, moving in a different direction altogether. They barely know each other and then, all of a sudden, they are in a world all their own, so close together, and so free. Their happiness is so real, so carnal you can gnaw on it. I see them there, motionless, marveling at each other, knowing that the future awaits them.

Liliana was the name I gave to my freedom.

[Laura Rosales]

One Monday, Lili trudged to class. What happened to you? I asked her, thinking she had taken a fall or had an accident. Liliana responded evasively, half-heartedly, trying to say something that I couldn't understand. It's that Ángel, she said. Ángel what? I dared to ask her. She had previously told me that, since she had started college, Ángel had become even more jealous than usual. He had failed his entrance exam, so he had no alternative but to keep working for the family business, which was in Toluca. Liliana was concerned that he felt inferior to her now that she was a university student in Mexico City. That was her in a nutshell: she was always worried about the pain of others. Ángel what? I insisted. It was then that she intimated that he had hurt her. I didn't know if I could probe even further or if it was better for me to keep quiet. Sex wasn't such an easy subject to tackle back then. A lot of girls had sex, it wasn't unusual, but talking openly about sex, at least between us, wasn't something we did. I managed to piece together from what she said that the day before she had gone to Ángel's house, that they had bathed together, and that they had had sex. They were dozing off when he woke her up, insisting they have sex again. Liliana did not explicitly say that he raped her, but she did tell me that in the end he had apologized to her.

On another occasion she came to school with a bandaged arm. When I asked her, she told me that she had slipped in the bathtub and injured herself on a broken glass. The explanation seemed reasonable to me, but I still kept wondering. Something was happening, but I couldn't put my finger on it. Something was out of whack, but I couldn't quite understand what it was. Her playfulness, her sense of humor, the way she walked through campus as if the world belonged to her, soon dispelled my concerns. She was so easygoing, so optimistic. I had no reason for concern. A little while later, Lili told me that she had broken up with Ángel, but that he would not let her go. He yanks me by the arm, Laura, she said, literally grabbing my arm, physically enacting her words. Her fingerprint on my forearm was reddish, and it only faded away little by little.

[Manolo Casillas Espinal]

I don't want to have any boyfriends, she once declared to whomever wanted to hear it. How come, I asked nonchalantly, as if I had not noticed the plural. Because then men think you are their possession, she said. And I won't take that. No way. I had not asked her anything, I had not even hinted at that possibility, but she must have known that that was my heart's yearning. She could read between the lines. She had a way of knowing what we only glimpsed about ourselves. I had fallen in love with her as soon as I met her in our fourth quarter, when we officially became architecture majors. She was outgoing and friendly, but she was, above all, very direct. Blunt at times. Fortunately, she was also charming, so we appreciated her honesty. She had a way with words, always speaking to us as though she were coming from a place we were only about to set off to. I longed for that world, the one she left behind in order to join us back on campus.

We started working in the same study group almost immediately. The program was very demanding from the start, so it was common for us to work entire nights or during the weekends and, because her apartment was nearby, it became our spot. We were all usually there, at Mimosas 658, working on blueprints or scale models, or simply sharing notes. I came to appreciate the way she approached architecture, how she would let her imagination run wild and come up with ingenious solutions to problems of perspective or projection. Architecture flew through her; it was not something intuitive, but rather organic.

If I close my eyes, I can see her clearly even now. Here she is, look at her. Her hair, long and straight, shiny under the sunlight, oscillating from left to right as she walks, usually in a hurry. Very tall, very slender, very much in her own world. Her black leather jacket, and the backpack on her back—a rebel. An avid reader. An intellectual. A woman who does not want to have any boyfriends.

[Othón Santos Álvarez]

The way she told stories. It must have been at the end of the second or third quarter; in any case we already had several team projects due. We were gathered together for lunch, nibbling our food and listening to her at the same time, as if under a spell. Liliana had visited the Teotihuacán pyramids over the weekend and was telling this colorful story of the whole journey. I don't remember the details, but I can recall how she convulsed with laughter, and how we, all around her, laughed to no end. We were almost in tears, and through those joyful tears I saw her at the very center of our attention: the leader of our group, without a doubt. Not only the smartest, but also the most focused and the most mature among us. So quick-witted and snarky.

We were mostly interested in getting passing grades, in preparing ourselves to get good jobs as architects and finally make some money, but that was not Lili, she always wanted more. Architecture was not a profession for her, but a way of exploring the material world around us, which bore living imprints from past worlds. She loved downtown Mexico City, for example. Everything related to our indigenous roots interested her. She never wasted an opportunity to visit ruins or pyramids, camera in hand. Liliana was very driven. She was especially good at planning and she drew very well too. Once, a professor asked us to develop blueprints for a market: the design, the façade, the distribution of the space. Lili's design was the best, of course.

We got to know each other quite well over time, especially because of our group work. At Lili's flat, where we usually met, we only had one drawing board. So, while someone drew, another built walls for the scale models, still another opened windows. That's how we worked together. We took turns sleeping. We spent whole weekends like that, half asleep, half awake, living in proximity. More than a group of friends, we were like a family. And a pretty close one at that. Still, there were issues we didn't touch: politics, for example. Or Liliana's shadowy boyfriend from Toluca.

As soon as we finished our work, we would all pitch in to buy beers or cigarettes. Then we went back to Lili's place and played some music, usually folk songs or some progressive rock in Spanish. We spent time telling jokes, talking about where we came from or where we wanted to go in the future.

Everything seemed so open to us.

[Ángel López]

I smoked whatever I could lay my hands on, and she smoked those stinky Raleighs that nobody liked. What's up, man? she'd greet me when we met on campus. She was super thoughtful: she surprised us with little letters, messages, drawings. Her handwriting was enviable, very unique, like the rest of her. She had style. Liliana was unassuming, hippie-like and, yes, very pretty. I thought she wasn't going to talk to us because we—Manolo, Othón, Gerardo, and I—were very working class. You could tell that we had no money: we only used inexpensive materials to make our projects, the kind you could buy at the corner store. Maybe that's why we sat in the back of the classroom, where the teachers couldn't see us and we could relax or even doze off. One day Liliana sat near us, and we realized that she was special.

I fancied Liliana, like Manolo, who was a close friend of mine. One day, Manolo and I concluded that he had a better chance of winning her heart, especially because he lived closer to her in Azcapotzalco. I was living toward the north of the city, quite far away. And frankly, he was more smitten with her than I was. Over time, Liliana became close friends with Ana, and they went everywhere together, although Ana was with Fernando. Or rather: Ana was dating Fernando while spending most of her time with Liliana.

On January 13, she made a cake to celebrate my birthday.

[Norma Xavier Quintana]

We both liked to wear black. Are you actually reading *Reader's Selections*? she asked me once, rolling her eyes. I tried my best to hide my religious, middle-class, conservative background in such a radical campus, but didn't succeed. I first noticed Liliana because she was very tall, but mostly because she was wearing pastel colors, very à la Flans, an all-girl band in vogue in those days. But we only became friends later on, when I switched to night classes. I had failed the Structures course, and Liliana didn't want to take the Installations class with the morning instructor, so we met in the late afternoon hours, when the sun was setting. By then she boasted this very long, lustrous hair, and had replaced all pastel colors with black. She never took off her famous motorcycle jacket. Once she challenged me: we would see which of the two of us could put up with wearing the same jeans for three weeks in a row without washing them. Neither of us won.

I skipped class with her, something I had never done before in my life. We would go for coffee or just lean against a wall, letting the world go by. She had ideas about pretty much everything, so many stories to tell. That's how I learned she had recently become a research assistant. And what is that exactly? I asked, curious. She read books, she said, wrote summaries, and handed them to the professor before a set deadline. I didn't know such a thing existed on campus, but I immediately wanted to become a research assistant myself. She said that, after graduation, she and Ana wanted to go to England. That was their plan, she said, as if it were no big deal. As if we could just pack our things and leave everything behind. I could not help but feel a bit envious

She assured me that all television stations were spurious.

It was through her that I got to know the other members of the study group, which behaved more like a family. Liliana, their leader. If she said something, that's what they did. Fortunately for them, she liked to make people happy. But she was not a hypocrite. If she liked you, she would give her life for you; otherwise, she wouldn't even look at you. When we worked together, she played a U2 cassette a lot, especially the song "With or Without You." She would play it again and again, obsessively, until everybody got fed up and forced her to change the song. She rejoiced in our company. In fact, she craved camaraderie. It was not unusual for her to ask her friends not to leave her alone. Or to stay overnight. And she was very clear about it: when she invited them to stay at her house, it was because she wanted company. Nothing else.

I had a car. I let her borrow it quite often. I gave her the keys and, when she was done, she parked it back where she found it.

This is how we became real friends, around the fifth trimester. I had a boyfriend who was from Cuernavaca, and he rented a room in a house here in Mexico City. A girl lived there too, and soon they got together. When I realized what was going on, I burst into tears in the classroom. Lili came over and hugged me. It's not worth it, she said. She handed me a piece of paper: *In the midst of winter I found there was, within me, an invincible summer*. This is your winter, she added. And it will pass. Don't cry for anyone.

[Leonardo Jasso]

Our professors thought highly of her. There was one professor who asked Liliana to join her as she went from drawing board to drawing board, rating our projects. As soon as she finished her assessment, the professor would ask Liliana for her own comments. Once when they approached my work station, Liliana was tough on me. Conscientious, but tough. I already liked her, but that made me like her even more. I wanted her to be my girlfriend for a while. But I was looking for an old-fashioned girlfriend, someone to hold hands with, and Liliana had other ideas. She used to say, for example, that the Bible was just a book full of amusing stories and that dating was what boys used to disguise their desire for possession and control. She didn't believe in any of that. She didn't want to be anyone's sweetheart.

Still, I didn't give up that easily. I took advantage of every single opportunity to talk to her. That's how I learned she had been a swimmer, which explained her lean, strong body. She told me her father was completing a PhD in some foreign country and that her only sister was studying in the United States. I assumed that was why she was so smart and diligent. I once surprised her in Toluca,

where I knew she went every weekend to visit her parents. I called
her out of the blue and insisted that we meet. She arrived in an
old car, and she took me to visit a spring in Almoloya de Juárez
where, as much as I wanted to, I could not make out the famous
line that was supposed to separate dirty water from clean spring
water. She took me to a clearing, in a nearby forest, afterward. I
used to camp here with my parents, she said. It was an area brimming with pine trees and tall oyamels that she returned to when
she wanted to spend time by herself.

[Emilio Hernández Garza]

Ah, how that girl loved going to the movies! We spent a lot of time
together when I managed a cafeteria in the Álvaro Obregón district for about a year and a half. She came every now and then, at
her own leisure, supposedly to help me out on the register, but I
suspected she was mostly looking for company. Although she did
not complain about the small amount of money she made ringing
up food. Or the pack of those hideous Raleigh cigarettes she usually took with her when she was done. She was not inconsiderate,
though. Never taking advantage of us being cousins. Iliana, a good
friend of mine from that time, and Liliana got along well. The two
of them would talk, while I was busy with work in the cafeteria,
watching them from afar.

She was such a smart aleck. Once we arranged to meet at
Parque Tezozómoc, near the metro station by her house. She was
late and I fell asleep on the bench. She woke me up with a great
laugh and told me that she had taken some photos of me looking
like a drunkard in Mexico City. She always walked around with
that little camera of hers hanging from her neck, taking pictures

of old buildings, desolate landscapes, hurried people crossing city streets, or slumbering cousins dozing off in public spaces.

Organizing movie marathons was our thing. On Sundays, especially when we arrived early from Toluca, or when my uncle brought her back at a reasonable hour, we watched as many movies as we could. We were so addicted to movies it was not rare for us to be at the movie theater all day long, watching films from 10:00 A.M. onward. We would buy a gigantic fruit cocktail at the market and sneak it into the theaters. Once we were done with the films, I'd invite Lili to eat at El Kioskito, a carnitas place I liked, although we'd also try the tacos de canasta by the Castillo de Chapultepec. We never missed the International Film Festival. I saw *Babette's Feast* and *Red Sorghum* with her. The last movie I saw with Liliana was *Dark Eyes*, with Marcello Mastroianni.

[Raúl Espino Madrigal]

Would you like to come home and stay the night? she asked. That's what she said, but I thought I misheard. She said it loud enough, enunciating every vowel and every consonant, and still I could not hear it well. Nothing had prepared me for that. We had come back together from a weekend in Toluca, after much insistence on my part. We met at the Toluca bus terminal and, once we got to Mexico City, I accompanied her to her metro station. We had had such a great time, talking and joking as we left behind the mountain pines and entered the city proper, and later, as we found our way through busy metro stations together. We were about to say goodbye when she asked me. I was so taken aback that I didn't know what to say. Liliana rendered me speechless with such ease;

she could say the sweetest and cruelest words, nothing in between.

I was standing there, stunned, thousands of thoughts racing through my head, when she added: I promise I won't rape you. I looked at her, bewildered. She brought up sex in such a relaxed way, nonchalantly even, and here I was half-paralyzed. Such a masterful move. Still, I didn't want to risk it. We had had a wonderful time that day, and my aunt, who lived near the Parque Hundido, was expecting me for dinner. I gracefully declined and, to my utter surprise, Liliana insisted. I don't want to be alone, she finally admitted. Please, stay with me. I can ask your aunt for permission if you want. I couldn't believe my ears. I could not believe how lucky I was. I naturally accepted. But no sex, she said, quite frankly. I had no problem with that.

We talked nonstop as we prepared to lie down on her full mattress. At one point, in between stories, I asked if I could stroke her back. She paused, giving the matter serious thought. It's a very important decision, she said. For all it could imply, she added. But she accepted nonetheless. After a while, we changed positions and she caressed my back. We spent a long time just like this, talking and cuddling and kissing. It was paradise. I don't remember how it came up, but at one point I admitted I had never had sex before. I was a bit ashamed, but it was the truth. How interesting, she said, refusing to elaborate further. I confessed I hadn't had any serious relationships, and that I was not really interested in casual sex. I really want love, I told her, to be in love. And Liliana looked at me with her enormous sad eyes, hardly blinking. This is perfect, I said. There will be time for more later, when we are ready. I did not want to put pressure on her. I wanted her to feel safe around me. In the diary I had started not too long before, I wrote, quite optimistically, that our relationship was finally taking off, and that the time would come for us to really be together. There would be time, I insisted, to love each other on a physical level as well.

Waking up next to Liliana was a dream come true. She left a string of kisses on my back at daybreak. Good morning, she said later, with a huge smile. I was truly convinced that we had finally moved on to that next stage and that we had finally become a couple, but that was not the case. I got up and scurried to campus for an early class, and when I saw her again she was as distant as ever. She wouldn't let me get close to her however hard I tried. That's how it was with her: a relationship of ups and downs, of sporadic peaks of affection and closeness.

[Iliana González Rodarte]

We never talked much, much less about personal matters, but in the hours we spent together while Emilio managed the cafeteria, and when she would visit us at the San Lorenzo Acopilco house, where we were roommates, I was left with the impression that Liliana was very worldly. She was interested in politics. She smoked a lot of cigarettes while talking about movies, but also about music. Once she told us that she had sung, or had somehow participated, in a big group performing with Café Tacuba, a progressive rock band that originated there at UAM. She looked so much like her mother! When we visited them in Toluca, she was always kind, very refined; an affable elegance running through her gestures and demeanor. The crockery. The coffee cups. The tall bookcases. How I wish I had talked more with Liliana about her personal life. If she had told me something, anything, I of course would have shared it with your parents. Perhaps that's why she didn't.

Liliana, in one image: the newspaper under her arm, the intellectual eyeglasses.

[Ana Ocadiz]

A battle of giants / turns / air into natural gas. / A wild duel / warns / how close I am to entering. / In a colossal world / I feel my frailness.

We were crazy about this song by Nacha Pop. We always emphasized the word *frailness*. Mine. Hers. And then we would talk
about our strength together. I don't remember exactly when, but
Liliana lent me a book that had been fundamental to her: *Milena,*
by Margarete Buber-Neumann. A book of black covers and
smudged pages. It told the story of the remarkable writer and ac-
tivist Milena Jesenská, who is now more often remembered, fortunately or unfortunately, as the mistress of Franz Kafka, a man
she loved very much. The story begins and ends in the concentration camp where Margarete and Milena met and, despite misfor-
tune and tragedy, despite hunger and cold, despite the awfulness
of those times, they became intimate friends. We were surprised
at the way in which they both challenged the authoritarianism and
hostility of their environment with a love that was full and light.
Milena, whose name means beloved, disobeyed the rules of the
concentration camp more out of habit and less out of principle:
instead of keeping to herself, or becoming dull or isolated or evil,
she lavished herself onto others with a determination that sometimes seemed like stupidity. But that was her dogma: love.

Liliana not only identified with a woman for whom friendship
was paramount, someone used to generosity, to showering everybody with attention and kindness (although Milena also demanded
everything in return), but she also recognized traces of our own
environment in the book—a world that, sometimes, in our darkest
moments, we thought of as a concentration camp. We were so
limited, or rather, the expectations for our lives were so narrow
that we often felt like we were bound by straitjackets. And I'm not
talking only about our parents. It was society as a whole. You had
to behave in a certain way. You couldn't give much of yourself,
much less freely; you had to be very measured. Closeness and
gain had to be calculated first. Liliana, on the other hand, loved

life, the street, cinema, her friends, architecture, Manolo, me, even Ángel. That was her superpower; and that, too, was her Achilles' heel.

I read the book in one sitting, and it impressed me so much that when I had my first daughter many years later I named her Milena, which to me was another way of saying her name. Of saying Liliana. That's what we were back then, Milena's girls. Her apprentices. We all became Milena's girls around Liliana, regardless of whether we were male or female. Milena's children. *I believe in terrible ghosts / from a strange place / and in the silly things I do / to make you burst into laughter. / In a colossal world / I feel my frailness.*

VI

TERRIBLE GHOSTS FROM A STRANGE PLACE

[Leticia Hernández Garza]

She met Ángel her first year of high school, maybe a bit earlier. She didn't like him at first, but he made her laugh. He was fun. And intense. He invited her to the movies. He lavished her with flowers and candy. He told her he couldn't live without her. And he was solicitous: he offered to take her wherever she needed to go in his souped-up red car. His vehement insistence ended up winning her over and, toward the end of high school, they started dating for real.

Ángel was always very jealous. He made a scene over pretty much anything. He once caused some drama when a swimming buddy gave Liliana a small gift. He couldn't bear it. He yelled at her, scolding her as though she was his daughter or wife. Little by little she realized he was trying to control everything she did, how she behaved, even who her friends were. They had been hanging out for a year when he first slapped her. Lili stopped talking to him for a while after that. I don't know how or why she got back together with him. At first Liliana saw this as a game, something harmless, a sign of his vehemence, but when she left for university, he became more violent. Liliana met people he was not able to supervise. Her world was expanding, while his was turning upside down.

[Raúl Espino Madrigal]

I was about to leave when I saw her running down the hallway. I had been waiting for her and was afraid she had stood me up. I was sad and annoyed, and worried we weren't going to make it to the movies. She was out of breath when she finally reached me. Someone came to see me, she said, panting. Someone I wasn't expecting. I was ready for her to say more, but she was still trying to catch her breath. I never knew what was going on with her and I resented that she kept me out of the loop when it came to her personal life. A relative of yours? I asked. When she caught her breath, she told me that it was a guy from the past. I don't exactly remember the words she used, but she didn't call him her "ex-boyfriend." Instead, she used some kind of vague turn of phrase like "someone I had a history with," or "someone who belongs to history," or "someone who appeared from the past." She didn't say his name. She didn't want to say more and I didn't want to hear answers that might have involved another man, so I didn't probe any further.

But then, as we stood there, she continued. I had no other choice, she said, more to herself than to me. She said this guy had showed up at her house unannounced and he wouldn't leave. She had to listen to him. He was extremely upset, and she had no other choice but to calm him down. You should have told him to go to hell, Liliana, I said, reminding her that we had plans. Why am I the one who has to be stuck here, alone, waiting for you? She didn't react. She seemed to be lost inside herself. And what's going on with you and this guy? I finally asked her, contrite. She looked me straight in the eye. I told you, he belongs to the past, she said calmly. He's history. He doesn't mean anything to me. We are in the present, she added. The past does not belong in the present, so it doesn't matter.

But then she admitted their encounter had been more serious than she'd first let on. The guy was carrying "one of those things that shoots bullets," she said, and I do remember hearing that exact phrase because it shocked me to the core. As she spoke, Liliana demonstrated by pointing her thumb and forefinger from inside her jacket. I froze, my head spinning. I went from being angry at her to worrying about her and asked if she was okay. She nodded. From what I understood, he threatened to hurt himself. Suicide? I asked, just to be sure. She nodded again. She had to wait for him to calm down and then, as soon as she could leave him, she ran to meet me because she knew I was waiting.

I didn't ask her what she did to calm him down. I didn't ask if he had left or where he was. It didn't occur to me to look around to see if he had followed her.

It was all very weird at the time. The mixture of anger and jealousy made it difficult for me to figure out who we were talking about. How could a guy like this appear out of the blue, and what did that mean for Liliana? The weapon was an issue in and of itself. Guns were totally foreign to me. I had never had any contact with them, not even remotely. Guns simply did not exist in my world. I was scandalized that Liliana could be involved in something like that, but she told me that I shouldn't worry, that everything was under control.

Are you sure? I am sure, she said.

I believed her.

What do we do now? we asked ourselves, realizing we were still there, sitting on the floor of the hallway, the campus empty all around us. You are safe, that's what matters now, I said. We paused, looking at each other. Do you think we can still make it to the movies? We couldn't help it. We checked the time and strategized our next steps: pesero, metro, taxi. We got up at the same time, and sped off to the cinema, knowing full well that we were still going to be late. We managed to catch a glimpse of *The Accused,* with Jodie Foster, which had just been released that week.

It must have been March. March 1989.

[Norma Xavier Quintana]

I never knew of any other boyfriend except for Ángel. Excuse me, I mean: Liliana's ex-boyfriend, not boyfriend. I don't think I ever got to see him in person. I was aware he sometimes drove her to her house in Toluca, that he sometimes picked her up at the university and, occasionally, he waited for her by the little apartment on Mimosas. I don't know if I'd only ever seen a photo of him, but I was able to recognize him. He usually came by on a red motorcycle, very noisy. Or in a black sedan. A compact car. What I do remember is that Lili wanted out of this relationship, but couldn't. The guy was very persistent. She was, or seemed to be, going steady with Manolo, but Ángel still insisted that she was his girlfriend. I never witnessed any violence between them.

[Ángel López]

I met Ángel a couple of times. A strange guy. We never spoke directly. He came to campus a couple of times and I saw him from afar. Someone told me that he was Liliana's friend from Toluca, and I figured that he was, or had been, her boyfriend. But she never introduced him to us as such. He was never at any of the parties we organized at Liliana's apartment. He was totally absent in the life that Liliana led here with us. She was very discreet.

Even when, much later, she started to go out with Manolo she was like this: no hugs or kisses in public, no holding hands. Nothing at all.

[Othón Santos Álvarez]

I don't have many virtues, but I am a good observer. Whenever any of my friends were down or depressed, I left them a message, a quote or a verse, to cheer them up. Lili was just like me, so we exchanged little messages all the time. There was this one time that I criticized Ángel's behavior, but she immediately put a stop to that. She was outspoken and talkative, but she knew how to set her own boundaries. Ángel's arrogance caught my attention, he had that motorcycle thing going on, his whole attitude. I didn't like him at all. He would park the motorcycle at Lili's apartment, placing it in the front courtyard. That's how I noticed he was carrying a gun. I'm from Necaxa, in the state of Puebla, and my family carried weapons, so I immediately recognized the bulge behind his pants, under his leather jacket, which fitted him very tightly. I went to Liliana, asking her about the gun, but she dismissed my concern and told me she didn't know anything about it. I tried to dissuade her from seeing him, but she wouldn't listen. Ángel was the kind of guy who'd half greet us and, if he did hang around, he'd isolate himself, suspiciously watching us from afar. Or, if he saw that we were still hanging out at Liliana's place, he'd leave for an hour or more and come back when we were heading out. He never made any attempt to get to know us or chat with us. I didn't trust him. Then he disappeared for a while, and it was during that time that Liliana went out with Manolo for almost two quarters. I only saw him a couple of times at the college. He would wait for Liliana in the parking lot and then they would leave on that noisy motorcycle, neither of them wearing helmets.

[Gerardo Navarro]

I was not aware Liliana had a boyfriend. In fact, I never saw her with anyone. The group was pretty much together all the time: here, there, and everywhere. We did homework together, we helped each other with projects, we ate together, and we even threw parties together. Every now and then that guy, Ángel, came by our campus to pick her up on Fridays, when she went back to Toluca. That was the only thing I knew about him: he was the guy who, on Fridays, would pick Liliana up on a flashy motorcycle. I saw him about three times and on none of those occasions did I notice any jealousy or violence between them. Liliana never spoke of him, in any case; she didn't even mention him. It was as if he didn't exist, or as if he was a ghost. Liliana was very reserved. We talked a lot, but mainly about school or movies, which she liked so much, or we joked around, but we rarely touched on such personal issues. If she wasn't with our group of friends, Lili was always with Ana, sometimes with Fernando. Usually with both.

[Leonardo Jasso]

I ran into him once when I was walking Liliana to her apartment. Classes had ended for the day but I wanted to keep talking, so I offered to walk to the metro with her. Lest something happen to you on the way, I joked, and she laughed. We made our way together through Azcapotzalco without giving it much thought. We got off at the Tezozómoc metro station, walking slowly, as I wanted to stay close to her for a while longer. As we turned into Mimosas, he was waiting for her in a black car. I stopped almost by instinct. I hesitated, but Liliana told me that there was no problem, that Ángel was just a friend. A friend from Toluca. And she almost pulled me by the elbow to bring me close to her side. When he got out of the car, Ángel looked at me sideways and, although he shook my hand, I felt a heavy vibe. I felt like I had to explain who I was or why I was there, but I didn't.

That day I understood that Liliana was not free.

[Ana Ocadiz]

I saw Ángel several times and spent some time with him, always with Liliana around. I got to know him here in Mexico City, except for that time we went to Toluca with him, a quick getaway that neither my parents nor hers knew about. I wouldn't say we got along well, but we were cordial to each other. I don't remember why he gave me a mixtape, I think it had a song that was popular then, but he added a passport-sized photograph of himself to the cassette, which was the same one that was used to identify him later. "You know I give you this with affection," he wrote on the back. March 1990.

One time, Lili and I were with him while he was delivering vehicle verification stickers that were fake, or shady at any rate, here in Mexico City. I was thrilled but afraid. We knew that he was doing something illegal, and I felt like we were accomplices to his crime just by being with him, but we never discussed it openly. We never said: Ángel is a criminal, a forger, he's really shady; but we thought it. At least I did. There was this air of risk around him; I couldn't explain it clearly, but it was a persistent feeling, and it made me uneasy, if not outright fearful. With the passage of time, I have come to see that we were young, naïve and well-meaning.

His possessiveness came across in his physical appearance: although he was not tall, he had strong arms and shoulders and legs, and had an unsettling presence to him. He was always somewhat conspicuous, without doing anything particularly outrageous, like that time he came to campus and walked through the design building. Something, I am not so sure what, made people turn as he passed by. It was obvious he did not belong there.

There were separations and reconciliations between them, but I never knew who was breaking up or why they got back together. He called her constantly. He looked for her, showing up unannounced. He kind of blackmailed her, threatening to hurt himself. It was his idea to deflate the tires of Manolo's car when he learned he was interested in Liliana. This was his way of letting him know that he had better back off.

[Emilio Hernández Garza]

I met Ángel in Toluca near the house where Lili's parents lived, in the little park across the street. I was getting out of a taxi and, in the distance, I saw that Liliana and this short, blond guy, who was wearing cycling shorts, were arguing. He was shoving her over and over, pushing her in the chest, forcing her backward. I ran to them, hit him hard and he fell. He tried to fight back, but I was much bigger. Liliana begged me not to hit him because he was her boyfriend. He had been her boyfriend in high school, but that was the first time I had met him. We had to calm down a bit before the three of us walked back to her parents' house. He had left his bicycle leaning against the fence. How can you go out with this little shit, cousin? I said when he was still within earshot. Don't you see this guy is a dwarf? I sneered. Ángel twitched again, but had to stay calm. He had no choice, and he left. Liliana and I went into the house and didn't say anything to my uncle or aunt. That Sunday she returned to Mexico City with me.

[Ana Ocadiz]

Liliana went out to buy some lottery tickets to give to Ángel for his birthday and, while she was there, she bought two more, one for her and one for me. It must have been mid-April. Then we went to the Azcapotzalco market to buy this dessert made of strawberries, whipped cream, lemon ice cream, and tons of honey. We really loved it, but it was huge so we usually split one. We were heading out when we saw a man selling birds, wire cages piled high up on his back, at one of the entrances to the market. The idea came to her immediately, lighting her eyes, and I understood it all at once. Lili bought a sparrow. Releasing the bird would be Ángel's extra birthday present.

We rejoiced, imagining her wings flapping through the air.

We rushed out of the market, with the sparrow in a brown paper bag, and went straight to the university. We had classes and research to do in the library, but during the day Lili would peek into the bag just to make sure the little bird was still alive. Time went by and Ángel did not show up, or he was late. We have to free her, Liliana told me in the early afternoon, flustered. I agreed. Where? I asked. Here? No way, she said, this is such an unremarkable place. We have to find somewhere special. She thought about it for a while and, suddenly, her eyes lit up. I know, she said. Follow me.

It didn't take us long to get to Parque Tezozómoc, which was not far from her house. Just one stop on the metro. She wanted us to do a little ceremony. Freedom, she reminded me all the time, was the most important possession in life. When we finally opened the bag, we expected the sparrow to fly off, but she didn't. The bird took a couple of steps on the grass, then she stopped and fell to her side. We tried to revive her, but we soon realized it was all over. Her death broke our hearts. She is in a better place now, I told Liliana, who remained motionless, in shock, as if something had been shattered inside her. She was about to be free, she said quietly as we walked toward her house.

She is free, I said, trying to reassure her.

VII

AND ISN'T THIS HAPPINESS?

The trip to Oaxaca. The famous trip to Oaxaca. It all started with my friends from high school, our stubborn desire to enjoy the summer at the beach. Puerto Escondido. Huatulco. Names like candy in our mouths. It suddenly occurred to me to invite Liliana as well. I suggested that she come with us, promising that everything would be fine, and that traveling together would help us a lot as a couple. I was feeling pretty confident at that time because things were going quite well for me: I had just won a national design award and, to crown it all, I was hoping to go steady with Liliana. I finally convinced her by the end of July 1989 and, since we had to buy tickets in advance, we went to TAPO, the bus terminal. It is now a fact we are going to Oaxaca together, I said once I had the tickets in my hand. Thrilled to the core. Smiling. Not so fast, Raúl, she replied. I have no idea what will happen in my life. I honestly can't promise you anything. A classic of hers, leaving me hanging, avoiding labels.

The day of our departure came, which incidentally fell on my birthday, August 9, 1989. But time passed and I did not hear from Liliana. We were supposed to call each other then go to the terminal together, but my phone messages didn't reach her. I didn't know what to do, whether to go look for her at Mimosas, like other times, or wait for her to call me. In the end, confused and angry, I decided to go to the terminal with my friends.

Where is your girl? My friends made fun of me when they saw me by myself. I don't know, I said, defeated. I begged them not to ask any more questions. Wait a minute, said one of them. Isn't that her? We turned around and, indeed, there she was,

Liliana, in the distance. I could not believe my eyes. She had shown up. I was instantly filled with joy, forgetting what had happened before. I ran to her, like in the movies, arms wide open, so euphoric I didn't even notice she was not responding in the same way. She was standing still, next to some backpacks. Are you OK? I asked when I finally reached her, and she nodded coldly, avoiding the cheek-kissing greeting. What's up? I finally asked, fearing her reply. There were some last-minute changes, she said. I waited, in silence. I'm sorry, Raúl, she began. Just say it, I said. I am going to Oaxaca, she said, but with my architecture friends. I am taking care of our backpacks, but they will be here at any minute. I was floored. I was speechless once again. I knew Liliana was never really into me, but I never imagined she would do something like this. But our tickets, I said, automatically, half stuttering, we bought the tickets. I changed mine a couple of days ago, she said, evading my eyes. My heart just stopped. I was crushed. It felt like I was in the middle of a very bad joke, unable to do or say anything, except it was no joke, it was my life. And it was for real.

It is my birthday, Liliana, I said, trying to appeal to her sentimental side. Make it my gift. I blatantly begged her to please make the trip with me. Travel with your friends, if you wish, but meet me in Oaxaca, please. She didn't budge. Could you at least give me a hug? I pleaded. She hesitated but ended up embracing me timidly. I closed my eyes. I was no longer in a busy bus terminal in Mexico City but in that other place I always traveled to when I smelled her. Her warmth. Her skin. Her closeness. I had lots of mixed feelings, but I loved her so deeply and her embrace truly felt like a gift. I bid her farewell before her friends arrived. And I walked away, feeling that every effort I'd put into trying to build a relationship with her had been utterly pointless.

[Ana Ocadiz]

Tents. Explorer backpacks. Cans of tuna and cans of jalapeño peppers. Very little money but, on the other hand, a true desire to go to the places of our dreams: Oaxaca, Huatulco, Puerto Escondido. We had all heard about them, but none of us had had a chance to visit them yet. We organized the trip at the last minute. We just brought it up when we were all hanging out one time, and it just took off. We would go, of course we would. Fernando, who at times was my boyfriend, and at times wasn't, said he was in; Leonardo, who was interested in Liliana, said he would go; and Carlos, a tall, blond guy, said he would join us too. We took night buses, trying to make the most of our holiday week, and save on lodging at the same time. And who cares about the discomfort or lack of sleep when you are twenty and your destination is utter beauty and absolute freedom?

[Raúl Espino Madrigal]

We arrived in Oaxaca City very early the next morning and walked directly to the hostel. My friends tried to cheer me up, but I felt drained, truly sad. We were just there, hanging out in the lobby, waiting for our room, when one of my friends glanced through the window and said: look, Raúl, there goes your girl. And, indeed, there she was, Liliana and her friends were walking down the street. I couldn't help it. I went out to talk to her. Come with me, Liliana, I said again. It's better this way, Raúl, please, she said.

It was not meant to be.

The next morning, before checking out the traditional markets, we went to the bus terminal to buy tickets to Puerto Escondido for that night. The idea was to take the bus overnight and wake up the next morning by the ocean. I was minding my own business while my friends bought our tickets, when someone pushed me from the side. I turned around, annoyed, when I realized it was Liliana, who had come to greet me. No way, I said laughing. What else could I do? We were both amused by the coincidence of running into each other there, since Liliana and her friends had come to the terminal to buy tickets too, but for Huatulco. I thought of you all night long, I told her when we sat down on one of those plastic chairs. So did I, she admitted. Does it make any sense for us to be in separate places when we are both thinking about each other? I asked. Wouldn't it be better for us to be in the same place? Those phrases summed up our relationship: wanting to be together without really being together.

I spent the whole day in the downtown district with my friends just walking around, marveling at the colonial architecture and the color on the walls. Here they go again, my friend said, pointing Liliana's group out to me. It was a curse or a sign: they were everywhere we were. We laughed and, obviously, they made fun of me to no end. I felt trapped with my friends, and believed Liliana was trapped with hers too. I wanted to untangle the situation, even if it meant doing something drastic or desperate. Go ahead, I said to myself. It is now or never. They were in a craft store or a shoe store, I don't remember. I went in and grabbed her by her arm. Cut the bullshit, Liliana. She asked me to lower my voice and dragged me to the sidewalk so we could speak away from her friends, somewhere a bit more private. Perhaps it was my attitude or my words, or perhaps she was not having a good time with her friends, but she finally agreed to join me. Liliana said yes, I will go with you, and a whole new world opened up for me. I want to go to Monte Albán, she said, adding that her friends had not wanted to visit the place the day before. I went there yesterday, I said, but I'd gladly go with you again. It's worth it, I added. And so, we coasted, the two of us, a man and a woman, off to Monte Albán.

It was the best part of the trip. We were in an incredible place, sharing a very quiet moment. After so much planning and after waiting for so long, I was elated to be in her company. At last, it was just the two of us. The area was full of tourists, but we remained in our own world, undisturbed, walking slowly between the pyramids, touching the ancient rocks, leaning against them at times. We climbed the steep steps of a pyramid and, wanting the moment to last forever, we found a spot to sit up there, on its cusp. The Valley of Oaxaca, which was very green and, at that time of the day, shaded by the golden light of the setting sun, emerged as a mirage. We remained there, mostly in silence, taking the moment in. A warm, gentle breeze surrounded us.

Together. We were together.

A man approached and, as were enjoying the panorama instead of looking directly at the ruins, he asked: do you like it? And Liliana answered: very much, speaking for both of us while looking into the immensity. I never liked her more. Between my shyness and her defensiveness, it was so difficult for me to get close to Liliana. This time I asked her to let me touch her hand. She smiled; the sun pricking her skin, her luminous hair, her enormous, gentle eyes. She extended her arms and clasped my hands with hers. Time stood still. We were sitting next to each other on top of an ageless pyramid, holding hands. Giggling. Murmuring words neither of us understood. I did not know what else I could ask from life. I felt blessed.

An eternal moment.

What a paradox, but such a thing does exist.

[Leonardo Jasso]

Liliana started the trip with us, but then, after a brief stay in Oaxaca, she vanished. It was all done with great mystery and secrecy. Some did not even notice she was no longer with us. But I had come on the trip in the hopes of getting closer to her, so I knew immediately. She left our group to spend time with some guy she was going out with. He was a tall, slim guy who had recently won a major design award. They talked a lot about him on campus. I missed her, but I didn't want to ruin my trip either. And so we continued toward the coast.

It was a huge surprise when Liliana joined us again on the beach.

[Raúl Espino Madrigal]

When it got dark, we returned to Oaxaca and met my other friends ahead of our trip to Puerto Escondido that evening. And we went straight to the beach upon arrival, as we had promised. It was dawn and we plunged into the sea. Then we proceeded to find a hotel and rented a large room for all of us. We ate something in the afternoon and, judging by her symptoms, it appeared that Liliana had caught a cold. We decided to rest, hoping she would recover soon. The town was bustling. A surf tournament was taking place and loud music hovered everywhere on the main street. We joined the festivities in the evening. People danced happily. Do you want to dance with me? I asked Liliana, holding my hand in front of her. But she was a bit listless. I don't feel that well, she said. You should find yourself a more suitable partner, she suggested. I stayed with her, enjoying the scene. I'm going to bed, she said a little bit later. I really shouldn't be here. She said it and, immediately, she was gone. Her independence always confused me. I'll walk you, I said, catching up with her. We went back to the hotel, where she took a couple of pills for her cold, and we fell asleep. We didn't even notice when my friends got back. Or when they went out early the next morning. Do you want me to bring you something to eat? I asked her when she woke up. She declined. I just need some time alone, she said. And I understood that she needed space.

When I went back to the hotel to see how she was doing or if she needed anything, Liliana was gone. She had left a little note, in her wonderfully stylish handwriting, explaining that she was not feeling well and that she wanted to continue the journey on her own. She didn't know whether she was going to continue traveling in Oaxaca or whether she was going back to Mexico City, but in either case, she had made her decision: She was not going to be with me. She left her share of the money to cover the cost of the room. I was crushed once again. Worn out. I was still holding the piece of paper in my hands, right there, in the middle of a room that had held her not too long ago, when I decided it was over for good.

I went back to my friends and, after a while on the beach, we saw that Liliana's group was around. And so was Liliana. I had been worried about her, fearing what could happen to a woman alone on the beach or on the road, so I was relieved when I saw her from afar. She looked happy and relaxed with her friends. She was her usual beautiful self. It was hard to see what troubled her inside at this distance. I approached her. Are you feeling all right? I asked, just concerned about her health, with nothing else in mind. I thought I at least deserved an explanation. I desperately wanted to hear what had been going through her mind. Why she had be-haved the way she did. What was troubling her, keeping her tied up inside. We sat on the sand. I looked at her and she stared at the ocean. I felt so ill last night, Raúl. I didn't feel right, she said. She hesitated, and then she added: It didn't feel right. I just want to leave everything behind, she continued. And then she paused. The sound of the ocean filled in the silence. I met my friends by pure chance on the beach, she said, looking me in the eye. I took her in, finding that place within me that belonged to her. They invited me to join them again, she said lightly. And that's it, she concluded. Was she half smiling, half resigned, self-deprecating herself? Was she aware that I would never look at her this way ever again?

That's it, I repeated.

It finally dawned on me. That was it.

[Ana Ocadiz]

We had a huge scare in Puerto Escondido. Liliana and I just got into the ocean without noticing the high waves. She was wearing long shorts over her bathing suit, and I had this wide, totally ri-diculous beach dress on, outfits that were totally unsuitable for the beach and very cumbersome, and much more so when wet. We had been ambling along the beach for quite a while, and we were passing an area of sharp rocks where surfers practiced when we decided to go into the water. But the waves were massive and the undertow began to pull us in. She was an experienced swim-mer, but there, in those turbulent waters, we were just a couple of crazy girls grinning at each other in utter terror. I seriously feared for our lives, but Liliana remained serene through it all. I was about to panic, but seeing her composed even though we were in real danger calmed me down. After a few tense minutes, we were able to swim out of the current and to the shore again. Her confidence got us back to safety. We never spoke about it. But her composure, her self-confidence, saved the day.

[August 1989]

I would like to hold this moment forever, perhaps even reach the sublime, and isn't this happiness? A moment, an image, a color, a gesture. I don't know where writing these words will take me. You know, Ana, I love you, and it's so easy to say it now, and it was so nice to realize it. Perhaps the sun, the sky so blue, the sea so close, the sand. A lonely log. Damn! It was so easy to feel it. I just reread what I have written and it looks like a declaration of love. And it makes me laugh. I hate getting corny, but I can't help it today. I don't think I'll ever send you this letter (a lie). I hope to give it to you personally. Maybe by the time I dare to do so, the moment will have been digested already. One way or another, I don't think I will ever be able to forget how happy I felt by your side, by the sea.

With love, Liliana.
August 1989. Puerto Escondido, Oaxaca.

[August 19, 1989]

I think you have gone on strike, dear favorite sister, for we have not received a letter from you, and we think it is a pressure tactic, is it?

I tried to write from Oaxaca and I couldn't, I suddenly found myself with so much before my eyes and my heart that I didn't know what could I write from all that. Now that I am back, it seems to me that they were the most beautiful six days of my life. I was in Oaxaca, the capital, in Huatulco, in Puerto Escondido. And finally, despite my misgivings, in Acapulco. Have you been to Oaxaca?

[August 24, 1989]

I'm cleaning my house. It's so dirty and I don't even know where to start. I'm also smoking, although I know I shouldn't. Also, I'm watching a silly soap opera. And everything is such a mess: a shoe over there, cooking oil, spicy sauce, my scissors, a pair of socks. And these foul smells: rotten water from old flowers, a clogged bathroom, the humidity.

And yet I don't feel bad.
In fact, I feel good. I feel very good.

[Ana Ocadiz]

Wednesday, October 4, 1989.

October 4, 1969 . . .

   20 years already. . . .

   Congratulations!

   *Today, all of us who know you and love you shiver in bliss
for we know we can enjoy your presence for one day more.*

   *I would like to tell you a thousand things, the thousand feel-
ings and thoughts that having you close triggers in me.*

   *You know? I have realized you are truly someone in my
life . . . I can chat with you about the things that happen to me,
about my fears and oddities, and you don't judge me, you listen
and support me. I want you to know that I am so deeply grateful to you for being my friend, and for the support you give me
when I need it.*

   *I also want to wish you the most complete happiness, peace
and health, not only today on your birthday but for your whole
life and forever . . .*

   *Oh, I hope you'll be my friend for another 394 years, OK?
Goodbye for now.*

With love
Ana.

[October 6, 1989]

My dearest and never underappreciated Ana:

First of all, I write on yellow paper because rose-colored paper is so cheesy (unofficial comment).

Guess what? I'm a little sad and a bit confused. May I tell you a secret? I think I'm in love. Back to the hole! And I don't know what I'm going to do to get out of this. Love hurts me, and yet isn't it that what makes us happy?

Anyway, that was not the important point. The important thing! The surprising thing! The extraordinary thing! The...Th... is that if you don't decide otherwise, we're going to Tampico. I hope to see you tomorrow at 8:30 p.m. at the north terminal, in front of the Tres Estrellas de Oro (if you find the three golden stars, let me know, and we'll steal them).

Well, this was meant to be a note and nothing more.

With love
Liliana.

P.S. After the Jehovah's Witness women pounced on me. After the man who sells gas on the street thought I was a married woman. After all those terrible things, I don't feel bad. I don't feel bad despite everything.

[Manolo Casillas Espinal]

I knew Liliana didn't want to have a boyfriend. She was adamant about it. I, on the other hand, wanted her to be my girlfriend. Or

I wanted to be her boyfriend. Either way. "I don't want scenes or complaints, Manolo," she'd say to me. "I cannot bear any kind of jealousy. I want my freedom above all." I'd listen to her, very patiently, as lovingly as I was able to, hoping she'd eventually change her mind.

I was supposed to take both Ana and Liliana to the bus station the day they were departing for Tampico. I swung by her house but, as she was not ready yet, I went in. There was the usual disorder inside: a book here, pieces of clothing over there. The luggage, open. "Don't go, Lili," I said to her out of the blue. She was on her mattress, carefully organizing a pencil pouch. "And why would I do that?" she asked, barely lifting her head. "Because I will miss you awfully," I said as I sat down by her side. I came as close as I could to her, tucking a skein of hair behind her ear. And then I kissed her. It was October. At about 5:00 P.M. In her home. Our first kiss. I was in utter disbelief when I dropped them at the bus station and even on my way back, when I touched my lips again and again with my right hand. I must have smiled like an idiot as I drove to the city to get back home.

We already spent a lot of time together, but we became even closer after that trip. We belonged to the same team, went to the movies together, talked to each other endlessly. As time went by, we moved from innocent kisses to some form of necking and petting. She enjoyed biting my shoulders and I, at times, would touch her breasts, her waist. We, however, never kissed in public and never held hands on campus. That's too corny, she'd say. We never had sex. Liliana was very careful, and remained afraid, although she never told me exactly about what, and I didn't want to put pressure on her. The idea of becoming intimate with her allured me, of course, but it was not my main goal. Getting to know her well and fully, little by little, was more important to me. Getting to know the whole of her, who she really was.

[Leticia Hernández Garza]

They were already covered in sand when I saw them. I assumed they went to the beach before coming home, but they stayed with us, at my parent's house, for about six days in Tampico. It was such an uncomfortable visit, especially because of Ana's excessive zeal. She would not let me talk to Lili alone, as we used to, and whenever I asked my cousin a question, Ana would go ahead and answer for her. She acted as if she knew Lili better than I did, even though I had known her forever. Lili was very naïve. Very loving. Very patient. Ana was obviously very possessive. Not at all a positive influence in Lili's life. In fact, Lili became quite isolated once she started hanging out with her. She didn't do anything without her. They went everywhere together, as though they were Siamese twins. Perhaps this was part of what Ángel was so angry about, I am not sure, but her presence was suffocating.

During that October visit, Liliana seemed to be suffering from an infection. I made an appointment with my doctor, and she was thinking of going with me, but at the last moment, without even notifying me, they left. They had already departed when I came home from work.

Liliana didn't even say goodbye.

[Ángel López]

They dated on and off. Sometimes they were together; sometimes they weren't. It was easy to know which one was which. When Manolo seemed sad, it was because he wasn't with Liliana; when they got back together, sparks came flashing out of his eyes. They loved each other; I have no doubt about that. I remember quite well Liliana's big gesture on Manolo's birthday that year. Lili arrived on campus with a large bouquet of cempasúchiles wrapped in newspaper. An absolutely enourmous bouquet. Where is the bastard? she asked. Who? Manolo, who else? Manolo popped out of the blue then, blushing violently. A bit mortified and a bit flattered, totally moved. It was such a grandiose gesture, totally Lili's style.

It was March 7.

[Othón Santos Álvarez]

They were such a hilarious couple. Manolo had a very funny personality, seeing the funny side of everything; and Liliana's sense of humor was sharp. Laughter followed them everywhere they went when they started going out together.

[Manolo Casillas Espinal]

I saw Ángel on campus only once but I made out his shadow down the street from Liliana's house quite often. He was like a ghost. A black cloud. You didn't need to see him to know he was there. I sensed he was nearby when I heard the noise of his motorcycle approaching. Liliana had hesitated before about their relationship. Sometimes she seemed to get along with him, and sometimes she didn't. But, after a while, she gathered enough strength and asked him, in no uncertain terms, to stop looking for her. I told him, she confided in me, how unnerving it was, how annoying it was, how disrespectful it was for him to show up at my house at will, on weekdays, without asking, without any kind of warning. I don't want him around me anymore, and he knows it, she said. I don't want to see him at all, she mentioned on more than one occasion. I commanded him, Manolo. You must believe me. I don't know what else to do. Then, to show how serious she was, she added: it's all over between him and me. We're done for good. One day, however, a group of us got together at Liliana's apartment and he arrived, uninvited. We were celebrating something or other, the atmosphere was festive anyway, but as soon as I saw him it put me in a foul mood. She had assured me that she had already given him an ultimatum but there he was, yet again, skulking around the corners of the apartment like a wounded party, throwing menacing glances at us. Who was this guy, anyway? Who did he think he was to impose himself on our parties, with that fury of his, so contained and resonant, so unspoken but also so real? Something in the way he moved, or rather didn't move, among us, the way he glanced at Liliana, monitoring her as if from a watchtower, seemed so unsettling. Clearly, he had no role there, in that house and with our group, and it wasn't that he wasn't worthy or that he didn't belong; it was that he didn't even try. I left the apartment fuming, convinced that Liliana had chosen him over me and, shortly thereafter, I started dating a girl from outside the university. I once took her with me to a conference in one of the university auditoriums, and Liliana and Ana got very angry when they saw us together from afar. A rather surprising reaction, since Liliana and I had kind of parted ways by then. But the next day, in yet another unexpected move, Liliana and Ana let the air out of the tires of my car, that old red Valiant Barracuda. I never understood why.

[October 27, 1989]

Dear Lety—

Oh, what an idiotic greeting, well, don't mind it, I do love you, you are my dear one, but the greeting is idiotic nonetheless. My cat is playing around, and I am drowning in memories. I'm tremendously sad, I even tried to get drunk, but I still can't do it. I can write, however, in my sixth quarter notebook. Ha. What an asshole I am. So many beers to drink, so many cigarettes to burn, so many tears to shed. Where has our childhood gone, Leticia? I don't see it anywhere. I look for those years in this absurd disorder, in the fear nighttime and loneliness bring forth to me... And the fucking cigarette went out. I'm smoking Delicados this time. I have not eaten, I have no money, and I am more drunk with sadness than with alcohol. Just longing for other times, for sunny afternoons, for dust, for summer vacations. I am alone, terribly alone. Time turns us into such monsters!

   I grabbed another beer and lost track of my thoughts.
   I just wiped the dust off my worn shoes.
   I don't expect to send you this, will I?

[October 31, 1989]

Dear Ana: Dearest Ana: Beloved Ana, Ana, what sounds better to you? Ana, anyway. Ana, again. Zaz!

Ana, yes, everything comes right on time. Even these twenty years managed to catch up with us.

I want to get it exactly right, but what can I tell you? Stoke something that you want to be stoked up, encourage those hidden dreams that will enliven mind and body. I couldn't say more than what you already feel, because all this is so deeply rooted inside of us, inside you, Ana, strong Ana, Ana love, Ana my child. Let's face our own desires with all our audacity, without paying heed to time (be it four centuries since Napoleon or two days after this autumn), without respecting distances (because, if necessary, we will fly from the most distant diamond mine in Africa to the very ice of the Arctic), without fearing barriers or obstacles.

Face your own desires with a premeditation so strong that it will make room for our beliefs and our shortcomings. What could we possibly fear? Wherever you decide to go, my support will follow you, as long as you don't give up because there is no responsibility more sacred and atrocious than that which forces us to be truly ourselves.

With love
Liliana

P.S. Ah, I forgot, Happy Birthday!

[Ana Ocadiz]

LYSM. Ana.

speckle that radiates a whole world of feeling inside me.
happy to keep counting on the support of that diffuse
to tell you that . . . I love you, and it would make me very
and sure I'm going to do it, although not to marry you, but
that at any time now I'm going to ask for your hand,
well-defined vagueness . . . well, well . . . it seems
and I understood (or so I believed) your essence and I observed
  your
I also left with you . . . I thought of you all the time . . .

to run and hug you . . . I saw you leave and I
to have . . . Lili . . . If you knew the desire that I harbor
toward a friend, the friend that I always wanted
that I could feel such a great and tangible love
present as a human being . . . you know? I never believed
screams, with all that you are, think, feel and you re-
madness, and your depth, with your silences, and your
I understood how much you mean to me . . . with your
how much I would have liked to stop that moment in which
ple . . . seeing you in the bus, saying goodbye . . .
that has already happened, and that lasts . . . yesterday, for exam-
when what remains is an image, a second
this . . . you know? Sometimes it is not easy to find the words . . .
(no chatter), I hope you are very euphoric when you read
it will be the attempt . . . Hello Lili . . . How are you feeling?
ple words? . . . Well, yes . . . Or that at least
Can you create three-dimensional coherence with sim-
range, full of sincerity, color, shape . . .
Hello, this is the healthy attempt to write a letter so st

Friday, November 24, 1989.

[I live off symbols]

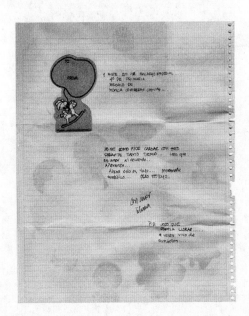

VIII

HOW I WISH WE WERE
NO LONGER FAIRIES IN
A LAND OF ICE

[April come she will]

Reconstructing the last months of Liliana's life is not easy. There was more to her than just the bright girl; the reliable and sometimes protective friend; the outspoken and quick-witted young woman who knew how to heal and hurt with words; the young student who was falling more and more in love with her field of study; the shrewd one, as some of her friends described her, the charismatic leader; the woman who was learning to believe in herself. In addition to all of these, there was the Liliana who, as much as she turned the world upside down, could not find the words to name the violence that followed her closely.

Perhaps there exists a diary, as one of her friends, not the closest one, claimed Liliana kept. I did not find it among her possessions. What I came across were numerous notes that she scrawled here and there in her notebooks, between thoughtful disquisitions on arch braces and house planning, art history and to-do lists. Misplaced between the pages of the notebooks or sealed in tin boxes or inside handbags and leather wallets, I found messages she received from others and messages she wrote to herself. They are pieces of a very complex puzzle that I will never quite finish putting together. One upon another, these writings are layers of experience that have settled over time. My task is to de-sediment them. With the care of the archaeologist who touches without damaging, who dusts without breaking, my intention is to open and preserve this writing at the same time: de- and recontextualize it in a reading from the present. Neither Liliana nor those of us who loved her had at our disposal the insight, the language, that would allow us to identify the signs of danger. This blindness, which was never voluntary but social, has contributed to the murder of hundreds of thousands of women in Mexico and beyond. As Rachel Louise Snyder has argued so strongly, what we did not know about domestic violence, about intimate partner terrorism, killed her. And killed us. At the beginning of the last decade of the twentieth century, in a country where aggressions against women were increasing at alarming rates, femicide violence arrived one night at my sister's house in Azcapotzalco, placed a pillow over her face, and took her life. Death by suffocation. But the work, the underground and constant work of violence, had started many years earlier, when my sister was just a teenager. And, Liliana, brave and loving, tried what so many women have done in her place: she opposed this violence, tried to escape it, denied it, attached herself to it, resisted it, deactivated it, negotiated with it. She did everything she thought possible and imaginable until, just a short time before the femicide that took her life, she left him. She removed herself from Ángel. Emotionally. Physically.

According to Snyder, and the chronology of increasing danger that she proposes for relationships characterized by intimate partner terrorism, women are at greater risk of losing their lives at the hands of their ex-partners in the three months after the separation, or in the three months after the predator realizes that, this time, the separation is real. Definitive. If this is true, if the conclusions reached by specialists based on thousands of quantitative data points and thousands of invaluable testimonies of women under duress mean anything, something must have happened in early 1990 between Liliana and Ángel, something new and resounding, something real enough to open the door wide to femicide violence. Something, perhaps, between March and April. Something in May.

[a system of notebooks and loose notes]

Her four notebooks were stored in a cardboard box among many other objects: brushes and stickers, pens, X-Acto knives, vellum paper and Fabriano paper, cards, books, earrings and bracelets, variously sized tin boxes. Two were letter-size Scribe notebooks and two were French-format notebooks, both spiral bound with small-squared graph sheets, which she used to take notes from the fifth to the eighth quarters, the last of which she did not conclude. The observations in these notebooks, many of them dated, became the backbone for a myriad of individual notes that appeared elsewhere. Liliana, a collector at heart, liked to store things, especially small, seemingly irrelevant, objects. She had, for example, organized chronologically the receipts for all the materials she had bought at the Lumen paper store since 1988: a thick sheaf, folded in two, which attests to her organizational skills and to her work as the archivist who not only paid attention to life's major events, but also to the more pedestrian aspects of the everyday. Some of the remarks in those notebooks, however, are undated. And that's when the color of the ink or the stroke of the penmanship helped me locate, at least approximately, the date on which they were written.

Once I had established the basic timeline, at least the most plausible, I took on the task of interspersing the many other notes that popped up on loose pieces of paper or napkins or metro tickets. Some of them came with dates, some didn't. I used the same method to orient myself: ink color, stroke type, subject matter. I also added the letters, as well as the individual notes or messages that she received during that period. Then I proceeded to transcribe everything, trying both to keep the timeline in place and to inhabit each of these traces. I took notes in turn, on small colored Post-its, which I placed next to the materials that I had organized in folders, in chronological order, on the rectangular dining room table when the desk space was not enough. Slowly but surely, Liliana unfolded herself freely in our midst, greeting us by the front door, in the study, and even in our bedroom. She was there, as real as the air we breathed.

What emerged from all that work was a map, or more precisely: a blueprint. Some of the lines marked the foundation and walls, while some others made space for a window or a skylight. The temptation to rebuild Liliana's life as a defenseless victim, powerless before the overwhelming force of the predator, was great. That is why I prefer that she speak for herself here in these pages: I can sense that, at every turn of the road, even in the darkest moments, Liliana did not lose the ability to see herself as the author of her own life. Like many women in her situation, Liliana tried everything—surrounding herself with a strong circle of trusted friends, falling in love in healthier ways, devoting herself to architecture, preparing herself for an independent life—but, at every turn, in the least expected moments, Ángel would show up, over and over again, telling her that he loved her, apologizing, assuring her that he was going to change. Ángel wasn't just asking, however. He was demanding a response, and if it wasn't what he wanted to hear, he would unleash a fury of jealousy, beatings, constant harassment, suicide threats, and, perhaps, threats against Liliana's own family.

Liliana knew the cycle all too well. She had been learning it the hard way for at least six years. Her own context bound her within the straitjacket of machismo, slashing her with the sharpest edges of a patriarchal system that, until very recently in our country's history, presented itself as the normal state of things; but Liliana, who sometimes described herself as sad or disappointed, a lonely girl eating slices of sorrow, willed herself till the very end not to fall. I must stand up, she said more than once. I know how to get back up again, she reminded herself when disappointment or anxiety took the best of her. I deeply believe in that Liliana. I deeply love that Liliana and all the Lilianas there were or there ever will be. But what counts here is her voice and her words. Her own words.

[Green Wave]

Volume number one is a spiral bound, letter-size, hundred-page graph-sheeted Scribe dual notebook. An image of the Statue of Liberty dominates the cover, the faint yellow of a full moon a bit to the right of her crowned head. Someone has inscribed the words "Quarter #5" on the top margins of the cover, along with playful, dark shades on the moon. A small spiderweb surfaces toward the lower left corner: a sign that Spider-Man was once there. The slant light of a Sunday morning allowed me to glimpse, quite by chance, some diluted letters in blue ink that had remained hidden for months: "I am bored. Othón does not hurry (HURRY UP!). Othón writes very slowly (I will shout). No, it's the library, I can't scream. (It's all done). 240789." The cover is already overflowing with symbols and, when the notebook is open, more spill out of its pages: loose sheets fall out, some bearing the handwriting I know well by now, some with handwriting I don't recognize. They are class notes, signs of an exchange that confirms a supportive network, camaraderie.

The first page features the words "Quarter #5" once again, and below the title is the class schedule, including the names of two professors:

Technological	7–8	B 17 Gabriel Jiménez
Interdisciplinary	8:30–10:00	EB 10
Operational	10–3	L013 Guillermina López
Theoretical	7–8:30	
Methodological	8:30–10	
Laboratory	10–3	

In highly controlled handwriting, using both pencils and ballpoint pens, the notes begin in earnest. There are sketches. There are more words, some in lowercase, and others entirely in uppercase to accentuate the importance of the subject matter. "Transitional architecture. Top quality arch-brace work. Waxed paper. Deadline: 10:15 A.M." Very soon, however, the flow of the class is interrupted and, with the same penmanship, as if it were the same topic, the first personal inscription appears on 130689, June 13, 1989:

... And yet
How I wish we were no longer fairies in a land of ice.
So much need for company.

Except for a list of names, perhaps the students she was working with at that time (Juan Carlos Sierra, Armando, Ana, Fernando, Eduardo), no explanation accompanies the sentences. The ellipsis and the adversative clause of the first line hint that the situation that has gone before was a positive one. And yet. In spite of. Despite that, there are wishes, everlasting yearnings, longings perhaps unfulfilled. Fairies come in all kinds of shapes and sizes but stand as quintessentially feminine in the popular imagination. Whether as demoted versions of angels or as variously rendered demons, fairies remain magical beings with supernatural powers, including, at times, sparkling wings. While their mischievousness or even malice have prompted others to flash charms or offer up prayers to fend them off, fairies often arrive at human scenes with unrestricted goodness in tow. They are resourceful and unselfish, like the fairy godmother or, like the tooth fairy, giving and helpful, even obsequious. What could these magical beings do in a bleak environment, glacial and hostile, among men and women rendered frozen by basic meanness and abject baseness? Fairy tales have accompanied the childhood of many girls, teaching them, however obliquely, the importance of being gracious, well-behaved, selfless. But well before she started this particular notebook, Liliana had tired of the stereotype for good. How achingly she wished to be something other than a fairy trapped in an increasingly inhospitable wasteland. Her craving for a world beyond fairies and fairy tales made her anxious for true companionship. She was sad but also restless; heartsick but also awake. Her desire for a different life, for a different love, was becoming a conviction.

Because the context of the note is not revealed, the note seems to come out of nowhere.

But writing doesn't come from nowhere.

It was an afternoon like any other. Liliana and Laura had met briefly on the walkway right in front of the library as they always did but she didn't seem her usual self. They were approaching the end of the quarter and the end of the calendar year, and that autumn of 1988 had been especially bright and dry, but Liliana's manner intrigued Laura. What's going on? Laura asked when Lili continued beating around the bush, speaking with great difficulty, half rambling. I think I am pregnant, she said at last. It was obvious she wanted to talk about it but did not know how, exactly. She was worried, anguished—that much was clear. She didn't know what to do but didn't want anyone to know either. More to the point, she didn't want to share it. I don't want to be a mom yet, Laura, she told her finally, I am not ready. We're only a year into college, she added, as an afterthought. A bit more than a year, Laura sighed, as if realizing it for the first time. The future, she said. So open. So huge. They were sitting on the stone pillars that had been silent witnesses to jokes, gossip, devastating one-liners. This time Liliana looked directly at the ground, trying to find a message in the dry grass. It'll be all right, Laura whispered. Whatever you decide will be the right choice. All decisions are valid, and all will ultimately be brave. I know, she said, unconvinced. She paused, then looked up to the sky, so annoyingly blue. I know it is my decision, and my decision only, she said. But I feel so lonely.

It was not easy to have an abortion in Mexico back then. Even today, the Green Wave mobilizations organized by Argentine feminists have made it abundantly clear that the struggle for abortion rights is far from over. Hoisting up a green scarf as a sign of support for pro-choice activists is as necessary now as ever. Even as women take to the streets, marching together as they demand access to free and safe abortion, there are still countless stories of girls standing, alone and frightened, at the entrances to clandestine clinics. At the time Liliana confided in Laura, middle-class women could often turn to doctors who, in exchange for some cash, were willing to perform abortions in dark, barely legitimate-looking clinics, but seldom without pouring tons of guilt and abuse on their desperate patients. Poor women had to resort to even more dubious methods that carried the risk of death, either from bleeding or from infections.

At a time when sex education consisted of the occasional lecture given in abstract and euphemistic language and accompanied by poor-quality illustrations, at a time when carrying condoms was condemned as a sign of moral depravity, unwanted pregnancies were common. While young people were roughly aware of available contraceptive methods, actually taking the pill or getting an IUD more or less implied that sex was not a temporary, one-time result of some youthful slip, but a regular practice. A new way of life. Many girls were not ready to admit, first to themselves and then to their partners, that they fell into that category. And contraceptives have of course never been 100 percent safe. Few young women spoke openly, much less at home, about their sexual yearnings, the hectic life of their hormones and their libido. Girls were supposed to be protected by a foolproof modesty, or by a discretion that would lead them to preserve appearances at all costs in case the former failed. They were to be fairies; fairies in an ever-hostile land.

Abortion was illegal in Mexico City until 2007, when the use of Zacafemyl (mifepristone) was authorized to terminate pregnancies of up to twelve weeks. As I write this, abortion has been decriminalized only in Mexico City and in the state of Oaxaca, and this since 2019 only. The states of Guanajuato and Querétaro authorize abortion only in cases of rape. For the rest of Mexico, abortion is only legal in cases of rape, or when the pregnancy involves a health or mortality risk for the mother. In some states, such as Yucatán, a mother's economic instability is allowed as legal grounds for abortion. For the rest of Latin America, abortion rights are granted to women only in Cuba, Guyana, and Uruguay, and as of December 30, 2020, after countless, ever strong, and massive popular demonstrations, in Argentina, where access to safe and free abortion has become the law. If Liliana lived among us, and became pregnant again, it would be wise of her to remain in Mexico City. Or move to Oaxaca or Buenos Aires. The situation has improved, surely, but in many ways, it is still quite the same. While it's unclear how many backstreet abortions are performed in Latin America, some demographers have used the "residual method" to estimate that as many as 450,000 women have terminated their pregnancies in Argentina alone each year, and criminalization continues to put women's lives at risk. While the religious right and a highly conservative patriarchal system—everlasting allies of machismo—would like to represent abortions as a moral matter, it is increasingly accepted that abortion is both an issue of public health and a human right. It is a decision that rests with women themselves, not to be legislated or prescribed by others. *Sex education to decide, contraceptives to avoid abortion, legal abortion to prevent dying:* the motto is as valid now as it was when chanted for the first time by Argentine feminists, green scarves held aloft in protest.

In mid-November 1988, Liliana wrote a note in free verse, a formal deviation from her paragraph-based writing, in which blank space erupts on the page with devastating effect. And there, with each broken line, the deep desire to break free forcefully contends with the nostalgia that assails her in the face of what is lost. The words chorionic gonadotropin—the pregnancy hormone that is detected with a blood test—written both on the last page of one of her address books and on one of the corners of her metro pass from the first week of December 1988, suggests that this text of broken lines and her abortion might have been linked. The lines vacillate between expressions of loneliness and abandonment, and the desire to fly away and start anew.

November 15, 1988

What if unleashing simply meant throwing your arms up
    into the air?
What if the spiraling course of time were nothing more
    than the evolution of an escalator that buries itself
    and survives?
Let's count the suns that did not come out
the things that destroyed what is full today
let's count infinity
the hands that did not touch us
the voids that we never fill.

Let's make these November afternoons accountable,
    the many
solitudes that surround us, ours
and the absent ones.

What do I do now?

Count the moments that didn't happen
the excluded loves
the shyest proximities
the many NOs
all that supplements what exists and is
this cubic, geometric, black-and-white landscape.
Count the air that is not here
the clouds that went missing.
Count the actions susceptible to observation
the distances
your absence so many times confirmed
let's count it.
How there are droplets coming out of the eyes

shallow clouds
this anguishing sweat.
I don't want to count them
not that way.
They fill me with the present
so resoundingly, so forever.
I am now, thus, part of your universe.

Let's count the things that are absent.
Count me among them.
Be my guest.

As with some of her texts, this one reappeared more than once, at times in sections, at times with minor modifications. But the original, the draft she worked on over the next few months, originated in that November when she feared the possibility of, or had just learned of, her pregnancy.

Liliana, who went through with the abortion alone by the end of 1988, was lucky. A doctor made her feel terribly guilty, but he didn't kill her. I can make her out in the distance right now, asking questions from those around her in utter despair, looking for information that was hard to come by. There she is, taking the metro and walking by herself on the narrow, cracked sidewalks of Naucalpan, a working-class district in the north of the city, trying to discern a number on walls full of colorful signs and flyers. I want to join her, even in that cold waiting room where she is asked, again and again, if she is sure. I am, she says, and I nod by her side. I take her hand, placing my arm around her shoulders. You're not alone, Lili. I am with you. I support you wholeheartedly. And, just as you have listened to me over the years, loving me as I am, I don't judge you. I am here for you. Know this, please.

Liliana had chosen a future that included neither children nor a permanent union with Ángel. Accompanied by herself and no one else, she licked her wounds little by little in the days that followed. She was discreet about her abortion, but did not hesitate to share her experience with Ana, and she recounted it too for Manolo when he tried to lure her into sex. In the early 1989 letter she wrote to Gabriela, an old high school friend from Toluca, she admitted that the abortion had been more traumatic emotionally than physically, and that it marked an indelible before-and-after in her life. Her UAM friends never learned the specifics, not even the exact date, contenting themselves with speaking of it as something that had occurred in "the past."

A couple of weeks after the procedure, on the same walkway where she had first shared her secret, Liliana told Laura that the deed was done. Their eyes met. Laura gently placed a hand on Lili's forearm, and they didn't talk about it ever again. I am late for class, she said. And Laura looked at her, as she had so many times before: there she was, leaving in a hurry, hustling through those long corridors, a free woman.

[I try to be honest]

The doodles and scribbles sprinkled among class notes in Notebook One come from the spring and summer of 1989. On the one hand, there are the drawings, numbers, and concepts of a diligent, attentive student, which corresponds to an improvement in her grades over this period; on the other hand, there are the hastily scrawled reflections of someone who was torn between the past and the allure of her new environment. Between one thing and another, Liliana aspired to something basic, but complex: to be honest. On June 16, 1989, she returned to the theme of desolation:

160689

I'm the girl standing on sadness.
I'm the one turned into apple cake.

A week later, she was writing to me about her academic passions in one of those notes that never quite managed to become letters:

June 27, 1989
Tuesday

My dear favorite and only sister:

I feel a bit guilty for not having written before (I think I always say the same thing, I don't remember), but I have had so much work. I have a feeling that this quarter will be very hard (and very interesting too). The project is now a vacation resort in Tequisquiapan, Querétaro, I am done with all the fieldwork, soon (today) I will start projecting. Finally, I am taking a History of Mexican Architecture class, and I am digging it. On Thursday we'll start visiting the sites. I think... rather I have plans to study restoration of historical monuments, you know, after graduation. Actually, that's what I think when I leave my Laboratory seminar (that's what the class is called) but when I leave Theoretical or Methodological class, I think a lot about graduate training in urbanism. I am not so sure just yet.

Ever since the summer of 1987, the month of July had marked an anniversary of trauma, as that was when Liliana first learned of Ángel's infidelity, causing a breakup that lasted a couple of months. July 1989 wouldn't be that different. At the beginning of the month, a cryptic note hints that her well-cared-for restraint was being broken down and an unsettling presence had appeared again, looming ominously.

030789

My privacy is being bombarded, my individuality. I feel watched over, constantly monitored. The loneliness that protected me is slowly cracking and that layer that I cared so much for is being pierced. I am myself the cause of this invasion (and this is the worst). I invade myself. I cannot stand it. Fucking maggots.

July 6 or 7 (I don't know if it's past 12), 1989

It seems silly to write to you, especially when I have so much work, but I feel weird, maybe I love you.

100789

While we go on living, as we swim in empty universes, day by day in this fish tank of scarcity, as far as the world does not lose its stupid gravitational center, it seems that everything is normal, even benign, but then, without warning, fear surfaces, instantaneous terror, when you barely perceive the other possibility—the one always longed for, the one always expected—that the other's unrecognizable face offers us, a

ghost, a cursed sorcerer haunting the uninhabited space of our
loneliness.

I'm still me, I'm still up on the apple cake, devouring sadness.

And yet, how much need for company.

Liliana recorded another traumatic breakup with Ángel in July
1989.

I wish everything was different, but we are so terribly
depressing, so devilishly complicated, that there was no other
way out. I'm sad, terribly sad, I want to escape from all this,
from the last three years, from my evil ways, from my lack of
understanding, from the memories of you. I don't know where
this was leading us. Still, despite all logic, despite reason. How
awful I feel. You were with Araceli two years ago. I believe all
our tragic moments have happened in july. There will be no
more july for us, no more discussions, no more respect. Why?
Why do things have to be this way?

See? I was trying to tell you. Nothing lasts forever and this
is what frustrates me. I feel enraged. But, beyond reason and
logic.

Memories. I drown in images, monsters without a face
engulf me. It's over. How many times did I tell you, Ángel?
Nothing lasts forever. And this rage, beyond logic, beyond
reason. It would be cruel if I said it's better this way. I cannot
get my head around it. Is this why it hurts so much? Could it
be that the terrible end of childhood has arrived? Could it be
that adolescence is over? Is it? Why, Ángel? Crazy Ángel,
good Ángel, angel Ángel. How not to repeat your name? There
is no room for resentment. There is nothing to hate. You will
never hear from me again. I am a blurry dot, slowly vanishing

on the horizon. Let's count the suns that did not come out. The shallow clouds. The suffocating sweat. Let's count the excluded loves.

The motifs kept coming back again and again, like in a morbid melody. Emotional imprints. The events of the summer of 1987 were woven into the lines she wrote over the winter of 1988. "Let's count the excluded loves. Let's account for what did not happen, for what did not become." The breakup ended a relationship that had unfolded not only over her two years in college, but over the years they were together through high school. And, by her own account, Ángel was at once desirable and vile. They knew each other all too well. They were fluent in all their private dialects. This time, however, the responsibility for the collapse fell not only on their individual personalities, but on something larger, something Liliana called *postmodernism,* a term in vogue not only among architecture students, meaning to convey, perhaps, *patriarchy.* In that same month, and unlike the previous separations that had been monothematic, compressed affairs, two more names appeared in her notebook: Raúl Espino Madrigal and Leonardo Jasso. In no uncertain terms, she told both these young men, whom she agreed to meet in the intimate and familiar terrain of Toluca, that she did not believe in dating, and that she did not want to be the possession of anyone. Her independence, what she called her freedom, had been a recurring theme in her writings from even before high school, but it emerges in these pages with newfound clarity.

300789

I am in between a masochistic and suicidal madman, a vulnerable and depressed pseudo-intellectual, and an empty-headed pseudo-preppy parrot.

300789

I wish that the answer to a what's going on? could come out as spontaneously as the question itself. I cannot. I can't say that I no longer love you, but I'm just not 17 years old anymore, maybe I am not as vulnerable as I was then, maybe I am even more so. I am so sick of everything. Postmodernism is at fault here. I am the product of my times, this is all a well-organized mess and I am the result of that mess. You make a scene in front of me. I make one in front of you. That's a postmodern relationship. Well, if at least you understood it like I do, it would be OK, but no, you have to come with all that (shitty) idealism about feelings, about fidelity, about specific cases. I'm so fed up with myself. I'm just a fucking bastard lying girl. There is no reason behind anything. I'm surprised you don't know this.

I would like to see you. Why not? Just because? Why not. Just because. Why not. Because not.

Ángel González Ramos. Leonardo Jasso Ortega. Raúl Espino Madrigal.

From the moment she began writing, Liliana was careful about revealing the real names of her characters. She became increasingly discreet over the years, at the explicit urging of her cousin Leticia, who recommended that she omit names in her letters so that prying eyes wouldn't get the message even if they were to open the envelope. Ángel's name figured quite frequently in her writings, as a kind of automatic gesture, but not those of other addressees. That is why the letter that she wrote and rewrote, at least twice, before sending it to Raúl Espino Madrigal in the summer of 1989, is particularly striking. Raúl had been smitten with her for quite a while by then, and Liliana, although tempted at times, had repeatedly rejected his advances. He seemed not to understand something that Liliana was very clear about: she was not into games, manipulation, schemes. At this point, she could spot them a long way off. Honesty was a fundamental concept in her personal vocabulary.

• • •

I did not intend to write to you, but I have a sheet of paper in front of me, so this might be the last time.

You know, right? I will never be with you. I will never belong to someone. And that, sometimes, makes me sad. I know you will interpret this as mere presumption, a sign of arrogance, but you must know it is not. I have fought so hard to be the way I am, to feel things as spontaneously as possible, not to condition my life. And the result is a constant state of uncertainty. You keep thinking that I am just showing off, but you do not realize this is just a response to your constant scheming and frustrated plans. That's all.

Maybe everything fell apart between us long before it began, when you let me read your diary for the first time and I felt disgusted to see that the person who I believed was seeking something akin to freedom was, instead, calculating opportunities, scheming, betting on a totally selfish love. I tried to forget it, or at least downplay it, but I couldn't. Yes, maybe that was it.

I didn't intend to write to you, but I have a piece of paper in front of me. I might not do it again.

I am trying to get to the point and be conventionally honest, you know that, right?

I will never be with you completely.

I am not, even remotely, the best person for you.

You will interpret everything I say as mere presumption. You are so terribly biased. You have divided the world between the holders of absolute truth, the unobjectionable; and the assholes. And me, Raúl? Where am I? In the middle, maybe right down the middle, blows raining down on me from both sides. I am exaggerating, indeed. But am I exaggerating?

I tried for a long time to get to where I am with very little help. You're going to say I am boasting, right? But do you really get it? Surely you'll think I'm taking the easy way out, but that's not it, I want this to be a way of life, and you have not been able to grasp that. I have no clue what gave you the idea that you could take me around on your arm. No, I feel like you don't get me. You believe everything is a desperate struggle to be different, but you believe this because that is your own struggle. But it is not mine. Mine is to be honest. Or at least to try. I try to be honest.

[What do you do if a bear attacks you?]

Liliana began the first year of the last decade of the twentieth century by writing a letter to her dear friend Ana Ocadiz. On white paper, typewritten, the letter invites reading and prevents reading at the same time. It is not easy to read a text in which all the spaces between words have been removed and all the letters of all the words have been joined in a continuous, run-on line. In fact, it is impossible to read such a letter in a rush, just passing your eyes over the paper. Liliana's deliberate opacity not only requires determination on the part of the reader, the willingness to read on despite obstacles, but also complicity. Even love. You always have to keep quiet about some things, Liliana had written when she was barely a teenager, you have to know how to eke out your information, your meanings, yourself. And here, writing down a message that wants to be read, and understood, but which, at the same time, resists easy or instrumental reading, Liliana was tremendously true to herself.

The previous year had changed her in many ways. But after the trip to Oaxaca in the summer of 1989, after kissing Manolo before leaving for Tampico in mid-October of the same year, after the passionate letters she exchanged with Ana, learning they loved each other dearly, the name Ángel came back. Blurred, muddled between the tangled words of the fourth line of the letter with which she greeted a new decade, the name was still there. "How can I get involved with someone else knowing that Ángel is still around?" And, a few days before the fall of the Berlin Wall, the ghost of his name haunted her once more, as seen on the first page of Notebook Two:

6 November 1989

...In spite of everything, I am here.

We find ourselves here, being part of a stupid nucleus. Are there exits? Doors? Maybe. If only there was a window.

What is happening? The world turns and turns, and I'm still here, as if nothing were happening, static. Still.

Why did Liliana keep returning to a relationship that, from the outside at least, offered her only instability and harm? In *No Visible Bruises*, Snyder suggests two alternative questions. The first: why does the predator come back again and again? The second: what is the most logical reaction when someone is attacked by a bear? The first question gives us space to explore the consequences of toxic masculinity in a patriarchal society, inviting us to consider how patriarchy deforms and hurts men, as much as it does women. The second question takes us directly to the center of a dramatic crossroads, a matter of life and death. A moment of decision. If a bear attacks you, do you attack him back, knowing that he can easily kill you? Or do you play dead and give in?

Victims stay because they know that any sudden move will provoke the bear.

They stay because they have developed tools, over the years, that have sometimes worked to calm down an angry partner: pleading, begging, cajoling, promising, and public displays of solidarity, including against the very people—police, advocates, judges, lawyers, family—who might be the only ones capable of saving their lives.

They stay because they see the bear coming for them. And they want to live.

When the institutional systems that are meant to protect women against domestic violence fail, and they do quite often and quite notoriously, they increase the material and symbolic power of the predator. In 1990, when no one was talking about intimate partner violence, when violence against women was still regarded as a crime of passion, when neither the victims nor their loved ones, nor even the abusers themselves, were capable of describing, and hence defining, and thus counteracting, the violence exercised in the name of love, under the guise of love, it was all too easy to be unaware of the mortal risk that such violence implied. In that opaque letter, so difficult to read, Liliana was talking about a game—a match she was aware she could win, or just as easily lose. A battle between giants in a city of fury. Until the very last moment, my sister thought she could win. She thought she could fend off patriarchy by herself and overcome it on her own.

[Fausto and La Kinski]

The census in Mexico is carried out once every ten years and, in the early months of 1990, Liliana and Ana decided to be part of the team of volunteers who traveled door to door, gathering data. They did the required training, then drew a map, and, following the recommendations of the bureaucrats in charge, headed to the area assigned to them on a cloudy Friday at noon. Together, which is how they did everything back then, they visited the buildings of San Pablo Xalpa, a housing complex adjacent to their university, to become familiar with the area before the real census, which would take place the following Monday, March 12. Once there, each looking for her own building, they realized with heavy hearts that they had to part ways.

When they met up again, Liliana was carrying a small white kitten in her arms. Ana looked at her, unable to conceal her surprise. What was Lili up to this time? You should have seen how these people opened the door of their apartment and just heartlessly threw her out, she said by way of explanation. In fact, they hurled her out so hard she tumbled down the stairs, she added with a bit of drama. I confronted them, she said. It's not ours, the tenants replied with contempt. You don't want her? Because I'm going to take her with me, she threatened. But they just shrugged and, without a dignified exit to hand, Liliana turned around with the cat in tow.

And what are you going to do with Fausto? Ana asked, reminding her about the neurotic, half-crazy cat that Liliana had adopted a while ago. Fausto would frequently attack them out of nowhere, and then, as if he hadn't done anything, as if his violence were a mere figment of the girls' imagination, he would sweetly snuggle between their legs as they watched television. What am I going to do? Liliana repeated with a big mischievous smile, emphasizing the *I*. What are you going to do, Ana María de los Ángeles Ocadiz Eguía Lis, with Clementina Camila Natasja O'Gorman, alias La Kinski?

Dumbfounded, Ana received the gift without really thinking about the consequences. Later, in a letter she typed while they waited for more instructions at the census office, a letter also made of words with no spaces in between them, she thanked Liliana profusely. She was going through some hard times, doing poorly in school, a dark mood overcoming her during the hours she didn't spend with Liliana. Most dear and adored Lilianita, she said. I love you very much. La Kinski came to brighten her loneliness in that far-off place of un-civilization, as she called the neighborhood in which she lived, a long way from the university campus.

[now you will see the world through my eyes]

Namibia achieved its independence on March 21, 1990. And, reflecting on the reunification of Germany, Liliana wondered: will the union of the Germanies hatch, again, the serpent's egg? That early spring, she made a long to-do list: "Cat vaccine, Cat food, Cat litter. Talk to Monica. BOTTLE. Fabriano paper. Paper for Methodological. TEC report (contract work). Pay electricity bill." And then, as if it were a bureaucratic order, she signed the note with her full name. She also had time to write down another message for Ángel:

SPRING DAY

I wish I were able to speak.

" I had patience.
" may you consider me equally cursed throughout the rest of
   your life.
" there were palliatives (for you).
" I was not one of them.

April surprised her with a letter from a former high school friend, a girl who had been on the same swim team and, in the reply that she wrote but never sent, she wondered what she was becoming. Liliana no longer recognized the innocent girl she had been just three or four years earlier. And she liked the change. In early April, she began visiting our cousin Emilio's cafeteria more frequently, looking for company as well as the little money she earned working the register. At some point, Ángel showed up and Emilio kicked him out as soon as he saw him, without even warning Liliana. Emilio had witnessed Ángel's aggression in Toluca and suspected that he was beating her. He also feared that he was armed, although he had no conclusive evidence of either. Just in case, he directed the building's security guards not to let that short, bad-tempered, blue-eyed guy come in when Liliana was visiting. They complied. Every now and then during the weekdays, instead of going back to Mimosas 658, Liliana joined Emilio and his friend Iliana in San Lorenzo Acopilco, just outside of Mexico City. She found solace there, and a camaraderie she rejoiced in while smoking cigarettes and telling jokes, talking about movies or drinking some wine. Through the large-paned windows in the living room, the electric lights of the sprawling city down below looked like fireflies.

I had left Mexico for Houston in the summer of 1988, but returned home for the Christmas holidays and, as soon as I finished the spring semester of 1990, came back the first week of May. Instead of going directly to our parents' house in Toluca, I stayed with Liliana in Azcapotzalco because I wanted to see old friends in Mexico City and, more important, I had to go to the Fine Arts Institute, where my first book, *The War Does Not Matter*, was being prepared for publication. Liliana and I jumped up and down, our arms interlaced, when I mentioned that I had an appointment with a photographer for my first ever author photo. Who would have thought, I said once we calmed down.

I knew it for sure, she replied.

I am not sure how many days I stayed with Lili that May, but I know I didn't notice anything out of the ordinary. Nothing in her demeanor or her voice, the way she talked or behaved, alerted me of any danger. I did not see any bruises. No scars. She hardly spoke of Ángel. When I asked her about *the Gremlin*, the code name we sometimes used to refer to him, she shrugged. Are you still seeing him? I ventured. Instead of replying, Liliana steered the conversation toward the future, her interest in traveling. Let's go to Florence, she said, lying on her back and lifting her long legs against the wall in a V shape. Let's go, I said, emulating her, my left foot near her right one. We closed our eyes and, in between sighs, we visited the Duomo, marveled at the art hanging from the walls of the Uffizi, made the sign of the cross before the main altar at the Santa Maria del Fiore Cathedral, and complained about how expensive all the food was, even the simplest of pizzas. We laughed. Mind-traveling is my only option, I said somewhat sullenly as we turned over and lay on or stomachs. For now, she replied, ever optimistic. I can always hijack an airplane, I said, half smiling. Stop it, she howled. You're seriously considering it, I can see it in your eyes, she said, truly amused. I can see you doing it, she said, pointing her index finger at my chin. In the morning, as we combed our hair in front of the tiny bathroom mirror, I asked her to let me use her glasses. Without hesitation, she took them off and gave them to me, and then continued brushing her teeth. I tried them on. Can I use them today? She rinsed her mouth hurriedly. For my sister's very first author picture? Her eyes, shining with pleasure and complicity. The joy, so unsparing. Hell yes, she said. We did not even pause to consider that we had different prescriptions. Now you'll see the world through my eyes, she said as I adjusted the frames. Now I will, I replied.

But I didn't.

During those days I spent at her apartment in such proximity, sleeping with her on her full mattress, talking endlessly about our plans, looking at our reflections furtively in the windows of the living room, greeting each other in the morning and bidding farewell when we went our own ways during the day, I did not sense the wings of danger fluttering between us. Did she feel them herself? Was she so blind or trusting, believing that danger had passed her by, unnoticed? Or was it the other way around? Was she so aware of the menace, so mindful of its consequences, that she chose to keep her cool, just as she had handled the heavy undertow in Huatulco, when she and Ana feared for their lives? Or was she ashamed? How could she admit, especially in front of her older sister, that a guy she despised had been able to maintain such a firm hold on her?

I left a message at her place on a large piece of paper, red ink and letters as bulky as a warning sign:

May 1990 (I forgot the day). MASA: It's about one o'clock and I'm just getting ready to go out. Let's see what happens today.

If I leave for Toluca, I'll call you tonight. If I stay, you'll meet
me here again later. Goodbye.

Your favorite sister.

In the only image that remains from that visit to Mexico City,
my first ever author picture, I am wearing my sister's glasses.

After a brief stay in Toluca, I had to return to Houston for the
summer session. As we prepared to leave for the airport, taking
turns piling my luggage into the trunk, my father took his old camera out, to capture the moment. Oh, not again, I said, doing what
I could to escape him. Over the years, he would make us pose in
the unlikeliest of places: dangerously close to overflowing dams,
centimeters away from an unfriendly bull at a livestock fair. We're
in a hurry, please, I said, a bit irritated. But he was determined.
Liliana stepped in. We'll do it on one condition, she said. Let's
make faces. What my father captured that day through the camera lens, under the annoyingly blue sky of the highlands, was a
happy pantomime orchestrated by his two grown daughters. Lili
and I stand in front of our old house, gesturing comically at each
other, and then, surreptitiously, in tacit complicity, at the camera.
Slim, with her hands inside the pockets of a long white skirt and
her ponytail down, Liliana watches me carefully as I close my eyes
and stick my tongue out toward the camera. In the next image, I
stare at her as she tilts her neck to the left and screws her mouth
toward one eye in a gesture that makes us both burst into laughter. Were we making fun of something? Perhaps. Probably of ourselves. Maybe of our father and his obsession with farewells.
Doesn't he know we'll be saying goodbye quite often from now
on? A beam of light beats on the white walls of the house, high-
lighting the golden hue of the brick columns that support the
canopy over the front door, as we carry on with the joke. Liliana,

suddenly quiet, squints as she looks at us. It is the bright, dry shimmer that overcomes the sky right before the rainy season begins.

It was the last time I saw my sister alive.

[unprotected]

In Notebook Four, behind the folded sheet that announced the beginning of the Interdisciplinary Seminar section, Liliana jotted down a list of songs listened to on the day she called our cousin Leticia, crying. The playlist was dated May 24, which was a Thursday. She was usually in Mexico City during the week, but since Liliana had no access to a personal phone in Azcapotzalco, it is doubtful she was calling from Mexico City. Perhaps she was elsewhere. Or perhaps Leticia's memory is flawed.

INTERDISCIPLINARY
May 24, 1990

My situation is absurd and tragic. Well, according to my limits.

Clown
Coming to You.
What a Beautiful Love.   Tears of Love
                                          Organ Grinder Friend
She.
Dear Pigeon.   Shades.
A Weird World.   Total Delivery.

Heart

Bitter Christmas

The rider

Four ways

Let's go

Very slowly

Love of Good

Moonless Serenade

Coming to You

Carabela

Bars Don't Kill

Kiss Me and Forget Me

Slave and Master

Renunciation

The Madman

In My Old San Juan

The somber, virile voices of Javier Solís and José Alfredo Jiménez have accompanied romantic breakups in Mexico for decades. They sang corny songs, songs of hurt, draped in shameless drama. While some songs vowed for revenge, most drew on everlasting love, the kind that never dies even if, or precisely because, it goes unrequited. The humiliated lover, left behind, basks in his pain, and pledges never to stop loving a woman who will remain, even against her wishes, his. Those were the songs that Liliana listened to on May 24, shedding tears.

On Saturday, May 26, Liliana noted at the top of a pastel-colored piece of paper, with unusually small handwriting, something that she had experienced a day after her tearful session with José Alfredo Jiménez's and Javier Solís's songs:

It finally happened yesterday. And today it seems to have disappeared. The euphoria passed away. There is no disappointment, I am still happy. Still. There you are, despite everything…I found you. So you are knowledge, you are, are you? Love and passion and desire for knowledge. You are you. You. Liliana.

The change was greater now. She was betting on herself, and not on someone else, after another breakup. She put faith in herself and her knowledge. Herself and her future. Maybe that May, Liliana was finally ready to let go. Perhaps that May Ángel also realized, at last, that she meant it this time. Maybe that May he knew that he couldn't control her anymore and was losing her for good. Four days later, Liliana described herself as unprotected for the first time in all the years she spent in Mexico City, a place known as a reckless, dangerous metropolis, but where she had felt at ease. It was a scant note, written on the last page of Notebook Four, a line in fine pencil handwriting, sealed with an exclamation point in purple ink:

May 30, 1990
It is, it was almost unbearable. On the metro, so unprotected. I'm at home, this space belongs to me!

There is nothing in her notebooks or in her loose notes to help unravel this puzzle. The threat, what made her feel exposed, open to attack, vulnerable to her core, clearly came from outside. The threat did not come from the public transportation system itself, but there it erupted forcefully, a defenselessness on which she did not care to elaborate and that, therefore, she did not let us see. Was she able to see it, in all its depth? A few days later, in a letter that she wrote to Raúl Espino Madrigal, but did not send him, she used the same term again: *unprotected*.

June 4 1990
I suddenly had the urge to go to my notebook and write (and write to you). Now I don't know what to say. I keep on looking for a letter you sent me, I can't find it...I feel bad, I know that you once wrote something on that piece of paper...I tremble,

and not because it's cold, I'm nervous, I think I'm finally understanding what happened to me in regards to you. I don't know
how to explain it, and understanding is hardly objective, but I
only feel tenderness, and I tremble, and it is not even cold.

Where the heck is that piece of paper? I don't hold on to
the past. At last I know that time passes ("and we are getting
old"). It has to be here!

My story is no longer hysteria.

I think of you, of you I think, thinking of you is what I do, and
it scares me because your image has always been accompanied by suspicion, anguish, mistrust. How I wish to visualize
you against a blue background without stains. Yesterday I
watched Santa Sangre, the movie, I'm still shaken up, buzzing.

How can I convince you that some things are not for mere
show.

" that I do not obsess over trifles.
" that I feel unprotected, so defenseless, how to tell you
   that... what?

I remember that day in Monte Albán, that moment, the only
eternal moment between you and me. Actually, I don't think it
matters anymore. I hate feeling like I want someone to truly
know me, for truly knowing someone is always risky. I once
loved you, possibly I still do. This is stupid and I don't give a fuck.

**[Do you know of someone who makes me yearn for so many
things?]**

... I still hear the waves breaking by our side, Ana, and I still
breathe in the smell of the sea, and yet we find ourselves in

another moment and another space. Do you realize? Things,
being the same, are different. The arrival of new people in
our lives, the arrival of new knowledge and feelings.
Perhaps we have changed: a year, a day, perhaps even a
second are just too much to remain static. I never told you,
maybe you never realized about all the pain that not having
you with me on the same path caused me. You will say: we
have not parted. But are you sure? You may think that the
university, or even our classes, are too pedestrian to really
change our lives or anything, but did we not get to know
one another in that time and space? Yes, I'm still hurt, still
irritated. Maybe that's why I have changed so much lately.
Have you felt it? I'm afraid I almost become violent at times.
Like yesterday, my silent shouting, the reproach that comes
out disguised as a simple "You're screwing it up, I don't like it."
And why didn't I scream "You are not with me," "You are not
sharing your anguish or happiness with me"? Why are you
not with me? Why didn't you fight hard enough for a class,
a simple class? Why? Yes, I am aware that the university
is not the only thing in the world and not even the most
legitimate one (paraphrasing Miquel Murillo), but wasn't that
what we chose? Sometimes I am judgmental, sometimes I
criticize you too much in front of my mirror. Sometimes I am
unfair. Aren't you the only one who should do it? I am so
selfish that I have come to think that my pain is greater
than yours.

The lack of longing scares me.....I think I should have never
said this............I do not know what to say anymore....I
want to apologize to you and scold you, caress you and hit

you, kiss you, feel you close, scream, pull your hair.....Do
you know of someone who makes me yearn for so many
things?

You know I love you. You know so well I love you.

. . .

How I am debating...whether or not it is a good idea to give
you this...I want to be truthful and honest. I want to be like
this with you.... With you I want to be like this.... Like this,
with you, I want to be.... To be with you, I want....I want
you.... Oh, shit! How come I want you?....Well...
    You know I love you. You know so well I love you.
    You know that I am fond of you.
    You know that I love you.

Liliana.

[in the shadow there is something that ended forever]

In addition to the presence of firearms or suicide threats, in addition to violent jealousy, constant harassment, and traces of physical and sexual violence, the Danger Assessment tool that Snyder analyzes in *No Visible Bruises* emphasizes the dangers of a victim becoming isolated. Little by little throughout 1990, Liliana's support group began to break down, although she did not lose it entirely. Ana, who had been her constant companion, her right arm, the closest and warmest presence in her life for the past year, was having trouble with a class and decided to switch to night classes, which dramatically reduced the time they spent together. "You are not with me," Liliana had reproached her in the letter that she didn't give her. Both Raúl and Leonardo had found part-time jobs that kept them away from campus, and they both began dating girls who, eventually, became their wives or long-term partners. I had been living in the United States for two years by then. And, right at the end of June, my parents embarked on their long-awaited trip to Europe. It was the first time that my father could afford my mother's airfare and, although it was a work trip that took them mainly to Germany and Sweden, they would take the opportunity to visit other cities together. It was a reward for a lifetime of sacrifices. It was, symbolically at least, the goal they had set for themselves more than twenty years earlier, when they left the cotton fields forever, and now they were, at last, about to achieve it. Manolo, who after a brief falling-out spent most of his free time with Liliana once again, drove the family's old white four-door Datsun to the airport, where everyone kissed each other and said farewell. I am so happy for both of you, Liliana said as she embraced them. Then, as they walked toward the gate, Liliana glanced at the distance that grew between herself and her parents. They turned back one last time and waved their hands from afar. Take care, Lili, they said. Manolo and Liliana drove the car back to Toluca, and then took the bus back to Mexico City. Though they were not officially together, little by little, they became a couple. They did homework together and walked together, although not hand in hand, around the university. He often picked her up at her house, before eight in the morning, in his red Barracuda.

In the early morning of July 16, 1990, when, according to witnesses on the street, Ángel jumped over the entrance gate to sneak into Mimosas 658, clearly trespassing, Liliana was not completely isolated, but, except for Manolo, she lacked the company of her closest network of friends and family. The risk index in the Danger Assessment would have been high in May, at the beginning of the eighth quarter, but now, already in early July, it had just gone up another notch. The risk index of a test that did not exist in Mexico, not even in the imagination, had just indicated that the risk was now lethal.

With some of her closest friends missing, her entire family out of the country, and her best friend preoccupied by academic and personal issues, Liliana, however, was not alone in Mimosas 658. On the upper floor, immediately above her apartment, lived the Álvarez family, and, during the week, their domestic worker slept in the room used for storage. How could a man murder a girl in such conditions without anyone hearing anything?

Still, June was not a bad month. According to Fernando Pérez Vega, Liliana had lost a lot of weight by then and, for the first time as a UAM student, she had left behind her leather jacket, bulky shirts and baggy pants. Instead, she started wearing dresses. There was one in particular, with small pink and blue flowers against a white background, that she wore with light ballerina flats, which highlighted her waist and accentuated her shoulders, making her look pretty and very slender. There was a freshness to everything she did. She walked faster, smiled more. In Notebook Three, she jotted down her options for MA and PhD programs. Right in the middle of June, she scribbled a note that she dated incorrectly, and interestingly, as 1986. Four years before. The handwriting was jagged and misshapen, huge by her normal standards, and spread over two columns with the French-style notebook held horizontally. Unlike so many other of her notes, this one was difficult to decipher.

160686

I'm still under the influence of alcohol, I am not writing like this because of that, but because the bus is jerking me around (I'm heading to Toluca). I am still lost in a cloud of subtle attentions. I don't know to whom I am addressing this, maybe to you, Ángel (Ángel, brother). Or to you José Luis (José Luis, a new dream?), or to you Sergio (so attentive in sensual matters).

I love each of you today. I love you all.

José Luis?

So far, none of Liliana's friends have been able to help us identify that pair: José Luis and Sergio, who spent time with her on a Saturday afternoon, a little before she left for Toluca. Written on the spur of the moment, the note exudes Liliana's excitement. She is a bit tipsy, a bit overwhelmed by a series of what she called "subtle attentions," impactful enough to make her forget her problems and even entertain the idea of a new love interest. In a radical departure, Ángel has become a brother in this letter, no longer figuring as a romantic or sexual partner. Is this the proverbial truth uttered by drunkards and children when least expected? Is this the wink, the crack, the unintended twist, that reveals an unprecedented emotional distancing? While the writing may be addressed to him too, therefore not excluding him altogether from her life, Ángel's role has significantly changed. Now he is family. Now he is a relative. Perhaps even an object of pity. Perhaps this feeling, this recasting of him as a brother, was behind Ángel's sudden and redoubled effort to win her heart back because some days later, on a note from June 25, Liliana wrote angrily and only in capital letters, with a

line that betrayed the weight of the whole body on the tip of
the pen:

june 25, 1990

I DO NOT UNDERSTAND YOU,
  I REALLY DO NOT UNDERSTAND YOU!
  ARE YOU PLAYING AT LOVING ME ONCE AGAIN?
  I DO NOT LIKE THIS!
  NOW YOU LOVE ME, TOMORROW WHO KNOWS?
  WHAT A COWARDLY SITUATION!

25
june twenty-fif

A few pages later, still using the same ink, although with a
more controlled stroke, Liliana wrote down the phrase of Albert
Camus with which he once consoled a betrayed girl:

In the midst of winter I finally found there was, within me, an
invincible summer.

Albert Camus.

Was she waking up? Had she found a way, this time, to console
herself and to counsel herself? Was her own winter finally coming
to an end? Below the note, which functioned as a kind of epigraph, Liliana let her unease flow, her language, the images that
populated her:

And the light will condense...
And it will fit in only one of my ears.

The blue will enter my mouth
And we will bathe in it.
It?
Blue is not an it, not even a she, a we...
Not "us."
No. Fat. Does fat kill fat?
Is this logical?
Is the stomach a cauldron?
A witch's cauldron...a witch with a wart on her nose.

On the roller coaster that was her mind, she wrote on June 28:

June 28

I have realized quite suddenly, I lie when I say "suddenly,"
because this has been latent in me for a long time: eyes, scenes,
hands, eyes, looks, the idea of who it is doesn't matter. Didn't I
see it like that last week? It is borne in one and in the other. I
don't really want love. Recurrent? June. June. June. Fantastic
June 28, 1990. June. June. June. June. June. June. June. June. June. June.

It's hard to know what happened then. Did she meet Sergio or
José Luis once again? Was she just rejoicing, thinking about what
had happened a week earlier? Was she with Ángel in a "recurrent"
but quite different new way now? The revelation, in any case,
broke free: the girl who had always taken the side of love against
all odds now questioned her position. If love, as she had argued in
a letter to Ana not so long ago, hurt her, this reluctance to love,
this "I don't really want love," placed her squarely on the opposite
side, perhaps the side of joy and freedom. Another love was possible. Another way to hem in bodies and desire. A day later she
received a gift—an unsigned note, written in green ink, an-

nounced: "Surprise." The use of quotation marks and capital letters gave him away. "For you who are very special. 06-29-90." The
wording, if not the handwriting, was clearly Ángel's.

Perhaps that sudden skepticism about love forced her to be
brave. Liliana seemed determined to take matters into her own
hands in early July. In the datebook that she used those days, a
small notebook with squared sheets and a brown plastic cover, she
wrote in her usual uniform and graceful handwriting:

Monday July 9, 1990

I want it to be a favorable day. I expect everything to work out
well tomorrow. There are many things to do and I fear that I
will not be able to finish them…I fear my bouts of anger, my
temperament. Operational review. Interdisc. paper. Wind
data…Atlas. Study for Laboratory. Paper for Laboratory.
TEC review. Construction work. Finishes. Installations.
Prepare TEC class. Make sketches and overheads.

If her friends' comments are to be trusted, that's the date Liliana finally broke up—for good—with Ángel. In the note, she fears
her own temper, but she does not fear him. As in the letter she
wrote to Ángel after their July 1987 breakup, she is willing to ac-
knowledge Ángel as an aggressive, short-tempered man, even a
bit foolish, but not as an evil person. She does not know, has no
way of knowing, that Ángel, who has repeatedly claimed to love
her so dearly, who professed loving her more than anything in this
world, is capable of taking her life. Liliana does not yet sniff the
reek of danger that trails after her.

Not long after, on July 11, Liliana received a brief note written
in pencil, and in capital letters only, on the back of a small flyer
announcing a cycle of *Mexican religious architecture from the*

16th century, yesterday and today (Genesis). Architect Carlos Lira Vásquez, Wednesday, June 13, at 10:00 hrs. K-001. The note, which was signed by Ángel, read: "WITH LOVE FOR LILIANA, JULY 11, 90."

I don't know for sure, even now, whether she met with him on campus that day or whether the note was left at her house, perhaps accompanying a gift. Judging by the choice of the stationery—a seemingly random piece of paper that may be found among many others on the walls of the buildings on campus—the gesture must not have been planned very far in advance. Because the message includes the words *with love,* I assume it went together with something else, perhaps chocolates or a stuffed animal. Perhaps some flowers. Love, lethal and repetitive, malignant and atrocious, was still there.

Liliana spent her last weekend in the Mimosas apartment, working with Juan Carlos Sierra and Manolo Casillas on a project that they had to turn in on Monday, July 16, very early in the morning. It was a demanding class, and they knew all too well that the final portfolio required long hours of careful work. On the morning of Friday, July 13, while waiting for the revision of her final project for the Technology TEC class, a seminar taught by Professor Alejandro Miramontes, Liliana had time to write in Notebook Four, all in purple ink, the following:

JULY 13, 1990

> Before TEC review
> from my drawing board, watching you

Gentle face
A child's face
Some full eyes

Freckles
Unruly hair
Moon hair
Skillful hands
How to confuse those hands with the expression of a child
    scribbling for the first time?
I could say your name
I could say that I love you today
But both would be a lie
Your name, love, would be fallacies.

Names change because love goes from one place to another, I
    will never consider it an absolute.

I love.
It doesn't matter the thing, the name, the time, or the space. I
    love.
I look back, and you're still there. That expression overwhelms
    me, haunts me, fills me. Moon hair.

    Who was that person who Liliana looked at, half distracted, half bored, as she awaited the evaluation of a final project? The lack of pronouns makes the task especially difficult. There is the mention of a child, and even then, the child is genderless. Ana was her only friend with freckles. Was her curly, tousled hair the moon hair Liliana was lovingly watching from afar? Were her hands, sweeping hastily over a blueprint, those she confused with a child's? I have no definitive answer. I still don't know who that person was, that person whom Liliana claimed to love now, after having questioned love so adamantly. As in the fight we'd had many years before, locked inside a car parked in front of a market,

Liliana put herself, without hesitation, on the side of love. But, by now, love has been transfigured. Her Achilles' heel, but also, as Ana claimed, her superpower.

Liliana spoke here, as she had ever since she was a child, of a love that was utterly free. Not the selfish love that tied couples together, but a love so grand, so absolute, that bowed down to no one, to nothing at all. A mercurial, changing love that tied and untied itself from the material world at will, such was Liliana's love.

Something was wrong, however. Or something had altered her all of a sudden, for on the morning of Saturday the fourteenth, Liliana wrote about her determination not to let herself fall, about her ability to get back up again. Perhaps her sermon about love, her insistence on a love that freely moved through bodies and minds, came as a result of the pressures selfish love attempted to impose upon her once again. It was then that she mentioned for the first time, and only in an oblique manner, a threat against her life.

In addition to traditional Mexican songs, Liliana listened to rock in Spanish, an emerging trend headed by Argentinian and Spanish bands, Charly García and Nacha Pop among them, and the New Song Movement, clearly favoring Cuban singers Silvio Rodríguez and Amaury Pérez. She also was partial to strong female performers, and Eugenia León soon became one of her favorite ones. In 1986, León released *Otra vez,* an album that combined traditional tunes with new compositions, which were generally thought of as Latin folk, or world music. A night before the crime, Liliana listened to and transcribed a stanza from "Don't You Go," a romantic song written by Pepe Elorza. While the lyrics have the singer begging for the lover not to abandon her, adamant about not letting go, Liliana chose to highlight three lines in which the forlorn lover hints at the existence of a life threat.

JULY 14, 1990

I just woke up.

I woke up nervous, sad…but I think and I repeat to myself that I can't let myself fall…I can't, for me and for you…what you said yesterday hurt me, you can't leave me just like that…I wouldn't allow it.

> "Because say whatever you want
> I am already part of your life,
> And you cannot attempt against yourself."
>
> (pretty song, huh?)

Just like Eugenia León in the song, Liliana had a hard time believing that a lover could make an attempt on her life. Wasn't she, after all, such an ingrained part of his life that any threat against her ought to necessarily turn into a threat against himself? The logic was impeccable; the somber irony with which she finished off the transcription, remarking on the prettiness of the song, less so. Rachel Louise Snyder convincingly argued that women receiving death threats from the men claiming to love them are asked to execute an impossible cognitive leap. Admitting the reality of the threat would require radically questioning the very narrative that made it possible in the first place. Was Liliana finally at that stage? Pretty song, huh? Liliana wrote in poignantly self-deprecating mode, fully aware of a situation her intellect could not come to terms with. Such a smart and snarky gal.

It was a Saturday. Liliana had spent Friday evening with Manolo, working at the Mimosas apartment. While they both knew they had to concentrate on the project, they did get distracted at times. This is what I think: Manolo sensed Ángel was trying to get close to Liliana once again, and wanted Liliana to assure him that, this time, she would choose him. This time things would be different. Or else. Liliana was being pressured on two fronts, both men claiming to love her madly. In the evening, when Juan Carlos Sierra invited them to a party in Echegaray, a middle-class neighborhood up north, they gladly accepted. They thought it would be a good way to relax before the final push, which would come on Sunday. They had fun for a bit, drank a couple of beers, and left the party early. Manolo dropped Liliana off at night, at approximately 10:00 P.M. When she woke up that July 15, at 10:30 in the morning, Liliana wrote:

JULY 15, 1990 10:30 a.m.

How I wish we were no longer fairies in a land of ice!
So much need for company.

Juan Carlos was tired and did not come to Mimosas that Sunday. Manolo arrived early, and they got to work immediately. They talked and joked every now and then as they continued with the project. They turned on the cassette player and listened again and again to "The City of Fury." Perhaps they downed a beer or two. Around 10:00 P.M., after dark, Manolo told Liliana that they had to stop. He felt satisfied that they had finished the project. They could improve a thing or two, but the main body of work was done. Stay, Liliana suggested. And we will leave early together tomorrow. Manolo hesitated. Was she committing to him now? Or was this just one of those invitations she issued because she felt lonely? I can't, Lili, he said. I promised my mom I'd come home tonight. Liliana looked disappointed but did not insist. She seemed tired, exhausted, and even then, when Manolo approached to kiss her goodbye, he found her beautiful. Don't be sad, güera, he said. I'll pick you up tomorrow, at the usual time. We'll bring this thing to campus together and then it will be the end of the quarter. You'll see.

It is difficult to know with certainty what Liliana did between 10:00 P.M. that cloudy, rainy night, and that still vague hour of dawn, when Ángel broke into her space. Judging by the ink in which they are transcribed, she may have used some of those late-night hours, when she was still alone, to transcribe the poems she was reading. She took up a squared page of Notebook Four to write out, word by word, "Presencia," the poem that José Emilio Pacheco dedicated to Rosario Castellanos, a poet who had died accidentally when trying to turn on a lamp while living in Tel Aviv. And, on the next page, she transcribed a section of Chaucer, as well as the poem "Luz y silencio," from the book *Los elementos de la noche*, by José Emilio Pacheco.

PRESENCIA

Homenaje a Rosario Castellanos

¿Qué va a quedar de mí cuando me muera
sino esta llave ilesa de agonía,
estas pocas palabras en que el día
deja cenizas de su sombra fiera?

¿Qué va a quedar de mí cuando me hiera
esa daga final? Acaso mía
será la noche fúnebre y vacía
que vuelva a ser de pronto primavera.

No quedará el trabajo ni la pena
de creer y de amar. El tiempo abierto,
semejante a los mares y al desierto,

ha de borrar de la confusa arena
todo lo que me salva o encadena.
Mas si alguien vive yo estaré despierto

(José Emilio Pacheco)

Cuando tendido en mi cama dormido completamente
  despierto
estaba para mí, pero porque no podía
descansar yo no lo sabía, porque ningún ser terrenal
(como yo supongo) tenía más dolencias
que yo, porque yo no tenía males o enfermedades

(Chaucer)

Todo lo que has perdido, me dijeron, es tuyo.
Y ninguna memoria recordaba que es cierto.

Todo lo que destruyes, afirmaron, te hiere.
Traza una cicatriz que no lava el olvido.

Todo lo que has amado, sentenciaron, ha muerto.
Porque en la sombra hay algo que acabó para siempre.

Todo lo que creíste, repitieron, es falso.
Cayeron las palabras en que empezó tu tiempo.

Todo lo que has perdido, concluyeron, es tuyo.
Una luz fugitiva anegará el silencio.

(j.e. pacheco)

The forensic report established July 16, 1990, 5:00 A.M., as the official time of her death. My parents were crossing the North Sea in a small plane at that time.

Presencia.

Homenaje a Rosario Castellanos

¿Qué va a quedar de mí cuando me muera
sino esta llave ilesa de agonía,
estas pocas palabras en que el día
dejó cenizas de su sombra fiera?

¿Qué va a quedar de mí cuando me hiera
esa daga final? Acaso mía
será la noche fúnebre y vacía
que vuelva a ser de pronto primavera.

No quedará el trabajo ni la pena
de creer y de amar. El tiempo abierto,
semejante a los mares y al desierto,

ha de borrar de la confusa arena
todo lo que me salva o encadena.
Mas si alguien vive yo estaré despierto.

[José Emilio Pacheco]

Cuando tendido en mi cama dormido completamente despierto
Estaba para mí, pero por qué no podía
descansar yo no lo sabia, porque ningún ser terrenal
(como yo supongo) tenía más dolencias
que yo, porque yo no tenía males o enfermedades

[CHAUCER]

Todo lo que has perdido, me dijeron,
es tuyo.
Y ninguna memoria recordaba que es cierto

Todo lo que destruyes afirmaron,
te hiere
Traza una cicatriz que no lava el olvido.

Todo lo que has amado, sentenciaron
ha muerto.
Porque en la sombra hay algo que acabo para siempre.

Todo lo que es fatal, repitieron,
es falso.
Cayeron las palabras en que empezó tu tiempo.

Todo lo que has perdido, concluyeron
es tuyo
Una luz fugitiva arraiga el silencio.

[j.e.pacheco]

The howling storm that shook the plane that night kept my mother awake.

IX

AN OBSCURE CRIME

If you pick up a flower, if you snatch a handbag, if you possess a woman, if you plunder a storehouse, ravage a countryside or occupy a city, you are a *taker*. You are *taking*. In ancient Greek you use the verb, which comes over in Latin as *rapio, rapere, raptus sum* and gives us English rapture and rape—words stained with the very early blood of girls, with the very late blood of cities, with the hysteria of the end of the world. Sometimes I think language should cover its own eyes when it speaks.

—ANNE CARSON, *Norma Jeane Baker of Troy*

[findings]

It rained that day. Manolo arrived at Liliana's house at ten past seven, just as he had promised. He had gotten up early, bathed, and combed that unruly mane of hair, which at times betrayed some of the reddish tint he'd had in childhood. He even had time to eat a good breakfast. When he got in the red Barracuda that his father had gifted him, he only thought, with great relief, that it was almost the end of the quarter. It hadn't been easy finalizing that last project over the weekend, but he was satisfied. He felt proud even, ready for whatever would come his way. Ready for the future. He had an Óscar Chávez song playing in his head as he parked his car in front of Liliana's house. How cheesy, he berated himself. And then he smiled. That's what she would say: how cheesy. He knocked on the entrance gate and Basilia, a petite young woman whom Liliana had introduced as the Álvarez family's new domestic worker, answered. Good morning, she said. He crossed the courtyard and opened the door to Liliana's apartment, which was closed but remained unlocked. He didn't see her up and about, so he called her name from the living room. They should get going. They had to turn in the project and they'd better be on time. On the other side of the room, in the space that was originally meant to be the dining room, spread Liliana's bed, and on it, but under the covers, he could discern the outline of her body. Everything else seemed in place. Nothing was in order, but there was no disorder either. Over time, he had become familiar with the rules of Liliana's mayhem and, knowing that they had worked late the night before, he figured that she hadn't had time to tidy up. Hurry up, güera, he said. It's getting late, he insisted when she did not react.

He glanced around the kitchen and saw that everything was as he had left it the night before. Her lack of response intrigued him. He approached her bed. Slowly. It was a joke. Maybe one of those pranks of hers, the kind of little tricks she'd play to make everyone laugh. It seemed strange to him that her whole body, including her head, was buried under the checkered cover. Lili, he said again, uncovering her face, ready for the laugh with which she would surely greet him. I caught you, she'd say.

Liliana's eyes were closed. Her mouth ajar. She was lying on her left arm and her straight hair, tousled, covered half her face. She seemed to be sound asleep, but there was something strange about her unresponsiveness. Lili, he said again. When he drew the cover farther down, he realized that she was fully dressed, her jeans on and her blouse buttoned up. Still, she did not react. Instinctively, he brushed his fingers against her cheek and an excruciating cold, a cold he had never felt before in his life, latched on to his fingertips and, in a flash, spread through every cell in his body. A sudden despair fell straight down his spine. He yelled. He screamed. He shouted her name and he called for help. Soon, both José Manuel Álvarez and Basilia were behind him, next to him, their breath heavy on his neck. Something is wrong with Liliana, he said. They looked at each other. They looked at her. Liliana is dead, he added without thinking. Without knowing for sure what he had just said. They didn't dare touch her as they stood there, looking down, transfixed around the bed. The landlord scrambled upstairs to call for an ambulance. Liliana is dead, Manolo murmured at the foot of the mattress. Incredulous. Completely paralyzed. Lili, he said again, squatting in front of her. Then he noticed the marks around her neck and the two bruises on her face. Her purple lips.

Things happened very quickly after that. The ambulance arrived. Manolo couldn't tell if the nurses attempted to revive her or whether they limited themselves to confirming his own verdict. There were other phone calls, this time to the police. Soon officers and forensic experts arrived. Who are you? they asked him. A classmate from university, he said. I was picking her up to go to campus. A classmate from university? they sneered back at him. While the detectives snooped around the room, he went upstairs to borrow the phone, trying to reach his cousin, Fernando Casillas, a lawyer. Abruptly, hurriedly, he told him what was happening. Were you the last to see her alive? he asked. It looks like I was. And were you the one who found her lifeless? Yes, he said. You're in trouble, he summarized. Do not answer anything until I arrive. Before leaving, the lawyer contacted Ana Ocadiz. Something happened, he told her. You have to go to Liliana's apartment immediately. Manolo, meanwhile, contacted Ángel López. He summarized the facts as best he could and asked him to come immediately as well. A few minutes later, on campus, Ángel López grabbed Gerardo Navarro by the elbow and pulled him away from the other students. Guess what? he said. Liliana was killed. You're kidding, he replied. No, I'm not kidding. Let's go. They ran into Juan Carlos Sierra on the way out and, after hearing the story, he followed them in another car.

The police began their interrogations both inside Mimosas 658 and on the street. Neighbors reported that they had seen a stocky young man with blond hair and blue eyes prowling the block during the night. They had seen the same man on their block before, at times waiting for Liliana in his car or rushing by on a very flashy motorcycle. Manolo told investigators that the man's name was Ángel. Her boyfriend? No, not really, he hesitated. She didn't want to see him anymore. Are you sure about that? Manolo began to connect the dots in his head, keeping his revelation to himself: perhaps Ángel had been hanging around Liliana's house all weekend and had seen them coming and going since Friday afternoon, unable to fathom what was going on behind the apartment walls that sheltered them from Ángel's view. Perhaps he had spied on them, and their closeness stirred his fury. What was Ángel to do, convinced as he was that Liliana belonged to him and to him only? What would a predator do but wait patiently outside her home, making sure she was alone and vulnerable, to attack her?

Manolo's mind was racing. Ideas came in a rush, sometimes in concentric circles, sometimes in reverse motion, sometimes fleeting toward vanishing points that made him run out of breath. Maybe Ángel had followed them when they went to the party on Saturday. Maybe on Sunday Ángel saw him getting into Liliana's flat a little after ten-thirty in the morning, and didn't see him leave until ten at night, and imagined them lying close together, their legs intertwined. What if what happened to Liliana had been his fault? he wondered. What if he was the cause of Ángel's jealousy and hatred? Overwhelmed by these thoughts, Manolo managed to overhear that Ángel had paid three thousand pesos to a couple of addicts on the block, guys he had gotten close to over time, who kept him informed of Liliana's daily comings and goings in exchange for drugs. He was keeping track of her, Manolo muttered to himself, and felt his pulse rise inside his wrists. During the night, a little before dawn, he overheard another witness say, Ángel found the gate to Liliana's house locked and asked one of the junkies to help him climb over the entrance wall, which was not particularly high, commanding them to create a foothold with their hands. Manolo turned to see the cloudy morning sky, then the street: even though Ángel lived far away in Toluca, he had managed to keep her under his watch. The pulse again in his wrists, temples, eardrums.

When Ana arrived, Lili's house was no longer a home, but a crime scene. She confirmed that the name that corresponded to the witnesses' description was Ángel González Ramos. Her light curls scattered over her head, a deep wound in each of her eyes. She wanted to see Liliana as soon as possible, to hug her, to prove that she had not lost her forever. It can't be, she repeated again and again. Is this true? Is this for real? She was willing to believe, even now, that it was all a practical joke or, at best, an elaborate misunderstanding. And who are you? they asked. She trained her eyes on them, regaining control over the trembling of her lips and voice. I'm her friend. I am Liliana's best friend. I am hers. While they made her wait in the courtyard, Ana overheard that, shortly before dawn, Ángel had borrowed a broom from a drunk in the house across the street to unlatch the gate. Once in the courtyard, he carefully removed one of the the glass slats so that he could open the door to Liliana's apartment from the inside. Did you know him? the police agents asked. Yes, she said. Could you describe him for us? they continued. I have a photograph at home, she said. If it would help.

When Gerardo arrived, in utter disbelief, sweaty, with a mouth full of thirst and terror, he heard about the neighbor across the street who lent Ángel the broom. If that neighbor had been asleep, none of this would have happened, he thought. No one paid any attention to Gerardo, so he entered Liliana's apartment, which had not been cordoned off, and walked it inch by inch. Liliana was on the mattress, just as Manolo had discovered her, fully clothed. Tennis shoes on, laces tied. At first glance there were no bruises on her face, but a subtle purple tint spread on her skin. Then, looking at her more carefully, Gerardo noticed that a button on her blouse was undone and the zipper of her pants half open. A stain surrounding her hips suggested that Lili had peed. Everything else was in order. It was Liliana's room, intact. He remembered it perfectly because he had spent many hours working, celebrating there. I got drunk for the first time here, he thought. And, at that moment, he burst into tears.

Manolo had become the main suspect in the crime and was taken to the police station for further interrogation. Meanwhile, the investigators who had already collected the information about Ángel took the photograph that Ana shared with them and asked her to accompany them to Toluca, to Pino Suárez 2006, where she and Liliana had once visited. A middle-aged woman answered the metal door. But when they inquired about Ángel, she told them that she hadn't seen him recently. Ana caught a glimpse of the black sedan Ángel drove those days, and looked up toward the roof of the multifamily compound. Days later, she learned that one of the neighbors claimed that Ángel had fled through the roof precisely when the police cars were approaching. He was caught off guard, not expecting that Liliana's friends would find her so early in the morning, only a couple of hours after he left. He did not think that the police, usually so slow and corrupt, would locate him so rapidly.

It was still early in the morning when *La Prensa* reporter Tomás Rojas Madrid arrived at Mimosas 658. Extremely thin, skilled in his trade, he observed the crime scene undeterred. He had seen so much bloodshed in his life, murderous rage, decapitated bodies. Still, news of a murdered girl, a university student at that, had potential. But the girl was fully dressed and the house was orderly. Not dramatic enough, he muttered. He listened to the police interrogations and asked his own questions, paying close attention to the answers. As the presence of a relative was required to identify the body, a group led by Ángel López took the road to Toluca, to inform Liliana's parents. They drove quietly, breaking the silence only to ask for directions. A hushed stupor kept them still on their seats, frozen within themselves, unable to articulate any sound or thought. The landscape was but a vanishing point they tunneled through. A horizon devouring itself. We've arrived, said Ángel López when he turned off the engine, but all remained motionless, hesitant about what steps to take. Let's knock on their door, he said, matter-of-factly, as if his hands were not shaking. At first, they knocked softly, but as no one came to the door, they increased the intensity and rhythm of their call. Ms. Rivera, he yelled, thinking that it was more likely for the mother to be at home at this time of the day. Who are you looking for? a neighbor across the street asked. Who are you? We're Liliana's friends from the university, they said. We need to talk to her parents. What for? she asked, suspiciously. Something terrible has happened, they said. She handed them the key and went into the house with them looking for a phone number, an address, anything that might help reach Liliana's parents. They searched furiously through the living room and the kitchen, trying to locate a datebook. They shuffled some notes scattered on the dining room table, reading too the list of errands left by the phone. They found nothing. I might have a number in my address book, the neighbor said at last, nervously, when they were about to give up. It's not theirs, she explained, but it may help us get to them. She dialed the number and waited; and it was only then, when listening to the ringing tones, that she realized the enormity of the task ahead of her. Her saliva swirled under her tongue, suddenly bitter. She contacted one of Liliana's aunts, a woman who lived in Tamaulipas and whom she had met recently, in one of her visits to the family.

I have some god-awful news, she said. Only then did Liliana's friends return to Mexico City. They were wrecked. The more they thought about what they were doing, the less real it felt. Their adrenaline ran out, and they were left there, like burlap sacks stuffed with heavy rocks on the seats of an old car, driving back to Mexico City. Only the murmur of the engine accompanied them as they smoked nonstop. Wasn't her sister living in Houston? one of them asked. Yes, they all recalled as they passed by the somber pines of the Marquesa National Park.

[1703 Albans]

The hour is confusing. It is too dark to be a summer afternoon and too luminous to be evening. The clash of knuckles against white-painted wood. Once, then once again. The whole strangeness of that action: knocking on the door. Nobody does that without a warning, not in the United States. No one shows up at the door of an apartment on the ground floor of a small building at the end of a cul-de-sac without first announcing their visit. Nobody except Jehovah's Witnesses or Girl Scouts who sell cookies at Christmas. Through the tiny peephole in the door it is possible to see the dark, straight hair of two women turning their heads from right to left. Restless. Gone astray, their eyes. Expensive leather bags hanging from forearms. Are you related to Liliana Rivera Garza? The first question, timidly spoken in Spanish, hints at something extraordinary. Something decidedly unusual. The two women work at the Mexican consulate in Houston. Their names and their positions get lost in broken sentences and glances that surreptitiously withdraw back into the interior of the skull. We are so very sorry, they say. They look down, and at each other, trying to decide who will utter the next sentence. There has been an accident. The silence that follows half-truths. The inability to continue. No, she is not in a hospital. It was. They whisper. Fatal. They have no further information. Their only mission on this July afternoon is this: notify the only relative anyone was able to locate. Our mission is to update you. To inform you.

Someone must enter the seven-digit number to make the first phone call. Someone must pronounce the words, carefully. Someone observes the tension that holds the cord in place between the telephone base and the handset. The tight distance between the two. Someone must deliver the news, which, in turn, will emerge from another black handset. Someone hangs up. Someone puts a couple of things in a carry-on and waits. Approaches the door. Starts the engine. Someone buys the ticket at the airline counter, offering personal information, immigration documents, and a check on which a nervous, almost illegible signature has been scrawled. Someone perches on the lonely seat at the gate and, a little later, on the aisle seat of an airplane. Knees bent and drawn together. Hands on thighs. Someone walks. Someone pushes away the hand that is trying to grasp her elbow in a quick, jerky movement. Looks straight ahead. Looks out the window and thinks, I once loved Mexico City with all my heart. Someone closes her eyes. I wish she'd had a great love, someone mutters, in English. Someone suddenly opens her eyes. The stiffness in the hands again. Jaw clenched. The whiplash of recognition that runs down the spine: realizing suddenly, knowing everything at once, not having the slightest doubt. Consciousness works like this sometimes. Someone connects the dots. Her eyes, someone remembers. Liliana's troubled eyes. All that winter sunlight splashing over her slightly tousled hair in the photograph, and on her face against the window, on her almost veiled face, those big eyes behind gold-rimmed glasses. Incredulous. Mortified. A burning question. Her eyes, my sister's eyes, and the jet engine. The fast pace of the flight attendants. And the stale air of so many passengers breathing in and out together.

[receiving a body]

Our cousin Emilio Hernández Garza received the news on Monday, July 16, at five in the evening. Ricardo Herrera and Oscar de los Reyes, who were lawyers and friends of his brother Fernando, had tried to catch up with him in the cafeteria but, by the time they arrived, he had already closed, so they went straight to the San Lorenzo Acopilco house that they knew so well. As soon as he made out their faces in the distance, he knew something serious was happening. Ricardo hugged him and said: I have some bad news. He felt a paralysis travel swiftly up his neck, freezing him in place. Then, as if the voice had come from another world, he managed to understand that, since he was the only close relative available, he had to go to Azcapotzalco to identify the body. His brother was in Michoacán but was already on his way back home.

His friends took him directly to the house on Mimosas, which by then was cordoned off, but Liliana's body had already been taken to SEMEFO, the government agency where the corpses of victims who died under suspicious or violent circumstances were kept.

Without much thought, he walked farther into the building while Ricardo and Oscar took care of the paperwork. What an icy place. His shoes slipped on floors covered in water, where corpses sometimes glided on the ground, unclaimed by anyone. It wasn't until one in the morning that he could see her. The girl who once photographed him asleep on a park bench and woke him up with a belly laugh. The girl he went to the movies with regularly, reveling in their shared obsession. The one who, one day, hung around his neck as they walked just to whisper, half serious, half joking, you're my favorite cousin. His cousin. She was stark naked, a body among other bodies, and yet as beautiful in death as she had been in life. Could he tell that behind her closed eyes she was resting, finally at peace? He could not detect a trace of harshness or horror on her face. No longing. No struggle. Fearing neglect, or the mistreatment the state agency was famous for, he waited by her side, without taking his eyes off her. His cousin. Who he had seen grow up. To whom, so many years ago, he had once written a letter that he was sure she still kept somewhere. When he asked the police what had happened they told him, carelessly describing the events in the crudest of terms, that the murderer had pressed a cushion over her face and suffocated her. Who could do something like that to a girl? they said. Something like what? he asked. Killing her first and raping her after, they said. Employees covering their mouths and noses, humming among themselves as they groped the arms and legs of the helpless bodies. His cousin.

Emilio received Liliana's body on Tuesday, July 17, at two in the afternoon. Maybe a little later. Maybe even a couple of hours later. He hadn't slept or eaten, but he had to go on. He wore the same shirt and pants from the day before, and the smell of sweat and the smell of sadness mingled in his armpits and groin. Thanks to a secretary at the morgue who allowed him to use her office phone, he learned that Uncle Aristeo was about to arrive in Toluca from El Poblado, and that some members of his own family, including his father, had gotten into a old, beat-up car to drive from Tampico. An old family neighbor, Rafael Ruiz Perete, also from Toluca, arrived in time to hire the hearse that would take Liliana to the family plot in a cemetery at the base of a volcano that our mother had bought years ago without thinking, without even imagining, that the youngest, her youngest daughter, would be the one to occupy it first.

[Do you want to see her?]

Someone is approaching in the crowd at the airport. Someone hugs her, his chin heavy in the hollow between her neck and shoulder. Someone is speaking. Shuts up. Sound filters through valves and drums made of flesh, of distance, of even more noise. It is impossible to recognize the words that jump out of half-open mouths. Teeth poke through lips that don't stop moving, but the sound that accompanies those words takes a long time to material-ize in the air. Television channels with interference problems. White noise. Someone is silent, numb. Someone refuses to ask questions out of fear of hearing the answers. Someone pushes her shoulders forward and hunches her back and touches her elbows with opposite hands. Someone says: let's go this way. Someone looks at the floor, the worn marble on the airport floor, and obeys. Let's get out of here. The night through the car windows. Take Constituyentes Avenue to leave Mexico City and drive toward To-luca. Soon, the city is left behind and the sparse hamlets on the mountains begin to appear. A little later, the pines and oyamels surge. And we are already, as if by magic, in the highlands. Huix-quilucan. La Marquesa. The National Institute for Nuclear Re-search. San Mateo Atenco. The Paseo Tollocan freeway. How many times have we traveled this road illuminated by streetlights and traffic signs? The branches of the willows touch the edge of the road cautiously. The weeping willows, do you remember? The willows that you liked so much. High up above: the variegated clouds within the night. The promise of rain that is the promise of summer.

There is an office. The door opens. A door made of rusty metal that once bore the color of old gold. Behind that door lies a dark room with low ceilings, which soon turns into many other rooms. The space gives off a musty smell, the reek of solid and useless instruments, of time contained. Then, suddenly, comes the scent. Something unknown, something without a proper name that goes for the nose and, abruptly, without asking permission or offering an explanation, forces itself through the nostrils, reaching with great impetus, with alacrity, the olfactory mucosa, only to slide through microscopic holes up to the olfactory bulb in the anterior part of the brain. How long does this whole process take? The limbic system. The hypothalamus. The cerebral cortex, the temporal and frontal lobes. What we call consciousness. What we call: fathoming. A chemical needle through the brain, the nervous system, the emotional spin. Everything is on alert. Do you want to see her?

Someone asks me that.

Do you want to see her?

[Tuesday, July 17, 1990, *La Prensa*]

Tomás Rojas Madrid immediately knew that this story belonged on the front pages of his newspaper. He had been working for the crime section of *La Prensa* for quite a while, and it took a lot to move or shock him, but seeing that girl there, all alone, on that mattress on the ground, made his heart shrink. University students were not murdered in Mexico City. Not yet. He had arrived early at the scene of the crime and, calmly, paying very close attention, gathered the material he would need to write his piece. He did it methodically, sparing no details. He had managed the time so well that he even had a chance to eat half a sandwich and drink two soft drinks before deciding on the title. It was a heinous crime, that was true, but he needed a catchy headline. If it had been a crime of passion, why was everything left undisturbed inside the room? No puddles of blood. No smeared walls. If the murderer had broken into the girl's house in the middle of the night with the help of a neighbor, how come no one had heard anything inside a building of modest dimensions, where sounds could resonate through shared walls? If she had been attacked or sexually abused, why was she all dressed up on her deathbed? An obscure crime, that's what it was. The adjective before the noun. A crime with many question marks. The editor of the newspaper decided to give the top headline to a story about an earthquake that had struck the Philippines the day before. But knowing *La Prensa*'s readership as well as he did, he left the title of Rojas's article on the lower right-hand corner of the front page: STRANGLED STUDENT.

OBSCURE CRIME. A young student was found strangled in her apartment.

A young architecture student was found murdered by strangulation inside the small apartment she rented in the north of the city, and the police are looking for the murderer among her friends.

Liliana Rivera Garza, 20 years old, was found in a bedroom at her home on Calle Mimosas, in the Pasteros neighborhood, at the edge of the Azcapotzalco delegation.

The crime was discovered around 8:00 in the morning by her neighbors, who were surprised that they hadn't seen her leave at her habitual time. They noticed that the main access door to the apartment was closed, but one of the windows had been smashed in by a blow.

José Manuel Álvarez, the owner of the property, and who lives on the second floor of the building, insistently called the young woman without receiving an answer, so he quickly decided to call the police. The young woman, who, according to her friends and neighbors, lived alone and worked to support her studies, was found dead when the authorities entered the room a short time later.

Liliana Rivera was strangled, and it is very possible that she was also assaulted, said the medical examiner of the precinct. Detectives from the homicide Prosecutor's Office of the regional delegation of the Attorney General's Office in Azcapotzalco investigated the crime scene and have not shared information as to whether there were traces of a struggle inside her bedroom.

Despite all this, the police have reported that the crime took place in the early morning hours, based on the coroner's assessment of the time of death of the young student.

What the neighbors cannot explain is why they did not hear breaking glass or the screams—if there were any—of the murdered young woman.

The agent of the public prosecutor's office arrived at the scene of the crime later and asked the experts to rigorously trace the fingerprints inside the room to determine whether or not the young woman was victim of an assault.

Liliana Rivera was well regarded by her neighbors, who indicate that she was well-behaved, receiving visits from only a handful of friends.

Suspicion is concentrated on her group of friends; maybe a jilted boyfriend stopped by to chat and took advantage of the opportunity to kill her, said one of the detectives who came to Mimosas 658.

The murder of this young student has caused quite a stir, because this area of Azcapotzalco is relatively tranquil, with frequent police patrols, but these types of events stoke fear among local residents.

Act 40/913 / 990-07 was filed in reference to the crime, the authorities reported.

[there's good corn in England]

Fernando approached Norma very slowly, biting his lip. Come here, he said, I have to talk to you about something. He put his arm around her shoulder and treaded on, as if protecting her from an invisible rain. She pushed him away a couple of steps down the road. Time turned around inside her veins. The trees on campus suddenly changed color. She looked at him again as if she did not know who this tall young man with black eyes and dark curls was. Why was he so close to her? It can't be, she said. Liliana couldn't have died like that. Liliana couldn't have died, she corrected herself. She immediately began roaming her own memory. Had there been some sign heralding the tragedy that she had missed? Liliana's tenderness burst out in front of her eyes, the many ways in which she was protective of her. From the day she gave her the Camus quote to the times she had made her laugh with silly jokes. People used to think that Liliana was tough because she was direct and, when the chips were down, she would not keep her thoughts to herself. But with her, with that girl from a religious background who once read *Reader's Digest Selections*, she had been sweet. Liliana was always tender with her, as if she had turned her into her own little sister. It can't be, Fernando. It just can't be. She began crying. She was like that for a little over an hour. Incredulous. Shaking.

Little by little, as she regained her composure, she remembered that, although Liliana never mentioned any violence or harassment directly, she did suggest that this guy existed, this guy from her past, someone she had a history with, a relationship: a guy so relentless and stubborn, always pressuring her to get back together with him. Had anyone been that obsessed with Lili? Someone who thought that if she wasn't his, she couldn't belong to anyone else? Was that it? So many trendy songs touched on the same subject, all those songs that Liliana adamantly hated. She recalled hearing Ana advise Liliana that she should leave Ángel. But, as much as she wanted to delve into those memories, what emerged from the fog were not revelations but images of Liliana by her side, talking, laughing, looking up at the trees, playing.

Her friend, her protector.

It was not long after that her friends from the university began to plan the journey to Toluca. They knew that the funeral and burial would take place there, in the highlands, and no one doubted that they would come. UAM authorized the use of an official school bus and a professor close to Liliana and her group of friends, architect Gabriel Jiménez, went along with them. The silence of funeral trips. Sometimes the windows turn into time tunnels. Norma brought her knees up against the seat in front of her and hugged herself under her jacket. On the other side of the glass Liliana stood with her little glasses, her hair down, her Puma tennis shoes. How is it that you and I, being so different, get along so well? Liliana had asked her the last time they had met on campus. Liliana was drinking a black coffee and, rather than sitting, she seemed to be sprawled on the cafeteria seat. I have to turn in a final paper, Norma told her hastily. I've got to go. But Liliana insisted that she stay. Let your friends turn it in for you, she said. You're not going to have more fun with them. And Norma stayed to smoke cigarettes and talk. Hey, after all this is done, we are going to do a master's degree, right? she said to Liliana, remembering what they had talked about in previous encounters. As soon as we graduate, we are off for England, Liliana answered, utterly convinced, raising her plastic cup. They were silent for a while. We're going to England to do a master's degree, she said again, smiling at her. And Norma, now on this uncomfortable bus seat that was taking them to the foot of a dead volcano, smiled in turn. How easily Liliana convinced her. What sort of magic spell did she hold over them, that made it so that Lili always got her way? The verdant summer road reminded her that Liliana had a proclivity for nature, the smell of the countryside. What are you going to do in England? she muttered. There's good corn, she had said jokingly. There's good corn in England, Norma. Don't you know?

[Wednesday, July 18, 1990, *La Prensa*]

STRONG LEADS IN SEACH FOR STUDENT'S KILLERS.

Liliana Rivera Garza was seen alive for the last time around 10:00 P.M. on Sunday; she was found dead by strangulation on Monday morning and, after preliminary investigations, the police indicate that there are strong leads that will allow them to catch the killers.

The young architecture student in the eighth semester was with some friends on Sunday and, in the evening, they left to let her rest.

In charge of the investigation, the deputy director of the Homicide Brigade of the Judiciary Police, Gonzalo Balderas, went to the scene of the crime, together with a dozen detectives, to inspect the room where the young woman was killed.

There are strong suspicions that an ex-boyfriend, deciding to eliminate her out of hatred, did the job on Sunday night. However, this hypothesis will have to be proven, police said.

Experts from the Federal District Attorney's Office will deliver an opinion this noon as to whether the unfortunate lady was the object of an assault or if she was strangled or suffocated.

It is extremely puzzling to detectives that the student's neighbors did not hear screams or other noises in the early morning hours.

Another detail that does not go unnoticed by the police is the broken glass in the door to the student's apartment.

[desperately looking for a corner]

People. There are so many people. The faces multiply incessantly. The drooping eyelids, the arms that are thrown into the air, the hands, trying to brush, touch, give solace. Is it possible to escape this siege? Is it possible to disappear all at once? Someone looks for a corner. Someone is desperately looking for a corner. A salient angle, the edge of all objects. If absolute lack of breath would be possible all of a sudden. Someone asks about documents, filing cabinets, family record systems. Someone requires signatures and places faded forms on small clipboards. Someone mentions the word money. Money is needed. Here is some money. How much money? Take this money. Someone wants to get a phone number, the name of an airline, the name of an international conference. Someone has to make calls. Calls have to be answered. Someone has to pay close attention to what happens in front of her eyes. Someone has to act as if she knows what is happening, where all this is happening, what is next. In the distance, on the other side of the windows, someone can glance at the sky, heavy with clouds.

Cirrocumulus. Cumulonimbus. And close by, the black hearse approaching, tiresome already, the slow rolling of old tires in a wandering line with no end in sight: cars, buses, taxicabs. Someone is looking for a corner. Someone desperately needs a corner.

They are young. They are appallingly young. They are so young that they continue to rejuvenate over the years. This is their virtue, and this is their tragedy. Sunspots, dry skin, chapped lips, which constitute signs of aging, emblems that say, I am alive, disappear under the onslaught of time running in the opposite direction. The future, which had already begun, begins again. Forward. Rewind. Forward. They still don't know what awaits them on the other side of the funeral, when the company and the incessant outpouring of stories and hugs come to an end. When the whispering stops. And the tears. What will happen to us when this circle of memory that we have woven in the corner of a room surrounded by windows falls to shreds? Someone sees them. What will happen when this extremely thin membrane, this mucus made of words and friction, melts in the open, under the indifferent light of the sun, in front of the vastness of the wind alone? Someone hears them. What will happen when you have to leave this capsule of mirrors and return to the other room in the center of which rests, solitary as an island, the coffin that contains her, the coffin that cuts her off from us? Someone smells them. The distance in which the action of the senses occurs, the distance that these senses inaugurate with their own doing is the only thing that fits in memory. The rest are scraps. Splinters. A piece of mouth. A hand. The stye on the tip of the hair. Acne marks. The wet back of the tongue. A cracked tooth. The eyelids, when closed. Someone says: she was loved. Someone says: the best architect in Mexico. Someone says: sometimes we chewed tiny flowers together.

Someone says: this is an injustice. Someone says: I will miss her. And many remain silent. Motionless. Wounded statues.

The rest, what is left as the wake dissolves and darkness envelops the earth, is this soulless space guarded by the peak of a dead volcano, five thousand meters high.

[manifesto]

AND WE DIDN'T WANT TO GO.

The gray coffin had been lowered, a noise announcing the bottom of the last repose of that grave.

In the midst of the silence, the stones screamed and mingled with the sobs of her friends who accompanied her to the last vestige of this life.

The sweat of the gravediggers dripped onto the casket lid. In their juggling, they arranged a gravestone and then another one and, as they hit each other, produced a stone timbre that stood out in that silence. Only those three men worked in haste, they were the only ones in a hurry, the only ones who wanted to finish their work.

A crowd of eyes that had seen her act, that had seen her love, surrounded that moat. Their eyes met, losing themselves later on the horizon. Others contemplated the darkness of the pit in that silence; others averted their eyes, unable to even look. Their pupils were drenched with the feeling of that loss.

A funeral prayer made the eyes of the audience overflow again. Those words acted like a whip that lacerated the hearts and made the tear ducts burst.

A few minutes had passed, but time was eternal. You could only perceive the sobs, sighs, and the whistle of the wind that came rushing down the volcano to say goodbye for the last time to this beautiful creature. We were spectators of silence.

Mother Earth, outraged to receive and house the mortal remains of that little girl, had been put back together. She had received her tribute and, with this, her History had been sealed.

The body of the earth had already hidden the last vestige of her traces. We were thus forever separated from her presence. Her spirit floated among us, comforting everyone present. She greeted us and smiled at us as usual, and we just couldn't believe it. Wouldn't admit it.

A tapestry made with colored flowers was placed on that piece of land, which signified the love that she gave us. Tormented too by sadness, they soon began to wilt. It was necessary to comfort them with improvised artificial rain produced by a water bottle to calm their anguish.

Immediately afterward, her friends talked to her, they held hands to form a circle of energy to remind her that she remained present, saying a prayer. The communication between everyone was real, the silence brought about by pain made a pathetic presence, and it was kept in each of the hearts pressed by a tachycardia that echoed in that luminous open sky.

AND WE DIDN'T WANT TO GO AWAY.

Apparently our farewell, as is traditional, had come to an end. It was like the blessing that marks the end of the ceremony, but.

But all the attendees stood firm, none wanted to step forward. Everything was quiet, there was no rush. A silent cry that marked the end.

AND WE DIDN'T WANT TO GO AWAY.

Cristina, her older sister, with a lump in her throat, articulated a thank-you to the company. We did not know what to do.

AND WE DIDN'T WANT TO GO AWAY.

The flowers were sobbing with sadness, but they were aware of their privilege: they would be her shelter. They would be with her always, always. They would accompany her to eternity in that piece of land.

One by one they said goodbye to Cristina. They did not know what to say. They babbled something in her ear and tried to comfort her with hugs. It was the only thing they could do.

Cristina was not left alone in that space. The sun, the wind, the flowers accompanied her at that moment, and the spirit of Liliana, with whom she talked, and with whom she made plans, as usual.

The indelible memory will remain latent in our hearts. A creature of the Lord was now gone, someone who gifted us with the opportunity to talk with an extraordinary being, someone exceptional who taught us so much, who awoke questions deep within us, and taught us to love our neighbors, thus illuminating our path in life.

Rest in peace. Meanwhile, we know your spirit will be present with us in the dynamism of a candle flame. Until we reach you.

I dedicate these lines to the parents of this most beautiful creature, who raised her with patience, love, and wisdom; to her siblings, to her loved ones, and to all of us, her friends, who have loved her so deeply.

IN MEMORIAM
GABRIEL JIMÉNEZ
July 18, 1990.
c.c.p. The rest of the world.

[Thursday, July 19, 1990, *La Prensa*]

A day after Liliana's funeral, Tomás Rojas Madrid, who had followed up on the case even when the story had moved to the inside pages of the newspaper, assured his readers that police had officially identified the murderer. While they had not yet disclosed his identity, the police were optimistic. They would soon find him.

KILLER OF STUDENT LILIANA RIVERA GARZA IDENTIFIED.

A group of heavily armed detectives is after the murderer of the student Liliana Rivera Garza; it is said that the murderer is hiding in a state near the capital of the country.

After the investigations of the agents from the Homicide Brigade of the District Judicial Police, the identity of the person responsible for the death of the young architecture student has been established.

The police have not wanted to reveal the identity of the murderer, for obvious reasons, so as not to give advantage to this individual, said one of the investigators.

As for Liliana Rivera Garza, it was reported yesterday that she did not live alone as the authority had initially announced, but that her parents are traveling in Europe and, so far, they have not arrived in this capital.

As the days pass, and after the investigations proceed, it has also been established that the murderer or murderers knew well the lay of the land when planning the murder of the young woman.

They knew the movements of the house well, and of Liliana's own neighbors, so they were able to catch her unawares on Sunday night.

If she did not cry out for help, it was probably because she was threatened with a weapon or she was familiar with the murderers, the police said.

In the corridors of the Judicial Police headquarters yesterday, the word was that the person or persons responsible for the crime would be arrested in a matter of hours.

[the ax; the knees]

The cruelty of children is legendary. When the parents' car slowly approaches the house, the neighborhood children come out to greet them. This is not in the script. This is not part of the plan carefully hatched by the family members who still take care of the housework and administrative affairs while waiting. Everything is ready. Everything is prepared so as to prevent a heart attack, a nervous breakdown, a stroke. When someone announces that they are already close, that the car has finally turned the last corner, the aunts and cousins and neighbors abandon their chores and leave the house slowly, very quietly. They cross the street, open the door of the neighboring house and, little by little, they begin to occupy all the available places in the room: the chairs, the armchairs, the benches, the arms of the sofa. The parents are returning from a long journey: from the North Sea to Mexico City. The Atlantic Ocean. The Sierra Madre Oriental. It was the journey to crown a lifetime of effort, a lifetime of sacrifice. They must be tired, but elated. They must be exhausted. But proud. Soon, that life of effort and sacrifice will be shattered forever. In a matter of seconds, they will cross a threshold that will deposit them in an unknown region. Everything will hurt. The voice. The memory. The circulation of the blood. The fingernails. The liver. The neck. They won't be able to do anything without hurting themselves. Teeth. The pharynx. The meninges. Soon they will join us in this other world of quicksand in which we have already placed our feet, sinking little by little.

Someone spies their arrival through the window. Someone can do nothing when the children on the block go ahead, throwing themselves against the vehicle that is still moving to scream at the top of their lungs, with a horrid uproar, she is dead, Liliana is dead, when they open the car doors. Their faces, incredulous first, then annoyed. Where did so many children come from? What are they all doing around the car, perching on the doors like little flies? But when the door of the house opens very slowly, and they see me, and I see them seeing me, I know that everything is impossible. I have to tell them what can't be said. I have to enunciate the words. Tell me it's not true, say her eyes, aware of the tragedy even before I open my mouth. But what the mother is able to utter is: What are you doing here? Shouldn't you be in Houston? Someone says: Liliana. And then stops, sobbing. Someone says Liliana is no longer with us. The ax; the knees. The gravity. The weight of the body.

A yowl pulls out of her stomach, and her larynx, and her palate. A yowl descends over the bookcases and the dining table and the stove. A yowl opens the doors, and hisses through the street and soon attracts the presence of sisters and uncles and cousins and neighbors. The yowling gathers us together. We are together still within that yowl.

[Saturday, July 21, 1990, *La Prensa*]

THE KILLER OF THE ARCHITECTURE STUDENT SURROUNDED.

Agents of the Federal District Judicial Police have laid a siege around the murderer of the young architecture student. The criminal has been identified and will be arrested momentarily, it was said yesterday.

Not only are members of the regional delegation investigating the facts, but detectives from the Azcapotzalco brigade, who have complained of too much work, are contributing to the investigation as well. The detectives of the precinct and the Special Homicide Prosecutor's Office have tried at all costs to evade questions from the media in the case.

Liliana Rivera, 20, was found dead inside her home in the north of this capital on Monday morning.

The young woman was strangled, and the crime holds many shadowy details so far, which the police authorities in charge of the investigation have not clarified.

THERE IS A WITNESS.

It has been established that there is a witness who can pave the way for the arrest of the murderer, but the police have remained tight-lipped in this regard.

One of the friends of the deceased girl has told the police that he left her in the apartment on Sunday night, at around 10:00 P.M.

The next morning, Liliana was found dead by neighbors who, surprised when she did not come out at the usual time, called the police who entered the apartment just to find out that she had died.

The event has created a commotion among the neighbors, for the street they live on has been somewhat quiet, although that does not stop bums and druggies from hanging out there, but they don't mess with anyone, they said.

The police opened up that line of investigation, but none of the junkies turned out to be the murderer.

[shapelessness]

This is the inaugural time. This is where the yowl first comes from. Someone conjectures as she opens the door to a room and, motionless, with her hand still around the knob, observes everything with meticulous attention: who am I now? The answer, if it exists at all, is slow to come. The answer does not exist. You have to approach the bed and sit there, bracing yourself, for a long time. You have to place your hands, however listless, on the bedspread, the pillow, the ragged dolls. You have to get up and stroke the clothes, books, notebooks. You have to feel the posters that line the wall: Marilyn Monroe, Che Guevara, the Golden Gate Bridge. And you have to stop in your tracks, at the very center of the room, to let the buzz of the stealthy walls enter your ears just to come out of them again. The minimal connection between all things in the world: longitudinal and transverse waves of sound, electromagnetic waves that challenge the vacuum, beta waves, alpha waves, theta waves. *To the ivory statues / one, two, and three like that / the one who moves dances the twist.* You have to absent yourself from yourself.

And when the ax comes—resolute, glowing, dexterous—to break your knees, to break the frozen sea that, suddenly, is the only thing left inside, you have to fall. You have to learn to fall. The full weight of the body. The solidity of the floor.

Everything is true. Everything is real.

Crying is a civilized act. But what happens there, in that room, is quite beyond the here and now of civilization. A scream is a high-pitched shrill sound that is emitted in a loud or violent manner. A scream usually expresses pain or fear. But this sound that roams the room alone, heard by no one, ripping its way through the stale air of static time, is something that comes from an unknown world and communicates in turn with worlds yet to be born. Whatever it is, it does not conform to a name. Names are rendered useless in its wake. A haunting shapelessness trailing behind you, breathing down your neck. You have to hold your abdomen and curl up in a fetal position on the floor. You have to hide your face. You have to beg.

Above all, yes, you have to beg.

[Tuesday, July 24, 1990, *La Prensa*]

The story made it back to the front page just a week after its first appearance.

This time the teaser announcing the content of the inner pages was inside a yellow box with black stitching, next to actress Irma Serrano's fierce face. Her red lips, her light eyes, and that circular black mole between eyebrow and eyebrow. After refusing to provide information on the murderer, the police had decided to offer not only his name to the media, but also his photograph. The optimism with which they had assured the public days before that his capture was imminent had already disappeared.

STRANGLER IDENTIFIED

Ángel González Ramos was identified as the person allegedly responsible for murdering the young student Liliana Rivera Garza. According to police, the student was killed by her ex-boyfriend, and he is eagerly sought throughout the country.

Conclusively, the police revealed yesterday that the student Liliana Rivera was killed by her ex-boyfriend, who immediately fled.

The murderer was identified as Ángel González Ramos, a suspect who is now on the most-wanted list of all the police corporations in this country.

The Chief of the A. Homicide Brigade of the Judicial Police, Gonzalo Balderas, said that there is overwhelming evidence pointing to Ángel as the person responsible for the crime.

As if to corroborate this hypothesis, Ángel González Ramos has been missing from his home since Monday the sixteenth of the present month, the day on which the crime took place.

"He does not have a very good record," said the police, in whose version of events Ángel entered the home of the young student, chatted with her, and killed her without warning.

That Monday, Liliana Rivera Garza, 20 years old, was found dead inside her home located at Calle Mimosas 658, in the Pasteros neighborhood.

Detectives, a forensic doctor, and the agent of the public prosecutor's office concluded that there was a possibility that she had been assaulted.

There were no signs of a struggle inside the room, so assault was ruled out from the start.

From outside the house, dozens of people watched the movements of uniformed police officers, personnel from the public prosecutor's office and the forensic service, and Chief Gonzalo Balderas and his detectives as they scrutinized the crime scene inch by inch.

A window was broken but it is not thought to have been the work of the criminal, because no one heard the sound of breaking glass.

Upon certifying the scene of the events, the agent of the public prosecutor's office drew up the act 40/913 / 990-07 against whoever was responsible and to the detriment of the student Liliana Rivera Garza.

Ignacio Perales, one of the commanders in charge of the criminal investigation, asked his team to go to the home of the ex-boyfriend, known as Ángel González, but he was no longer there.

Strangely, Ángel González has not been to his house since that day, and detectives point to him as the author of the brutal crime.

Such an assertion is not based on a simple hypothesis, said Gonzalo Balderas. There is a witness who saw Ángel, one of the most wanted alleged murderers in the country, entering Liliana's apartment that night.

[if you break, break going out not in]

What exactly happened that dawn at Mimosas 658 after Ángel forced his way into Liliana's personal space, surreptitiously and uninvited, after paying three thousand pesos to a street junkie? No one can say for sure. It's all guesswork at this point. Only the murderer knows, and he has decided to keep this information to himself since the summer of 1990, when he went on the run. Only the full compliance of justice, whose system issued an arrest warrant against Ángel González Ramos on November 29, 1990, "for the crime of homicide, provided for in article 302 and punishable by imprisonment in article 307 of the Criminal Code," will be able to lift the veil of this "obscure crime."

The questions that journalist Tomás Rojas Madrid posed again and again in his articles for *La Prensa* are as valid now as then: given the brutality of the crime, how is it possible that no one living close by, living on the second floor of the same building, heard anything? There was the clatter caused by a broomstick that, late at night in a dim light, tried to reach the latch of a metal door. And the smack of the feet landing on the concrete after jumping over the gate. Why didn't José Manuel Álvarez, the landlord, react when he saw Ángel González Ramos arrive at his private property at about 2:30 in the morning, leaving in a hurry around 5:00? If witness testimonies are to be trusted, both Manolo Casillas and Gerardo Navarro overheard that Basilia, the domestic worker, confirmed she had heard some sobs, a low cry, without establishing a precise time of the event. Who cried and why? Perhaps they were low and brief sounds, but wouldn't the silence of dawn have amplified them?

In a twist, the newspaper article from Wednesday, July 18, the day Liliana was buried, described the killer's actions as driven by hatred. Was Ángel looking for Liliana that summer night with a concrete plan to kill her, to end her life forever and thus fulfill the mandate of toxic masculinity? Or did Ángel act according to the fierce but still ambiguous idea of teaching her a lesson, imposing the pedagogy of cruelty on her and her body, providing her with an exemplary punishment that would leave her alive, but forever marked with the imprint of his possession? The silence that did not awaken the neighbors would support the first theory, the fact that he paid for the junkies' help, revealing his identity, would support the second. The result, either way, is the same. Ángel exerted horrifying lethal violence on my sister's body guided, as the journalist Rojas noted, by hatred. Gender hatred. The hatred against the independence and freedom of women. Hatred against Liliana, the girl who always sided with love.

Answers are few and the facts remain incontrovertible. For some thirty years, I have missed Liliana every day and, within every day, every hour of every day. And within every hour, every minute. Every second. Grief is a double-edged sword for those who have lost loved ones, loved women, due to acts of intimate partner terrorism. As Snyder has analyzed in *No Visible Bruises,* survivors often blame themselves, their negligence, or their blindness with unprecedented harshness. They did not protect what they most loved; they did not notice what should have been blatant before their eyes; they didn't stop the predator. The pain that is not detached, not even a millimeter, from guilt and shame gets stuck before mourning can begin, staying in a formless limbo where words lose meaning and the connection with others and with the world fades slowly. Families flee inward, hiding even from themselves. What right do they have to demand justice when they themselves were not able to protect their very own from danger?

The system in charge of blaming the victim, moreover, starts working when things are still fresh and it does not stop over the years. It is a methodical and crushing machine, whose blades mince any interpretation that veers from its verdict. It is there, working perfectly, among those who whisper: if only they hadn't let her go to Mexico City; if she hadn't started dating at such a young age; if she had been more judicious; if she had waited for marriage to have sex; if she had not had an abortion; if she had not been on the wrong path. If she had not been free. And the well-greased machine continues to work, no matter how many years have passed, among those who point out that the parents spent a lot of time outside the house, the mother had a job, the father did not give her enough money, the boyfriends besieged her, even women wanted her. And why did they take so much time to re-open the case? The machine operates silently but effectively in the murky looks and the feigned smiles, in the rehearsed choreography of commiseration with its limp protocols and saccharine ceremonies. The careful pat on the back, the embrace that lasts a bit too long, the handwritten note that gets lost in the mail. Above all, the unyielding machine is at play among those who feel safe and, sighing with relief, erect a moral line that swiftly divides us from you. It is in the imperative, inescapable, overwhelming demand that the victim be blamed and that you blame yourself with her. It is in the imperative, inescapable, overwhelming demand to exonerate the murderer at all costs.

One does not learn to be silent; one is forced to shut up.

One is forcibly silenced.

How many siblings do you have? I never knew how to answer this seemingly innocent question. The mere possibility of hearing the question shook me to the core. And the answer, when I decided to provide one, was nothing more than gibberish in crescendo: I once had a sister, but I no longer had one; I no longer had a sister, but I would have a sister forever; I have a sister; I would have a sister only if. After the first awkward moment, if the questioner lacked manners or empathy or a basic understanding of human relationships, the questions followed: was she older or younger? Fearing that, later, the inquiry about how, when, why would begin, I usually chose to hide my eyes and walk away. Eventually, I gave up. I said that I had no siblings so as not to cry, so as not to give explanations, so as not to give a false sense of mutual trust, so as not to create a situation in which I had to defend myself and, above all, defend her. Or I didn't answer at all, feigning sudden deafness. Changing the subject is a skill that is learned over time.

It's been like this for many years.

In his poem "To a Sad Daughter," Michael Ondaatje talks tenderly to his sixteen-year-old daughter. Bittersweet and nostalgic, the poem covers the typical tropes of the relationship between parents and children when adolescence arrives: the parting of paths, the search for their own identities that separate teenagers from home, their justified rebellions or futile resistance. Liliana would have found it corny, I'm afraid; but perhaps she would have given in a little to the unquestionable affection that shrouds the lyrical voice. Although the father refuses to give advice, he has to accept, one might say grudgingly, that the poem is, in its own way, a first lesson. A guardian's advice. *Want everything,* he tells his daughter. *If you break / break going out not in.* I still have the impression that that summer of 1990 Liliana was trying to get out. After so many years of gaslighting, after the years in which Liliana learned to tame the furious bear by acquiescing to his demands, after years of resisting, struggling, scuffling, negotiating, Liliana was most definitely on her way out.

She wanted everything and she loved everything. Demanding the impossible was her calling. And this lesson, which we learned at home, which our parents taught both of us, was later reinforced in books and poems, plans and buildings, songs, complicated clouds, university campuses, trips, infinite gatherings, close friends. When we broke down, when the patriarchal machinery crushed our bodies and hearts, laying siege to the past and the future, Liliana was, indeed, trying to get out. I have no doubt about it. Liliana was already out, believing deeply, honestly, provocatively, that a radically different life was possible.

Another kind of love.

In a narrow and tricolor paper bag that once contained a Christmas present, Liliana kept the letter that she never sent Ana, a couple of notes torn from notebooks, and the letters that I wrote her from the United States. In my last letter, dated March 9, 1990, I described my new life in great detail, disclosing my utter surprise and dislike for a university system committed to quantitative production and eschewing social responsibility. Toward the middle of the long letter, I told her that I had gone to the movies to see *Camille Claudel,* with the beautiful Isabelle Adjani as protagonist, about: "a brilliant sculptor who Rodin fed on for years and who was eventually confined to a mental health facility for a long time, about 30 years. No one acknowledged her work while she was alive; in fact it did not start to gain recognition until the 1980s. The film impressed me in so many ways: the depiction of Camille's feverish vocation being the top one. But I did pay attention to the caring attention of her father, his trust in what he called Camille's talents and, naturally, I could not avert my eyes from her destruction. I am convinced many women have believed and still believe that our goal as artists, as creators of all sorts, is self-destruction—that romantic bomb. I was filled with rage at that crime, and at so many others that we cannot discern in our midst, and immediately realized that, when I left Mexico, I was escaping from those voices that encourage you: this is an abyss, don't you see it? Dive in. Throw yourself into the emptiness. I do not want an ending like that for me or for you, or for anyone else for that matter. Self-destruction and disenchantment do not constitute an example of a true and fiery romanticism but of a romanticism that is murderous. Because we are here, indeed, full of talents, not to feed the vampiric mastery of others, nor to fall blind into the abyss of madness, nor to carry a stone like Saint Jerome. We are here with the enchanted weight of existence, and its lightness, the placid lightness of dreaming for we have yet so many things to say, do, think, rethink, re-create. Our point of view is new for a history that has denied us, erased us, usurped us, hundreds of millions of times. We have to stay; we are here to stay: Enough is enough! Neither the dogma of love, nor that of fame or of money will be able to destroy something much firmer and more innocent at the same time within us: the foolish, timid, unleashed desire to live fully. If we do so, if we live fully, we'll be creating another life, something more beautiful, something more just. That's what our voices and our hands are for."

Raúl Espino Madrigal recalled that, once, while frolicking on the grass in the lush gardens at UAM Azcapotzalco, Liliana lent him a book. A postcard sprouted out of its pages, unexpectedly. It was yours, he told me. You had sent it to her. A black-and-white photo with some naked hippies on a tram. On the back, you wrote: "One day you will come here and we will have the time of our lives together."

The actor River Phoenix died in 1993 and Selena, the famous Mexican American singer, was killed in 1995. When I found out about their deaths, I immediately imagined them together. Liliana, River, and Selena, and the naked hippies, on the slopes of a gentle hill, barely touched by a subdued green, from which it is still possible to glimpse the lapping waves of the Pacific Ocean. There are empty plates, huddled, smeared by chocolate frosting, on outdoor picnic tables. Half-empty glasses of red wine. Some nibbled apples. Cats and dogs prowl in their midst: Fausto is there, as neurotic as ever, chasing a lizard. La Kinski sneaks into the frame every now and then, shy and cautious, as someone who has known rejection before experiencing love. Muffled voices float, indistinctly, in between the warm gusts of wind. The distant echo of shared laughter. It is the early evening of a summer day shrouded by a fine golden light that, little by little, gives way to darkness. I can still hear their whispers from afar.

And they are still alive.

X

OUR DAUGHTER

[Ilda Garza Bermea]

Liliana lay crosswise in my uterus. Instead of settling head-down, already preparing for labor, she chose the transverse lie. We lived in Monterrey at the time, solely off the scholarship that the Tec de Monterrey had awarded your father. We struggled to make ends meet, barely having enough money to pay the rent, so the very idea that the childbirth might require special care worried us. A very kind doctor, aware of our hardships as newcomers to the city, opted for a more natural method: he settled Lili upside down inside my belly with his own hands and, when he finally succeeded, he placed two rolled towels alongside my abdomen. And then the good doctor bandaged me, trying to prevent our second daughter from taking the transverse position once again. This is how I spent the last months of my pregnancy, with a towel on each side of my stomach and completely bandaged, from the torso down to my hips, during the suffocating, terribly humid summer of Monterrey. Imagine that.

[Antonio Rivera Peña]

I missed your birth because I was in high school classes in Matamoros, but I was right on time to be there for Lili's birth in Monterrey. They wouldn't let me go into the delivery room, but I was the first to see that both your mother and your sister were fine after all the effort. We could have named her after one of your grandmothers, but neither your mother nor I suggested the name

Emilia or Petra for our second daughter. Liliana was unique from the start, she carried a name that no one had used in the family. A radically new experience.

Your mother says that she chose Liliana's name because, in those days, Carlos Lico—a popular singer back then—sang a lovely if sentimental song that he dedicated to his third or fourth daughter, whose name was Liliana, the title of the song. I believe I was the one who chose the name, but I couldn't say why I liked it so much. Maybe we both reacted to the filial feeling of the song lyrics: *Your little lovely face bears the sweetness of the angels of heaven when you sleep. Liliana, my love.* And I still know the entire song by heart. Lili was very attached to your mother from the start. Unlike you, who were always skinny, Liliana soon became a plump and rosy baby. But that did not weigh on Ilda, who carried her everywhere she went. Liliana, who used to suck the thumb of her left hand, would settle into your mother's arms and pull one of her earrings with her right hand. She did it so consistently and for so long that it ended up ripping Ilda's earlobe in two.

[Ilda Garza Bermea]

I shouldn't have spied on her, much less driven around the patio of the kindergarten where we had enrolled her. But I went and drove the car around the little school, going very slowly around the back patio, where I assumed she would be. Lili saw me and started crying. I couldn't stand it and went in for her to take her back home, hence abruptly ending her career as a kindergarten student in Delicias, Chihuahua.

[Antonio Rivera Peña]

Who ate a whole watermelon in one big gulp? I asked her while stroking her belly when she was a toddler. It was a code, the sign that unleashed our laughter together. A game between the two of us. I used to call her my chubby one. Or roly-poly. And this amused her for a while, but as the years went by, Lili begged me not to call her that anymore. She blushed, totally mortified. That slender, tall teenager, who was already starting to swim on a local team, didn't like to remember that she had once been a plump little girl.

[Ilda Garza Bermea]

She was always so good, so noble, so empathetic, I am not exaggerating. And she was like that from childhood. She was born that way. She'd take a bite out of her mouth in a snap to give it to whoever needed it. She could never bear to see the pain of others without trying to remedy it herself. I don't want you to feel bad, but you were never that way. Remember her notebooks, all so neat. Her impeccable room. The way she took care of her clothes, her dolls, herself. She thrived on company, closeness, conversation. I am so glad I had time back then to heat up your socks every morning before both of you woke up, tugging them over your heels when you were barely responsive. I always felt very responsible, accomplished even, when I took both of you to swimming lessons, often staying there, looking over you, admiring you both in fact, as you trained. Remember how happy we were when I applied mayo or olive oil to your hair during the weekends, the little bathroom turned into a luxurious spa all of a sudden? Unlike you, Lili was always very punctual. How she suffered when we took both of you to school at the same time when we lived in Toluca. And to top it all, taking you to high school first, before dropping her off at elementary school. Terrible idea. What an injustice. I still believe that she was so stressed every morning that she ended up developing stomach cramps. A case of infantile colitis.

[Antonio Rivera Peña]

When she grew up and was able to move around in the kitchen, she had no qualms about making me coffee. Especially for my dad, she would say to me, carefully placing the steaming cup on the table. No other daughter had done that for me before. None did it afterward.

[Ilda Garza Bermea]

Little by little I realized that they were becoming sweethearts. Liliana did not openly say it to me, but rather we began noticing that he came looking for her very frequently. He rode his racing bike sometimes; and, others, he drove an old car. He did not mind taking Lili around on her errands. He took her wherever she had to go, and dropped her off afterward. It made me feel safe. It was a sign that he cared about her, that he was aware of her needs, and was willing to make himself useful. Still, he never set foot in our house. He was never her formal boyfriend. To us, he was nothing more than a smitten suitor.

[Antonio Rivera Peña]

When I left for Sweden to complete my PhD—and if there is something I regret in my life it is this trip, what was I thinking? What was all that for after all?—her letters kept me alive. Unlike you, who only sent me a letter from time to time, Lili never stopped writing. It didn't matter if she had exams or was on holiday, if she was participating in a swimming tournament or the weather was foul. She wrote about everything with great ease on those pages. Her wanderings. Her doubts. Sometimes she even complained about her mother or a friend, or about you. But they were happy letters, very intimate letters, letters that meant we were close. When I absented myself from home to finish that degree that I pursued out of time or at the wrong time, and that now, all these years later, seems so unimportant, her letters became my life clock, a way of measuring flesh time.

[Ilda Garza Bermea]

But how he made her suffer in high school! I don't quite remember when they broke up for the first time, or if it was in fact the first time, but Lili shed so many tears for him. I once ran into her in the park behind the house. I was getting some exercise when I saw her from afar, approaching with her long strides down the street. She looked extremely upset, distraught even. She did not face forward, but downward, looking into the asphalt, crying. She couldn't stop crying. I instinctively went to her and hugged her tightly. Crying isn't the word I'm looking for: whimpering maybe. Her sobs didn't even let her utter a word, and this broke my heart. I started to cry with her. She couldn't understand why things had to be this way. She asked for my advice and I, thinking it was one of those girlish romances that she'd forget soon, told her not to obsess over it. It was not the end of the world. A new love would arrive sometime soon, perhaps even her true love.

[Antonio Rivera Peña]

I can't regret that trip enough, having left for all those months.

[Ilda Garza Bermea]

A sister of mine came to visit us while your dad was in Sweden. I needed to take her to the airport in Mexico City and, since I didn't drive in the city, Liliana asked Ángel to drive us there as a personal favor. He was very solicitous, very correct, and said that he'd gladly do it. That was the first time he entered the house and he looked a bit put off, a bit intimidated. As we did not think highly of him, Liliana was suddenly happy because she felt we could no longer look down on him. Maybe that's why, when your dad wasn't here and Lili asked my permission to go with him to the movies or to go for a ride on his bike, I let her go. Later on, when I realized that he drove to Mexico City to pick her up on campus and bring her home, I was thankful. We had always had a healthy respect for Mexico City, such a sprawling metropolis with an iffy reputation. The city was very imposing and Lili so young, so trusting. I felt reassured knowing that she was not taking the bus.

[Antonio Rivera Peña]

I confronted Ángel several times for several reasons. But once, I almost came to blows with him over his appearance. He was so scruffy when he came to see her, showing her, and us, no respect at all. Sweaty. Disheveled. Liliana was already in college and, for us, it was a true luxury to have her back at home, if only for the weekends. Your mom always bought flowers and cooked something special for her. Seeing Lili, even for a few hours, made us happy. We were always in a good mood around her. He crossed a line that day. I couldn't take it anymore, and I couldn't help it either. I saw him through the window: he was on the sidewalk, beside the lawn, in his cycling shorts, a dirty T-shirt, all shabby. I rushed out immediately. This is no way to visit a girlfriend, I said. I told him that, when I was young, I would put on my best clothes to go see Ilda. A clean shirt. Shiny shoes. Combed hair. I also told him that if he wanted to come by our house and visit Liliana, he had to show more respect for her and for us. Instead of apologizing, he was furious. I was already yelling at him and, as I am short-tempered too, got ready to throw the first blow. Liliana came swiftly between the two of us, trying to calm us down. Please, Dad, she said. Ángel, please. I went back into the house swearing, truly angry, rather sulky, and Lili came after me. She said that she would talk to him. This won't happen again, I promise, she said. Everything is under control, she added. She was clearly mortified but, at the same time, seemed so serious and stern in her resolve. Then, after a short pause, she said: Please, respect my life too. I am an adult now, I know how to handle things. Trust me. I looked at her, so brave and grown up. Her gentle eyes. She deserved a better boyfriend—I was sure of that, but in my eyes no one, no man would have been good enough for her. I love you, she said at the end. I really love you. I heard her, but later I realized I really didn't pay attention to what she was actually telling me. It took me a while to understand that she was threatened. It finally dawned on me that Liliana must have been under duress all those years. I am sure Ángel not only threatened to hurt himself but to hurt us, her family, as well. I am convinced that's what happened. I gave Liliana, and you, a lot of freedom. I have always believed in freedom because only in freedom can we know what we are made of. Freedom is not the problem. Men are the problem—violent, arrogant, murderous men.

[Ilda Garza Bermea]

Mom, where is Dad? she would often ask me as soon as she got home. Is Dad OK? She'd search for him around the house and, if she couldn't find him, she looked worried. Your dad is fine, Lili, don't worry, I'd say. He is fetching some sweet bread for the merienda. Or he stayed a little longer at the lab today. Or he will be here at any minute.

She would only relax when she saw him walk through the door.

[Antonio Rivera Peña]

No, I can't tell you how I felt. I can't even tell myself. Do not ask me that.

[Ilda Garza Bermea]

One day, desperate because we had no news from the police, I asked Doña Benita, the woman who helped me clean our home, to go to that family's house. We heard the murderer had fled, but I had my suspicions. I was convinced then, as I am now, that his family was protecting him. We hatched a plan. Doña Benita would knock on their door and introduce herself as a migrant worker down on her luck. I have a sick child who needs urgent care, she would say. Please, give me a job, even just for today. I can wash clothes or do the dishes. I can clean your bathrooms. I am good at ironing. The ploy was outlandish, it's true, but it ended up working. She spent a whole morning in that house, ironing and keeping an eye out for him. You should have seen it, Doña Ilda, she said once she made it back home. It's a madhouse over there, she said, exhausted. People come and go as they please, yelling at each other, calling each other names. I couldn't even keep a count of how many of them were there. Young people and old people. Some young men, some women. And they do know how to shout! They curse at each other all the time. You son of a bitch. You jerk.

Dumb-ass. Motherfucker. But that young man that you pointed out to me, I did not see him there.

[Ilda Garza Bermea]

We did all we could. One day, we received a tip that a girl who had been Ángel's girlfriend in Toluca might have known his whereabouts. We didn't need to think twice. You came with me, remember? We drove together to the UAEM campus where Ángel had been admitted as a communications student one year earlier, and together we faced her. I don't remember her name, but her face endures in my memory: a pretty, slender girl, long wavy hair, eyes full of fear. You know where he is, I yelled at her, demanding an answer. You know where this coward has gone, I insisted. Were we next to a classroom, all eyes on us as I yelled? Perhaps. Please, tell us where he's hiding, I implored before giving up. It is the heart of a mother begging.

[Antonio Rivera Peña]

Don't ask me, please. I cannot repeat them. The words that the police agents used to describe our daughter's life, our daughter's body, dirty her. I won't repeat them.

XI

CHLORINE

They, like us, are alive in hydrogen, in oxygen;
in carbon, in phosphrous, and iron;
in sodium and chlorine.

—CHRISTINA SHARPE, *In the Wake*

I started swimming again when, after living in Mexico for five years, I returned to San Diego in the summer of 2008. The last time I had trained in a pool was about twenty-six years earlier, just before entering college. More due to lack of sports facilities than by choice, swimming and pools disappeared from my life as books, political discussions, field practices, and activism rushed in. When I joined the YMCA in San Diego I planned on using the cardio equipment, maybe some weights, but mostly I was interested in the sauna. I didn't notice the pool until later. And when I did, it took me even longer to get all the gear—the swimsuit, the goggles, the swimming cap. When I finally got into the water for the first time I only swam two hundred meters, but I came out exhausted. The water felt strange: hard, compact, as if I were swimming uphill. I went back to floor exercises. Sometimes, if I had time, I would run a little on the track. But from then on, I avoided the pool.

In the fall of 2012, I spent half of my sabbatical year at the University of Poitiers. I decided to take my son with me on a trip that began in France and ended with the spring semester in Oaxaca. We stayed in a university apartment that was quite far from the office assigned to me in the Latin American literature studies building. Instead of going to my office every day, I spent my mornings at home, writing. My host at the university, Cecile Quintana, called me on the phone one afternoon in late September. She was worried because she had not seen me in a while and suggested that we meet at the pool where she swam. Do you like swimming?

She picked me up at the apartment and, after providing me with an old bathing suit, and buying the goggles and cap at a nearby machine, we went to the changing rooms and the showers before going through a narrow passage where different-colored towels hung on stylish hooks. There were plenty of swimmers at that hour. A team of beginners trained at the narrow end of the pool while another team, consisting of more seasoned swimmers, did the same along the right side of the pool. Logic told me that they must continually collide with each other, but the reality was that they swam in such a way that the training continued without any interruption. Visitors were allowed to use a couple of lanes on the left side of the pool. How many laps do you swim usually? Cecile asked me. I haven't swum in centuries, I said. I swim about forty laps every time I come, she said casually. Don't worry, I'll wait for you in the stands if I get out before you do, I said, chuckling.

If I had swum alone, as I had done in San Diego, I would surely have given up almost immediately. Soon, I was out of breath and, instead of gliding through the water in rhythmic strokes, my body twitched underwater, producing a series of clumsy, lackluster movements. I even gulped down some water and, at that point, I thought I'd drown. If I hadn't been next to Cecile's lane, keeping an eye on her elegant swimming style as she passed by my side over and over again, in complete control of herself, I would have jumped out of the water right away. I barely swam three hundred meters that evening, but once under the shower, as I closed my eyes and rinsed my hair, that distance felt like a real feat. I was drained and strangely exuberant. Delirious even. An unprecedented joy ran through the muscles of my body. When Cecile suggested that I buy tickets to come swim with her every week during the fall, I decided I would. That night, when I got home, I had to ask Matías to help me pull my shirt over my head because I couldn't lift my arms. We made fun of my age and my being so out of shape as I twisted my body to make his task easier.

As I had promised Cecile, I swam on a regular basis from then on, sometimes once and sometimes three times a week. She would pick me up, we would talk on the way, and then we would dive into the pool to swim in those crazy lanes where no one, miraculously, crashed into anyone. My physical condition improved rapidly and, little by little, as I paid close attention to my stroke and kick, I realized that swimming was something I knew quite well. I remembered how proud I had been of my style: my arms flying, my neck swinging from left to right, my breathing patterns, rhythmic and even.

It must have been in November, or at any rate when the weather outside had reached freezing temperatures and the warm water in the pool gave off a spectral mist in the last hours of evening, that I came out of the water so suddenly, impelled by a nameless force. I was going to go to the locker room, but I couldn't make it. Instead, I sat on the wooden bleachers, cap and goggles in hand. I remained there, very still, frightened, water dripping everywhere. Almost out of breath. I watched the swimmers come and go and, without a warning, I burst into tears. I didn't make a sound and the tears were easily mistaken for water, but I still covered my mouth with my right hand.

Her name crossed my lips without giving me time to think about it. I said: Liliana. And then I heard it. I was paralyzed. The smell of chlorine, which flooded the place, entered my nostrils fully and filled me inside. This is something I always did with you, I said. And I heard what I said. Disoriented, not knowing what to do, I dove into the water again instead of going to the locker room. I touched the bottom with my feet and, pushing them against the floor, I propelled myself hard toward the surface. Liliana, I said as I came up. Liliana Rivera Garza. And I repeated her name under the water, filling my mouth with chlorine water, while trying to touch the floor of the pool again.

I have said on numerous occasions that one swims to be alone. But that's only half true. Sometimes it is necessary to go alone, to swim by oneself, next to no one, in order to join a communion in the water. In geology, residence time is a concept used to measure the duration or persistence of a substance or a portion of material or a body in a specific location, such as the ocean, earth, or atmosphere. It could be water in a pool. Sodium, for example, has a residence time of 260 million years. Liliana will reside here, with me, as long as I plunge into the water, when I stroke and kick, and breathing becomes fleshed memory.

I managed to swim twenty laps in a row in the pool in Poitiers that autumn. Afterward, I didn't miss a single opportunity to swim. I swam every day we spent in Oaxaca, walking for half an hour to reach a small local resort whose main attraction was a twenty-five-meter pool. The water came from up the mountain spring and was unbearably cold. Still, I managed to swim forty laps a day there. I swam in the university pool when I got back to San Diego. And I swam in each and every one of the pools that were close to the places where I was invited to give talks or writing workshops. Is there a pool near the hotel or the auditorium? I asked first, even before I inquired about the honorarium.

Sometime before she became an architecture student, on one of those afternoons when boredom and laziness got the best of her, Liliana complained about how the chlorine in the pool dried out her skin. She did not say, although it was also true, that all those years of training, at least three hours a day in the water, had damaged our hair, giving it a rough texture and that suspicious yellow luster. Nor did she mention the smell of our bodies. It was so obvious, so persistent, that over time it became our natural perfume. We smelled of chlorine back then; chlorine was the smell of our being. That's what our childhood still smells like now. Chlorine is the sign we remain together.

She has persisted in carbon and phosphorus, in sodium, and in chlorine.

I remember her powerful kick. The way the bathing suit revealed her girlish belly before she turned into a lanky teenager. The marks left under her eyes by the tight goggles. The way we ran, ghost look-alikes at night, when the pool began to give off its warm steam. The rubber flip-flops. Speedo. Arena. Nike. The screams that came out of our mouths when we placed ourselves under the violent jet of the cold showers once we were done bathing. Her flip turn: heading into the wall, somersaulting and pushing off again. The time she got a glimpse of my pubic hair and asked me: am I going to have that soon too? The way she arched her back to slide just inches under the water. How she held her breath. The wrinkled tips of all her fingers. The way we compared our swimming times after a competition. The noise of the whistle. The first time I saw her learning to breathe out under water. Laughter, above all. I remember laughter. The glimmering reflections of the sunlight on the surface of the water we shared.

Swimming was what we did together. We dashed into the world each on our own, but we came back to the pool to be sisters. This rectangle of water was the space of our most intimate sisterhood.

It still is.

I injured my right shoulder almost a year and half ago, and I had to suspend my visits to the swimming pool. The rotator cuff. A bad tendonitis. Instead of swimming, I started writing this book. If the wound heals, I will swim once more.

I want to meet her again in the water. I want to swim, as I always did, in my sister's company.

ACKNOWLEDGMENTS

My sister built a meticulous archive of herself during her time on earth. This book is based on notebooks, letters, notes, newspaper clips, photographs, blueprints, address books, and calendars found among her possessions, which remained untouched for almost thirty years. The documents, which revealed the past as an unfinished process, did not communicate, however, directly with the present. The determination and technological expertise of Saúl Hernández-Vargas, my husband, played a key role in unlocking their many secrets. His tireless efforts led us to locating, and later contacting, many of Liliana's closest friends: Ana María de los Ángeles Ocadiz Eguía Lis, Manolo Casillas Espinal, Raúl Espino Madrigal, Othón Santos Álvarez, Gerardo Navarro, Ángel López, Fernando Pérez Vega, Norma Xavier Quintana. Months later, after reading a tweet in which I mentioned Liliana's name, Laura Rosales contacted me. I interviewed all of them over the phone, transcribing rather than recording our conversations. A rewrite of their testimonies is included in chapters five, six, and seven, although they were also useful, as indirect references, in other chapters.

My conversations about Liliana have been numerous and constant over the last two years. While I did not formally interview my parents, Antonio Rivera Peña and Ilda Garza Bermea, talking with them was crucial to writing chapter ten of this book. Confi-

dences from cousins Emilio and Leticia Hernández Garza, which I transcribed based on phone and in-person exchanges, served as the basis for some scenes and transitions throughout this book.

I received legal advice from Héctor Pérez Rivera and Karen Vélez during the early stages of this research. Thanks go to lawyer Andrea Medina, for suggestions made at a crucial point during my investigation. I am especially grateful to lawyer Sayuri Herrera, head of the Mexico City Public Prosecutor's Office Special Unit for Femicides, for the many conversations we have had and the sound advice, legal and otherwise, I have received from her.

My everlasting gratitude to journalist Daniela Rea, who for the first time took my sister's name to the International Women's Day demonstration on March 8, 2021, in Mexico City. Photos and videos from that event belong to her.

Raúl Espino Madrigal designed the font, based on Liliana's own handwriting, that was used in this book to transcribe her letters and notes. Amaranta Caballero, poet and designer, offered an early treatment for the Spanish-version cover of this book.

The Liliana Rivera Garza documents are housed as a part of the Cristina Rivera Garza Papers at the Nettie Lee Benson Latin American Collection, at the University of Texas at Austin. Heartfelt thanks to Daniel Arbino for his careful handling of these materials.

On page 3, the verse *"here, under this branch, you can speak of love,"* comes from the poem "Limit," by Mexican poet Rosario Castellanos. On page 58, *"Toluca, which means unfortunately,"* belongs to my poem, "Los bárbaros se quedan a cenar" / "And the Barbarians Stayed for Dinner," in *La más mía* (*Tierra Adentro*, 1998). On page 100, the lines *"If I had illusions / if there were crazy passions, reasons"* ("si tuviera ilusiones / si existieran razones locuras pasiones . . .") belong to the song "Distante instante / Distant Instant" by Rodrigo González. On page 151, *"A battle of giants / turns / air into natural gas* . . . ("lucha de gigantes / convierte / el aire en gas natural . . .") belongs to the lyrics of "Lucha de gigantes / Battle of Giants," a song performed by Nacha Pop. On page 167, the title "And Isn't This Happiness?" which I took from a letter Liliana wrote to Ana Ocadiz, was also used by Jin Shengtan, a Chinese man of letters from the Ming dynasty.

Unless otherwise indicated, all translations from the Spanish included in this book—letters, newspaper articles, personal notes, poems—are the my own.

PHOTO: © MART CALVO

CRISTINA RIVERA GARZA is the award-winning author of *The Taiga Syndrome* and *The Iliac Crest*, among many other books. A recipient of the MacArthur Fellowship and the Sor Juana Inés de la Cruz Prize, Rivera Garza is the M. D. Anderson Distinguished Professor in Hispanic Studies, and director of the PhD program in creative writing in Spanish at the University of Houston.